BUSINESS ISSUES, COMPETITION AND ENTREPRENEURSHIP

STATE REGULATION OF SMALL BUSINESS

IMPACT OF REGULATORY FLEXIBILITY

BUSINESS ISSUES, COMPETITION AND ENTREPRENEURSHIP

Additional books in this series can be found on Nova's website under the Series tab.

Additional E-books in this series can be found on Nova's website under the E-book tab.

BUSINESS ISSUES, COMPETITION AND ENTREPRENEURSHIP

STATE REGULATION OF SMALL BUSINESS

IMPACT OF REGULATORY FLEXIBILITY

LINDSAY LOCKWOOD
AND
PAUL GARRITANO
EDITORS

nova publishers
New York

For permission to use material from this book please contact us:
Telephone 631-231-7269; Fax 631-231-8175
Web Site: http://www.novapublishers.com

Library of Congress Cataloging-in-Publication Data

ISBN: 978-1-62948-193-7

Published by Nova Science Publishers, Inc. † New York

CONTENTS

PREFACE

Chapter 1 – The Regulatory Flexibility Act of 1980, as amended, established a process of analyzing and mitigating impacts of federal regulations on small businesses and other small entities. In the ensuing years, states began adopting regulatory flexibility legislation (or executive orders) of their own. In 2002 the SBA Office of Advocacy launched a Model Legislation Initiative utilizing a model state regulatory flexibility bill, which incorporated many elements of the federal legislation in simplified form. The model legislation was published for general use in 2005, along with supporting commentary and materials, and a guidance document to assist states in implementing regulatory flexibility legislation was published in 2007.

About half the states adopted regulatory flexibility legislation in the period 2002 – 2007. By the end of this period, SBA data showed that 45 states and territories had some form of regulatory flexibility legislation or executive order, and about 20 of those included all of the elements in the model legislation. SBA's Model Legislation Initiative wound down at the end of the Bush administration, although progress continued at the state level.

This study revisits regulatory flexibility at the state level with two general purposes:

- Assess the implementation of state regulatory flexibility laws; and
- Document further developments of state regulatory flexibility programs.

The study drew on available public documents. It examined the legislation of each state and traced the rulemaking process from notice through regulatory flexibility analysis and review.

State regulatory flexibility programs differ greatly in many dimensions. The study identified elements of what might be called regulatory flexibility infrastructure. Almost all states were missing at least some of these elements, and the quality of design and apparent effectiveness of implementation of individual elements vary greatly among states. The range of practices and best practices provides a structure for summarizing the findings of the study.

A statutory basis is necessary for a durable regulatory flexibility program. Executive orders that are not subsequently enacted as statute tend to fade away when the governor leaves office. The statute should establish the institutions and basic processes for regulatory flexibility analysis. SBA's model legislation provides a useful framework, but it is rather basic and some important elements are not conveyed by simply adopting it. The better state statutes spell out procedures and responsibilities and define institutions in greater detail.

Language is important. Actions that are merely authorized ("may") often are not done. On the other hand, "shall, where possible" creates a triage issue. "Affects small business" is the most common state requirement for a regulatory flexibility analysis, but most state regulations that affect small business have minor impacts. The federal Regulatory Flexibility Act has a two stage process, but state laws tend to read as if the same full analysis is required for all regulations. In some cases the effect seems to be that little attention is paid to regulatory flexibility analysis of any regulation. Some states have specified thresholds – usually in aggregate dollar terms. Better crafted methods are sometimes used for the related issue of holding a hearing.

Notification and provision of public information on proposed regulations is an important part of rulemaking infrastructure. Almost all states post notices on line, but the quality ranges from the simplest pdf reproduction of a hard copy *Register* to highly integrated, searchable online systems. The key is to provide both a clear summary notice and access to supporting documentation. This can be accomplished by hyperlinks in a pdf notice, but many states provide inadequate links or do not post most documents. The *Register* (hard copy and on-line) is typically published by a centralized agency; individual departments (except for environmental agencies) usually have little or no information on their web sites. Almost all states have a requirement to send notices to parties that have made timely requests, but only a minority have web pages where such requests can be made on line. Even fewer have web pages for making comments on line. Most states publish hearing schedules in some form, but information often is fragmented.

Relatively few statutes call for pre-NPRM involvement of stakeholders, and the mechanisms are usually optional. Since such involvement is often informal, so that it was difficult to assess, but consistent early involvement does not seem probable.

Guidance on regulatory flexibility analysis is a weakness of most state programs. Overall guidance on rulemaking rarely more than mentions regulatory flexibility analysis. Evidence of training on regulatory flexibility was rarely found. The most common form of guidance is checklists or templates for reporting analysis. These do little more than repeat – but do not elaborate on or explain – the statutory requirements. The best of these require some degree of thought and explanation in responding to a question paraphrasing the statute. Adopting SBA's model legislation does not provide guidance. Its discussion of disproportional impacts is in the Findings preamble, which state laws never incorporated. Only two or three states have discovered on their own this fundamental basis for regulatory flexibility analysis. More thorough guidance is needed.

The function of small business regulatory advocate is an essential element in the regulatory flexibility infrastructure. Fewer than one fifth of the states have such an advocacy position or office, which was usually established by statute. An advocate works with agency staff – from early in the rulemaking through the public hearing process - to inculcate regulatory flexibility principles and practices. In addition to advocacy as usually defined, this function provides informal (and sometimes classroom) training – including the sort of guidance that usually is otherwise lacking. A knowledgeable advocate may well have a better understanding of regulatory flexibility than anyone else involved in rulemaking. Advocacy is a long-term process; an advocate builds relationships and persuades and motivates agency staff.

Review of proposed rules is best done by a small business regulatory review committee. Where they exist, such committees are usually established by statute and typically are made up partly or entirely by representatives of the small business community. These committees review proposed rules, sometimes are active earlier in the rulemaking, usually are involved in review of existing rules, often serve an advocacy function, and occasionally provide guidance and training. Review committees generally can require agencies to respond meaningfully to their comments and may develop working relationships with agency staff. In a few states, the Governor has essentially delegated his authority to the committee. Because business people are busy, strong leadership and staff support are important for a committee to be successful.

Legislatures in most states review proposed and existing rules. With one exception (Illinois), however, they have no discernible interest in impacts on small business. Their concerns are generally restricted to statutory authority for a regulation, consistency with legislative intent, and consistence with other regulations or statutes.

States have various provisions for review of existing regulations, which apply more broadly than – and usually do not explicitly address – regulatory flexibility. Periodic review of all rules is a best practice. Some states enforce this with sunset provisions every five to ten years. The consistency and thoroughness of these periodic reviews was not clear. In a few states a review committee can initiate review of specific rules, and this can help focus on small-business issues. Short-term intensive reviews do not appear effective. A few states have sunset periods of less than two years, with the result that all regulations are renewed in a single omnibus bill, and only a few are sporadically subject to actual review.

Some states (and some agencies within states) have an ombudsman function. The ombudsman works with businesses that are having difficulty with a regulatory agency to resolve issues concerning existing rules. This function provides feedback and information that can usefully complement the activities of an advocate or review committee.

A few states have conducted broad reviews of regulation ("red tape") through surveys, focus groups, roundtables, and other meetings. Findings have been fairly similar and unsurprising, but the exercises have provided information for policy and administrative purposes and have been useful in raising consciousness and focusing agency attention on issues of regulatory burdens. One consistent finding – that poor "customer service" contributes greatly to what is broadly understood as "burden" of regulations – indicates that regulatory flexibility issues extend beyond regulatory development and the rulemaking process.

Executive branch support for regulatory flexibility is essential. At a minimum, regulatory flexibility must be regarded as a legitimate activity in its own right. It should be a policy priority to make the regulatory flexibility infrastructure effective. Legislatures, having initially passed the legislation, rarely follow up on regulatory flexibility. Regulatory flexibility also must be recognized as an activity that is distinct from other small business assistance and, as such, be given support and resources at the departmental level. Lacking executive support, statutory regulatory flexibility programs in several states have ceased to function.

The nature of executive involvement makes a difference, as several new Republican governors illustrate. Ohio and Maine put substantial emphasis on regulatory flexibility in its recent reforms. Michigan and New Jersey were not focused on regulatory flexibility, but they made serious attempts to reform the rulemaking process in ways that seem to benefit small businesses. Arizona and Florida, by comparison, went about rescinding and reducing regulations as quickly as possible. Ironically, regulatory flexibility is vulnerable to a "regulatory reform" campaign. These governors opted for gubernatorial control of rulemaking, as opposed to use of established functioning process. By taking the review and approval powers into their own offices, they pushed aside two of the best designed regulatory flexibility infrastructures found in this study.

Chapter 2 - When government takes small businesses into consideration in developing regulations, it saves time and money for a vital sector of the nation's economy, our small businesses. This primer on the Regulatory Flexibility Act (RFA) is designed to be used by those interested in the basics of federal regulatory compliance with respect to the RFA and Executive Order 13272. For more detailed guidance on the RFA, federal agency rule writers and policy analysts should refer to the Office of Advocacy's step-by-step manual: *A Guide for Government Agencies: How to Comply with the Regulatory Flexibility Act* (www.sba.gov/advo/laws/rfaguide.pdf).

The chief counsel for advocacy of the U.S. Small Business Administration has been designated to monitor agency compliance with the Regulatory Flexibility Act.

In: State Regulation of Small Business
Editors: Lindsay Lockwood and Paul Garritano
ISBN: 978-1-62948-193-7

Chapter 1

RESEARCH ON STATE REGULATORY FLEXIBILITY ACTS*

Small Business Administration, Office of Advocacy

EXECUTIVE SUMMARY

The Regulatory Flexibility Act of 1980,[1] as amended,[2] established a process of analyzing and mitigating impacts of federal regulations on small businesses and other small entities. In the ensuing years, states began adopting regulatory flexibility legislation (or executive orders) of their own. In 2002 the SBA Office of Advocacy launched a Model Legislation Initiative utilizing a model state regulatory flexibility bill, which incorporated many elements of the federal legislation in simplified form. The model legislation was published for general use in 2005, along with supporting commentary and materials, and a guidance document to assist states in implementing regulatory flexibility legislation was published in 2007.

About half the states adopted regulatory flexibility legislation in the period 2002 – 2007. By the end of this period, SBA data showed that 45 states and territories had some form of regulatory flexibility legislation or executive order, and about 20 of those included all of the elements in the model legislation.[3] SBA's Model Legislation Initiative wound down at the end of the Bush administration, although progress continued at the state level.

This study revisits regulatory flexibility at the state level with two general purposes:

- Assess the implementation of state regulatory flexibility laws; and
- Document further developments of state regulatory flexibility programs.

The study drew on available public documents.[4] It examined the legislation of each state and traced the rulemaking process from notice through regulatory flexibility analysis and review.

* This report, released May 2013, was developed by Microeconomic Applications, Inc. under a contract with the Small Business Administration, Office of Advocacy.

State regulatory flexibility programs differ greatly in many dimensions. The study identified elements of what might be called regulatory flexibility infrastructure. Almost all states were missing at least some of these elements, and the quality of design and apparent effectiveness of implementation of individual elements vary greatly among states. The range of practices and best practices provides a structure for summarizing the findings of the study.

A statutory basis is necessary for a durable regulatory flexibility program. Executive orders that are not subsequently enacted as statute tend to fade away when the governor leaves office. The statute should establish the institutions and basic processes for regulatory flexibility analysis.[5] SBA's model legislation provides a useful framework, but it is rather basic and some important elements are not conveyed by simply adopting it. The better state statutes spell out procedures and responsibilities and define institutions in greater detail.

Language is important. Actions that are merely authorized ("may") often are not done.[6] On the other hand, "shall, where possible" creates a triage issue. "Affects small business" is the most common state requirement for a regulatory flexibility analysis, but most state regulations that affect small business have minor impacts. The federal Regulatory Flexibility Act has a two stage process,[7] but state laws tend to read as if the same full analysis is required for all regulations. In some cases the effect seems to be that little attention is paid to regulatory flexibility analysis of any regulation.[8] Some states have specified thresholds – usually in aggregate dollar terms.[9] Better crafted methods are sometimes used for the related issue of holding a hearing.[10]

Notification and provision of public information on proposed regulations is an important part of rulemaking infrastructure. Almost all states post notices on line, but the quality ranges from the simplest pdf reproduction of a hard copy *Register* to highly integrated, searchable online systems. The key is to provide both a clear summary notice[11] and access to supporting documentation.[12] This can be accomplished by hyperlinks in a pdf notice, but many states provide inadequate links or do not post most documents. The *Register* (hard copy and on-line) is typically published by a centralized agency;[13] individual departments (except for environmental agencies) usually have little or no information on their web sites. Almost all states have a requirement to send notices to parties that have made timely requests, but only a minority have web pages where such requests can be made on line. Even fewer have web pages for making comments on line. Most states publish hearing schedules in some form, but information often is fragmented.[14]

Relatively few statutes call for pre-NPRM involvement of stakeholders, and the mechanisms[15] are usually optional. Since such involvement is often informal, so that it was difficult to assess, but consistent early involvement does not seem probable.

Guidance on regulatory flexibility analysis is a weakness of most state programs. Overall guidance on rulemaking rarely more than mentions regulatory flexibility analysis. Evidence of training on regulatory flexibility was rarely found. The most common form of guidance is checklists or templates for reporting analysis. These do little more than repeat – but do not elaborate on or explain – the statutory requirements. The best of these require some degree of thought and explanation in responding to a question paraphrasing the statute. Adopting SBA's model legislation does not provide guidance.[16] Its discussion of disproportional impacts is in the Findings preamble, which state laws never incorporated. Only two or three states have discovered on their own this fundamental basis for regulatory flexibility analysis. More thorough guidance is needed.[17]

The function of small business regulatory advocate is an essential element in the regulatory flexibility infrastructure.[18] Fewer than one fifth of the states have such an advocacy position or office, which was usually established by statute. An advocate works with agency staff – from early in the rulemaking through the public hearing process - to inculcate regulatory flexibility principles and practices. In addition to advocacy as usually defined, this function provides informal (and sometimes classroom) training – including the sort of guidance that usually is otherwise lacking. A knowledgeable advocate may well have a better understanding of regulatory flexibility than anyone else involved in rulemaking. Advocacy is a long-term process; an advocate builds relationships and persuades and motivates agency staff.

Review of proposed rules is best done by a small business regulatory review committee. Where they exist, such committees are usually established by statute and typically are made up partly or entirely by representatives of the small business community. These committees review proposed rules, sometimes are active earlier in the rulemaking, usually are involved in review of existing rules, often serve an advocacy function, and occasionally provide guidance and training. Review committees generally can require agencies to respond meaningfully to their comments and may develop working relationships with agency staff. In a few states, the Governor has essentially delegated his authority to the committee. Because business people are busy, strong leadership and staff support are important for a committee to be successful.

Legislatures in most states review proposed and existing rules. With one exception (Illinois), however, they have no discernible interest in impacts on small business. Their concerns are generally restricted to statutory authority for a regulation, consistency with legislative intent, and consistence with other regulations or statutes.

States have various provisions for review of existing regulations, which apply more broadly than – and usually do not explicitly address – regulatory flexibility. Periodic review of all rules is a best practice. Some states enforce this with sunset provisions every five to ten years. The consistency and thoroughness of these periodic reviews was not clear. In a few states a review committee can initiate review of specific rules, and this can help focus on small-business issues. Short-term intensive reviews do not appear effective. A few states have sunset periods of less than two years, with the result that all regulations are renewed in a single omnibus bill, and only a few are sporadically subject to actual review.

Some states (and some agencies within states) have an ombudsman function. The ombudsman works with businesses that are having difficulty with a regulatory agency to resolve issues concerning existing rules. This function provides feedback and information that can usefully complement the activities of an advocate or review committee.

A few states have conducted broad reviews of regulation ("red tape") through surveys, focus groups, roundtables, and other meetings. Findings have been fairly similar and unsurprising, but the exercises have provided information for policy and administrative purposes and have been useful in raising consciousness and focusing agency attention on issues of regulatory burdens. One consistent finding – that poor "customer service" contributes greatly to what is broadly understood as "burden" of regulations – indicates that regulatory flexibility issues extend beyond regulatory development and the rulemaking process.

Executive branch support for regulatory flexibility is essential. At a minimum, regulatory flexibility must be regarded as a legitimate activity in its own right. It should be a policy priority to make the regulatory flexibility infrastructure effective. Legislatures, having initially passed the legislation, rarely follow up on regulatory flexibility. Regulatory flexibility also must be recognized as an activity that is distinct from other small business assistance and, as such, be given support and resources at the departmental level. Lacking executive support, statutory regulatory flexibility programs in several states have ceased to function.

The nature of executive involvement makes a difference, as several new Republican governors illustrate. Ohio and Maine put substantial emphasis on regulatory flexibility in its recent reforms. Michigan and New Jersey were not focused on regulatory flexibility, but they made serious attempts to reform the rulemaking process in ways that seem to benefit small businesses. Arizona and Florida, by comparison, went about rescinding and reducing regulations as quickly as possible. Ironically, regulatory flexibility is vulnerable to a "regulatory reform" campaign. These governors opted for gubernatorial control of rulemaking, as opposed to use of established functioning process. By taking the review and approval powers into their own offices, they pushed aside two of the best designed regulatory flexibility infrastructures found in this study.

I. INTRODUCTION

A. Background

1. Federal Regulatory Flexibility

The Regulatory Flexibility Act of 1980[19] established a process of analyzing and mitigating impacts of impacts of regulations on small businesses and other small entities. This process includes publication of a regulatory agenda (5 USC 602), an initial regulatory flexibility analysis (5 USC 603), a final regulatory flexibility analysis (5 USC 604), and a periodic review of rules (5 USC 610). The provision on judicial review (5 USC 611) was amended in the Small Business Regulatory Enforcement Fairness Act[20] to allow judicial review of compliance.

2. State Regulatory Flexibility

The Office of Advocacy's mission concerning effects of government regulation on small business is not limited to the Federal government. State governments are within the Office's purview. Yet, lacking any statutory authority, the Office's role is necessarily limited to advocacy.

Model Regulatory Flexibility Legislation

In December 2002 the Office of Advocacy launched a Model Legislation Initiative utilizing a model state regulatory flexibility bill,[21] which had been developed. This model legislation was published for general use three years later, together with supporting commentary and materials.[22] A guidance document to assist states in implementing regulatory flexibility legislation was published in 2007.[23]

SBA's model legislation tracks provisions of the Regulatory Flexibility Act.[24] The model legislation is simpler and clearer, however - stripped down to the essence of regulatory flexibility. The model legislation does not contain much in the way of procedures. Procedures are described in a guidance document, which emphasizes flexibility. Rather than set notification requirements, for example, the guidance emphasizes the importance of outreach and of involving the business community as early as possible. It offers a variety of strategies and techniques as options – including a state regulatory register (which is required at the Federal level under 5 USC 602 and 5 USC 609) – and gives examples from a number of states that had started regulatory flexibility programs.

Adoption of Legislation

As of 2007, summary SBA data[25] indicated fairly rapid spread of state regulatory flexibility legislation. About a dozen states had legislation at the time of the model legislation was first released.[26] Fourteen states first adopted legislation from 2002 through 2005, and three other states may have done so in that period.[27] Eleven more states, ten of which were reported as considering bills in 2005, adopted legislation by 2007. Two states first adopted legislation between the 2007 *Guide* data and the latest SBA data. In addition, three states had executive orders on regulatory flexibility.[28]

Out of 54 states and territories,[29] the last available SBA data showed that 45 had legislation (or an executive order) on regulatory flexibility. The SBA lists were divided into "active" statues and "partial or partially used" statutes or executive orders. The distinction is whether all five provisions that SBA considered key were included in the statute or not. From these data, it appears that judicial review and periodic review were the two provisions most often lacking. Of the 45 states and territories, 19 reportedly had complete legislation (5 of which initially had partial legislation but passed additional legislation), and 26 had partial legislation or executive orders. Six states, five of which reportedly considered bills after the model legislation was released, and three territories had no regulatory flexibility legislation.

Ebbing of the Model Legislation Initiative

Activity on the Model Legislation Initiative appears largely to have ceased after 2008. This would hardly be surprising; all but one state had at least considered legislation, and advocacy efforts doubtless appeared to be encountering diminishing returns. Changes in administration tend to bring new priorities. Most of the Regional Advocate positions, which were key links in the Initiative, became vacant and many remained so into 2010, so that continuity was lost. The Model Legislation Initiative page was archived when SBA redesigned its web site, and there is no obvious link from the new site. The web site includes only a list and two fact sheets,[30] and they have not systematically been updated. A detailed list of citations to state statutes, which also is archived, is dated 2005.

B. Study Objectives

State regulatory flexibility laws identified in the five-year-old SBA data have been in effect long enough to be fully implemented and establish a track record. The Model Legislation Initiative played a significant role in adoption of some state regulatory flexibility legislation (or, in a few cases, executive orders). This study has two general purposes:

- Assess the implementation of state regulatory flexibility laws; and
- Document further developments of state regulatory flexibility programs.

Assessment of implementation entailed creating profiles of state regulatory flexibility requirements and practices, which vary considerably. SBA's model legislation served as a useful benchmark, as its provisions are stated with elegant simplicity and clarity. Similarly, the *State Guide* provided a benchmark for some elements of process that are found in the Regulatory Flexibility Act but not in the model legislation. As specific best practices are identified, they also were implicitly used as benchmarks. The findings provide the Office of Advocacy with useful information for future policy and targeting future advocacy and assistance efforts.

State action on regulatory flexibility did not wind down along with the Model Legislation Initiative. There has been a surge of regulatory reform. Over the last ten years, several dynamics have been at work in different states, including:

- Initiatives for new regulatory flexibility programs;
- Withering away of some regulatory flexibility programs that were started;
- Measures taken to enhance existing regulatory flexibility infrastructure and practices;
- Initiatives to overhaul the rulemaking and review processes, some of which had little no explicit relationship to regulatory flexibility; and
- Backlash against regulation based more on philosophy than analysis, which – on the whole – did more harm than good to effective regulatory flexibility practices.

C. Analytical Approach

Information was collected from print (i.e., on-line) sources. This was appropriate in that openness and accessibility of information is itself an important aspect of implementing the process. Use of on-line information was a limitation because in most states some type of useful documents were not on line. In such cases, however, the documents – while "public" in a legal sense – usually were not easily accessible,[31] so that collection and review was beyond a study of this scope. OMB rules prohibit original collection of information from more than a fraction of the states without approval of a formal information collection, and this also was beyond the scope of the study. Documents generally were available from enough states to show patterns and the range of practices.

Conceptually, information collection was organized and driven by assuming two roles:

- A small businessman trying to weigh in with his opinion on a rule, who is looking for
    - Regulations that may affect him,
    - The specifics of a particular regulation,
    - How he might comment and otherwise make his concerns heard, and
    - Any recourse if concerns of small businesses (like his) are not being considered.
- A new regulatory agency staffer trying to learn about the process, who wants to know
    - What the regulatory flexibility law requires,
    - What he has to do to comply with the law,
    - Where he can get assistance, and
    - What rulemaking resources are available.

This dual approach was fruitful in identifying and providing information on practices themselves and experience with the responsiveness of the system.

In collecting the data and performing the preliminary analysis, each state was studied individually at one point in time. The process began with a review of statutory requirements[32] for the major components of regulatory flexibility in SBA's model legislation,[33] including elements that were not in the model legislation.[34] The review also covered provisions requiring notification, publication, and opportunity for public comment on specific rules[35] and for review by a legislative committee, executive branch agency, or independent commission.[36]

The review then turned to the state *Register* to assess the format, accessibility, and content of public notices. These notices sometimes included documents such as impact analyses. Beyond that, the course of the review depended on the organization of the state. Other sources[37] were examined for information on:

- On-line materials or references to inform stakeholders about the rulemaking process and opportunities to participate in it;
- A state register and/or other notices and elements of a program to provide information on and track specific regulations;
- Status information on specific rulemakings outside the *Register;*
- Procedures for involving the public during the public comment period and prior to the notice of proposed rulemaking (NPRM);
- Guidance and training materials targeted to agencies and other information describing standard regulatory flexibility practices;
- Regulatory flexibility analysis requirements such as timing and triggers for analysis;
- Procedures and criteria for reviewing proposed and existing regulations;
- Adjunct positions such as small business advocate or ombudsman;
- The committee or commission that performs review;
- Schedules, agendas, minutes, and other information on meetings and public events (e.g., training or regulatory hearings);
- Links to the Governor's office or other information on involvement of the Governor;
- Documentation of examples of regulatory flexibility analysis and its practices from past and ongoing rulemakings; and
- Information on regulatory flexibility outcomes on specific rules.

In some cases, where information should have been available on the internet but was not, a contact was made to try to locate relevant public information.[38] In a small number of states,[39] such a conversation evolved into a more general background discussion.

Individual reports for each state included the statutory provisions, a discussion of practices (including strengths and weaknesses), an updating for recent developments (if appropriate), and an overall assessment. The study report is based on a comparative analysis of the individual states.

II. State Statutory Requirements

A. The Benchmark: SBA Model Regulatory Flexibility Legislation

The first state regulatory flexibility legislation was enacted in the mid 1980s, shortly after the federal Regulatory Flexibility Act of 1980. For the last decade, state legislation has been strongly influenced by model regulatory flexibility legislation developed by SBA. The Office of Advocacy presented the draft model legislation to the American Legislative Exchange Counsel (ALEC) in December 2002 (although a few individual states used the language somewhat earlier). ALEC adopted it as a model bill for consideration by state legislators.

This model legislation (Appendix A) serves as a useful benchmark for describing and assessing state regulatory flexibility statutes. The model legislation is patterned after the federal Regulatory Flexibility Act but is considerably streamlined. It includes the following elements:

- **Findings.** The findings include the central rationale for regulatory flexibility: Uniform regulatory requirements that ignore "differences in scale and resources" (i.e., size) of businesses can impose disproportionate costs that have adverse effects on competition, efficiency, innovation, and productivity.
- **Section 2. Definitions.** This section defines "agency," "proposed regulation," "regulation," and "small business." "Small" is defined as being:
  - Independently owned and operated, and
  - Smaller than a certain size defined in terms of employees or revenue.[40]
- **Section 3. Economic Impact Statement.** "Prior to the adoption of any proposed regulation that may have an impact on small businesses," an agency must prepare an economic impact statement that:
  - Identifies and estimates the number of small businesses affected,
  - Projects recordkeeping and other administrative costs and expertise required,
  - States the probable effect on impacted small businesses, and
  - Describes any less intrusive or less costly methods of achieving the purpose.
- **Section 4(a). Regulatory Flexibility Analysis.** Each agency "shall" prepare a regulatory flexibility analysis; "shall... consider" regulatory methods that accomplish objectives, "consistent with health, Safety, environmental, and economic welfare," and minimize impact on small businesses; and "shall consider without limitation:"
  - Less stringent compliance or reporting requirements for small businesses,
  - Less stringent compliance schedules or deadlines for small businesses,
  - Consolidation or simplification of reporting requirements for small businesses,
  - Establishment of performance - rather than design or operational - standards, and
  - Exemption of small businesses from all or some requirements.
- **Section 4(b).** Each agency must notify a designated state review agency,[41] and that agency will "advise and assist" in the regulatory flexibility analysis. This requirement mirrors federal requirements to notify and receive guidance from the SBA Office of Advocacy.
- **Section 5. Judicial Review.** An "adversely affected or aggrieved" small business has the right to judicial review of an agency's compliance with these requirements.

- **Section 6. Periodic Review of Rules.** Rules must be reviewed periodically with respect to minimization of small business impacts to determine whether they should be continued, amended, or rescinded. The review must consider the:
- Continued need for the rule,
- Nature of complaints or comments received from the public,
- Complexity of the rule,
- Extent of overlap, duplication, or conflict with Federal, state, and local rules, and
- Degree to which relevant technology, economic conditions or other factors have changed.

B. Statutory Requirements for Analysis

The analytical elements of regulatory flexibility analysis – the economic impact statement (SBA Section 3) and the Regulatory Flexibility Analysis (SBA Section 4(a)) – are the elements most often found in state legislation. There is, however, considerable variety.

- The wording of state legislation varies from verbatim quotation of the SBA model legislation to rather different language conveying the same concepts (most often found in the early legislation).
- Some regulatory flexibility legislation is inserted into the Code as a separate module, and may conflict with (or at least be a variation on) other requirements of the state Administrative Procedures Act; in other states it is better integrated into the state APA.
- In some states these sections stand more or less alone; in others they are surrounded by more other elements of SBAs model legislation and complementary provisions in the state APA.

Related rulemaking procedures, such as hearings and legislative review, are covered by state APAs.[42]

1. Definition of "Small Business"

Most states have definitions of "small business." Most states use employment size standards, but relatively few also include revenue size standards. Other factors also enter the definitions. Size standards can be summarized as follows:

- Among states that use an employment size standard,[43] the level of employment varies considerably. Specific standards include:
  - Fourteen states[44] use size standards of 75 or fewer employees, with six using a standard of 20 or 25 and six using a standard of 50,
  - Nine states[45] use a size standard of 100,
  - Seven states[46] use a size standard of 150 to 500,
  - Two states[47] cite SBA standards,
  - California sets industry-specific size standards,[48]
  - Two states[49] allow use a higher size standard if appropriate to the regulation, and
  - Texas also has a "micro-business" size standard of 20 employees.

- Some states specify that the standard applies to full-time employees, a few specify full-time and part-time, and many do not distinguish.
- Some states include the conditions of independent ownership and non-dominance in the field; some include one but not the other; and some make no mention of this.
- Several states include a requirement that the business is located in the state[50] or that a majority of employees work in the state.[51]
- Some states include "for-profit" in the definition of "small business;" most do not. Minnesota has a size standard (10 employees) for small municipalities.
- Two states do not specify size standards but allow agencies to define size classes appropriate for a specific proposed regulation, and two other states allow flexibility.[52]

2. Adoption of SBA Model Legislation Provisions

Direct Adoption of All SBA Language. Some states[53] adopted legislation that uses the language of both Section 3 and Section 4(a) of the SBA model legislation more or less verbatim.

Direct Adoption of Regulatory Flexibility Analysis Language. Other states[54] adopted SBA's Section 4(a), regulatory flexibility alternatives, more or less verbatim, but not Section 3. This may not be a serious omission. Arizona expanded the language to include more, or more detailed, impacts, for example, and Connecticut retained the ideas but changed the language. Even though Section 4(a) explicitly lists types of regulatory alternatives for small businesses, however, the focus on small business impacts may be lost.[55]

Economic Impact Analysis With a Shortened List of Alternatives. Four states[56] use their own language in setting out analysis requirements, and this does not include the full list of alternatives found in SBA Section 4(a).[57] Other useful provisions may compensate. New Jersey and New York have among the most detailed requirements for economic impact analysis. New Jersey has a separate statutory regulatory flexibility analysis process for small municipalities. Nevada's statute puts heavy emphasis on public participation, including workshops.

3. Partial Adoption of SBA Model Legislation Provisions

Economic Impact Analysis Requirement without Explicit Alternatives

Some states adopted the substance of all of the components of Section 3 – sometimes verbatim and sometimes expanded. This included the requirements to delineate and assess the impacts on small business and to consider alternatives that would reduce burdens on small businesses. There are several variants with respect to the requirement implementation of regulatory flexibility analysis:

- Two states[58] have requirements for assessment of impacts on small businesses, but there is no institutional environment supportive of regulatory flexibility analysis.
- Two states do not list explicit alternatives (except exemption) but have a stronger imperative than just consideration of regulatory alternatives.[59]
- Three states[60] have statutory requirements for a regulatory review board located in the executive branch development agency. These probably insure the implementation

of regulatory flexibility alternatives as effectively as an explicit statutory mandate – depending on how effectively these provisions are implemented.[61]

- Three states[62] have limited economic impact analysis requirements (or more extensive requirements that do not mention small businesses) and then adopt a system of tiering, under which an agency may divide the population into classes (including size, among other possible classifications) and adopt different standards for each class.

Minimal Provisions with Strong Administrative Support

Two states have provisions that summarize the components of regulatory flexibility analysis too briefly for any detail or nuance. Neither statute seems capable of commanding much attention on its own. Both, however, have excellent institutional support.

- Massachusetts has an extremely active Assistant Secretary of Economic Development, who reports directly to the Governor. She serves as reviewer, advocate, educator, and liaison on a relatively informal basis.
- The Texas Attorney General provides some of the clearest guidance found in any state and gives unusual emphasis to substantive analysis as a required part of rulemaking procedure.

Other Provisions

Other states begin with a finding that small businesses are adversely affected and then proceed along different paths:

- Two states[63] refer regulations with adverse small-business impacts for review – one to legislative committees and one to a Small Business Regulatory Advisory Committee. The reviewing bodies may comment or provide input, which the agency must consider.
- Two states[64] mention small business only once and almost incidentally.

Forms of Relief

Some states have adopted measures that provide relief after a rule has been promulgated.

- Minnesota requires analysis of impacts but has no requirements for regulatory flexibility alternatives. Instead, the statute has provisions that apply to individual cases:
  - A temporary exemption, based on an impact threshold,[65] and
  - A variance, based on circumstances of the petitioner.
- Hawaii and Washington provide a waiver for first-time minor or paperwork infractions.[66]

4. No Regulatory Flexibility Analysis Requirement

Seven states[67] do not have a regulatory flexibility analysis process. The requirements to analyze economic impacts are sometimes quite extensive,[68] and a few states include regulatory alternatives (for business as a whole). Nebraska has a statutorily authorized negotiated rulemaking process. Statutes in these states, however, do not mention small businesses. Wyoming, on the other hand, has no requirements for economic impact analysis of any kind.

5. Additional Provisions Concerning Impacts Found in State Legislation

Most states adopted requirements for impact analysis that go well beyond the elements of regulatory flexibility analysis. In some case the regulatory flexibility analysis elements were integrated into a larger list of requirements; in other cases not. Requirements for the economic impact analysis included the following:

- Fiscal impacts – typically reported in a "fiscal note – is the most widespread concern. Statutes require analysis of fiscal impacts on local government jurisdictions,[69] costs to the agency itself,[70] and/or fiscal impacts at the state level.[71]
- A statement of whether the regulation is mandated by federal law or regulations and/or a justification if the rule exceeds the federal mandate is required by some states.[72]
- Analysis of employment impacts is required by some states.[73]
- Analysis of other market impacts, such as the effect on competition was required by some states.[74]
- Quantitative analysis, such as an explicit cost-benefit analysis, (including elements such as discounted benefits and a baseline), or direct comparison of costs between alternatives was required by some states.[75]
- A discussion of a regulation's impact on matters such as public health, safety, and the environment is required by some states.[76]
- A description whether and how small businesses were involved in the development of the rule is required by some states.[77]

C. Statutory Requirements for Oversight by State Review Agency

The SBA model legislation includes designation of a "department or council that exists to review regulations [which] shall advise and assist agencies in complying with the provisions of this section." Only a minority of states with regulatory flexibility requirements have such a department or commission, and some of these have broader oversight of regulations that does not always address regulatory flexibility issues. In almost all other states without such a review agent, regulations are reviewed by the legislature. There are states where it appears that the legislature would rather retain its control of the rulemaking process. When a department is designated, it almost always is the department concerned with commerce and/or economic development. Independent commissions are usually attached to and supported by this department.

Individual states have more varied organizations than SBA's model legislation suggests. Their functions may include assistance, advocacy, and/or and review of the completed rule.[78]

- Some states[79] follow the SBA model, designating an agency and giving it the general responsibility to advise and assist agencies in regulatory flexibility activities
- Some states[80] have statutes that spell out the agency responsibilities in more detail.

- Texas is the only state where the Attorney General's responsibilities go beyond review of a rule on legal and technical grounds. In Texas:
  The attorney general, in consultation with the comptroller, shall prepare guidelines to assist a state agency:
  1. in determining a proposed rule's potential adverse economic effects on small businesses; and
  2. in identifying and evaluating alternative methods of achieving the purpose of a proposed rule."[81]
- "The [Virginia] Department of Planning and Budget in coordination with the agency shall... prepare an economic impact analysis of the proposed regulation."
- Colorado has an umbrella agency – the Office of Policy, Research, and Regulatory Reform, within the Department of Regulatory Agencies - that oversees all aspects of rulemaking and is well positioned to integrate assistance and review.
- Some states[82] have a Regulatory Review Council that is appointed by the Governor, by the legislature, or jointly. Members may be small businessmen or a mix of businessmen and senior agency personnel. These councils review rules and make recommendations or comments. Arizona's Council has authority to block a regulation. Some hold hearings. Some do impact analysis of their own. Some file annual reports with the legislature and/or Governor. They may also act on requests for review from the small business community.
- Some states[83] have an Office of Small Business Advocate, whose functions will be discussed further below.
- Some states[84] have an independent advisory commission on small business, generally made up of small businessmen, which reviews rules, has an advocacy role, can serve as a liaison between the business community and the agency. The purview of such commissions is usually fairly broad, covering all aspects of a regulation that may affect small businesses. In some cases the commission files an annual report. Such a commission provides "input" and comments but does not have authority beyond the respect it is able to command. Advisory committees at the departmental level are an alternative.[85]

D. Statutory Requirements for Periodic Review

SBA's model legislation provides for periodic review of rules by an agency. The provisions include the general purpose of further minimizing burdens on small businesses, specification of the frequency, and criteria for review.[86] SBA's criteria generally summarize the motives for review and are sometimes quoted in legislation. Periodic review of rules, however, is not unique to regulatory flexibility. Most states have some form of periodic review of existing rules, and there are various ways to structure periodic review.

- Some states use SBA's approach of review by agencies at fixed time intervals.[87] Most of these states use the five-year review cycle. Some states[88] quote SBA's language almost verbatim. Some require refilling the rule or specify the notice-and-comment procedure for a rulemaking.[89] Some require a report to the legislature. 90

- Statutes in some states require agencies to develop a plan for reviewing rules[91] or to prepare a list of rules for review – either on a five-year cycle or for rules that have become "obsolete" – and submit the list to the legislature.[92]
- In some state rules that have generated complaints or concerns are referred to the agency for review. Such a procedure involves a review board or other body with which public comments may be filed.[93]
- In some states[94] the legislature or (occasionally) the Governor directs agencies to review specific rules or to produce a schedule for review of rules. This is done at the discretion of the requestor; the statutes provide no criteria.
- North Dakota gives agencies explicit statutory authority to review rules at any time. This option, of course, is always implicitly available to an agency.
- In Wisconsin the Small Business Regulatory Review Board does the review and reports to the legislature.
- Automatic expiration of rules (sunset) is an option used by a number of states. Sunset review has two variants:
    - Rules expire on a fairly conventional review cycle (four to ten years). To retain a rule, the agency must readopt it, using the same procedures used to adopt a new rule.[95]
    - Rules expire within two rules of adoption and must be renewed by legislative action.[96] The legislature passes an omnibus bill reauthorizing all rules scheduled for expiration that year. In practice, a rule is actually reviewed only if a legislator objects to its inclusion in the omnibus bill.
- Two states[97] require an agency to do a general annual review of rules. In Arkansas the review specifically focuses on new legislation and rules that may require changes in existing rules.
- In some states[98] the legislature does the review of existing rules. Where a procedure is specified, it is the same procedure the legislature uses to review new rules. Only one state has a review cycle (5 years). In other states rules are "subject to review" by the legislature, they are reviewed "as time permits," or the statute says nothing about timing.

E. Statutory Requirements for Judicial Review

States generally have not adopted procedures for judicial review of regulatory flexibility analysis. States have, in their Administrative Procedures Acts, provisions for review of regulations and rulemaking. Criteria for review tend to be related to compliance with statutes and general procedural requirements, which typically do not include the quality of analysis or decisions based on the results of analysis (which tend to be considered policy, rather than law).[99]

It was not possible to review any judicial cases involving regulatory flexibility analysis. Court records simply are not indexed in a way that makes such a search possible. Given all of these considerations, judicial review was not considered further in this study.

F. Observations Concerning Statutory Requirements

Implementation of the statutory requirements are discussed further below, but some observations can be made about adoption of SBA model legislation provisions into state laws.

- Adoption of the SBA model legislation is no guarantee of a regulatory flexibility program; that is only the first step. The specifics are helpful. Without something like them, it is too easy for the focus on small businesses to be lost among the APA procedures. Specifications such as the regulatory flexibility alternatives (Section 4(a)) and criteria for periodic review (Section 6(c)) are helpful in keeping the analysis and review processes from slipping into meaningless generalities.
- The conceptual rationale for regulatory flexibility analysis – disproportionately large impacts of regulation on small businesses – is in the "Whereas" clauses of SBA's model legislation. It is almost never included in state legislation.[100] Yet this rationale is both a unifying policy principle and a part of the analytical calculus that might make it easier to explain regulatory flexibility analysis to agencies. Disproportionate impacts also is a key concept in keeping broader regulatory reform from ignoring small business.
- Size standards of 20 to 50 employees are more appropriate for regulatory flexibility analysis than SBA size standards. Many states realize this. Regulation-specific size classes are quite innovative. None of this makes much of a difference, however, because state analyses are rarely detailed enough to use – or refer to – size standards.

Very few states have designated an agency that really advises and assists in regulatory flexibility analysis. The majority of states make no such designation. Agencies that are designated tend to lack focus either because they oversee regulation as a whole, or because they concentrate on other aspects of small business development than rulemaking. Where an agency does provide effective assistance, it typically creates a new unit to do so.[101] Independent small-business review councils and agencies with a specific advocacy mission are the most likely to have the appropriate focus.

III. Guidance for Rulemaking

State statutes rarely get more detailed about regulatory flexibility analysis than SBA's model legislation. Implementation of the practice, however, requires guidance.

A. Elements of Guidance

1. Agencies Providing Guidance

Most states provide guidance for rulemaking. Guidance may be provided by the executive or the administrative branch. In the executive branch the Secretary of State or another administrative agency usually provides guidance. In two states the economic development department provides guidance. In two others an independent regulatory review commission provides guidance. On the legislative side, guidance is usually provided by a staff office with a name like Legislative Reference Bureau. In a majority of states, the office that provides guidance also publishes the state Register.

2. Background Materials

Some states – including those that provide the most detailed guidance on rulemaking – provide background information. At times this information is similar to – and may actually be – information provided to the general public. Types of information found in pamphlets, fact sheets, and other documents and on websites of agencies that provide guidance include:

- General background information on rules and rulemaking;[102]
- A Frequently Asked Questions page;[103]
- Discussion of the different types of rules (regular, emergency, expedited, temporary);
- Flowcharts of the process of rulemaking (sometimes at two levels of detail);
- Schedules for filing and publication (sometimes including a scheduling calculator);
- Narrative discussion of the steps in the rulemaking process;[104]
- Checklists for required documents and activities;
- Links to executive and legislative entities involved in the rulemaking process;
- Forms (or links to them);
- Information on where and how to file forms;
- Advice on involving the public, such as "appoint an advisory council and obtain public input" or involving the public prior to the NPRM:

> The rule drafting period is the amount of time used by the agency to draft the proposed regulation and solicit input from interested parties as appropriate. Interested parties may include the public, industry associations, or persons or groups affected by the regulation. Because it is difficult to significantly change a regulation once it has been set for hearing, the drafting period is an important phase in the development of a regulation.[105]

Arkansas' FAQ Sheet (Appendix B) provides another example.

This sort of orientation information can be helpful, but (except for advice to involve the public) it does not get into the subtleties of regulatory flexibility.

3. Manuals and Related Guidance Documents

Most states have manuals on how to develop and publish a regulation. The Manual usually is published by the agency with whom documents are filed or the agency that compiles the Administrative Code. (e.g., the Secretary of State, the Office of the Revisor of Statues, or the Legislative Reference Bureau). The publisher of the Manual typically has a particular interest in ensuring that the regulations are properly prepared for publication. Moreover, statutes often phrase requirements as something that must be done "before filing." Although organization and emphasis vary among states, manuals provide the following sort of information and guidance:

- **General Background.** This information orients the user to the rulemaking process. Individual topics may include:
    - A discussion of the purpose and nature of regulations, compared with statutes,

- A clear summary description of the steps in creating regulations, sometimes including references (even hyperlinks) to statutes and other types of sources,
- An overview of agencies involved in rulemaking (e.g., of the Office of Secretary of State and the Joint Committee on Administrative Rules) and their functions,
- A description of the state *Register* and its structure,
- A description of the state Administrative Code, and
- A discussion of the role of the agency Regulatory Coordinator (if there is one).

- **Procedure.** Manuals usually include step-by-step instructions that can cover almost every requirement in the State Administrative Procedures Act.[106] Where alternate procedures exist (e.g., for emergency rules), they are discussed as well. Guidance includes:
  - Identification of notices that must be filed,
  - Instructions on how to file (including use of on-line filing resources, if any),
  - Other requirements for provision of documents (e.g., to the legislature),
  - Other required activities (e.g., hearings), the procedures to be followed, and the conditions that may require them (or allow them to be omitted),
  - The sequence in which activities (e.g., filing or hearings) must be done,
  - Timing requirements, both minimum elapsed time between actions and deadlines,
  - Rule-writing procedures, such as incorporation by reference, and
  - Rule review procedures and the agency's responsibilities during the rule review process.

  Most of the procedures described reflect statutory requirements; some are from the state Administrative Code.
- **Content and Format.** This guidance pertains to individual notices, statements, or other documents that must be prepared. It covers the information that must be included in documents and requirements (or suggestions) for formatting and detail. The presentation usually includes sample filings, forms, and/or templates, as well as narrative discussion. This guidance typically closely tracks statutory requirements.
- **Style.** The Manuals usually provide detailed guidance on how to write a regulation, much of which comes under the general heading of Style Manual. Guidance (which can be extremely detailed) covers topics such as:
  - Format of assorted documents,
  - Numbering of sections and subsections,
  - Annotation,
  - Grammar, syntax, and punctuation, and
  - Exact wording to be used in specific situations.

Because a major purpose of these Manuals is to help agencies fulfill the statutory requirements, they follow the statutes closely – sometimes including the APA as an appendix. Many extensively quote the statutory language, which can be rather clumsy for purposes of guidance. The best of them do extensive editing of statutory language for readability and clarity.

As a rule, manuals and guidance documents provide no more information on regulatory flexibility analysis than the requirement to file one. This essentially provides a checklist item, but not guidance. As is illustrated by the *Louisiana Administrative Code Handbook*

(Appendix B), the guidance on regulatory flexibility analysis can be little more than how to say one is not needed. California provides another example. The checklist (Appendix B) contains a question about the existence of small business impacts,[107] but does not mention alternatives analysis. All four sample documents provided as guidance include explanations stating that alternatives were not needed or available. The wording of California's narrative description of the contents of two of the documents that an agency must submit is almost an invitation not to adopt alternatives.[108]

Some manuals or guidance documents do little more than quote or paraphrase the statute. Tennessee (Appendix B) provides an example. Ohio's Manual includes a chapter on Rules That Affect Individuals, Small Businesses or Small Organizations, but this chapter is almost entirely about procedures.[109] Kentucky is particularly disappointing because the statutory language describing tiering (Appendix B) is unusually detailed. Although the guidance on economic impact analysis in general in the *Kentucky Administrative Regulation* is moderately extensive, guidance on tiering is no more than:

TIERING: Is tiering applied? (Explain why or why not)"

A few guidance documents begin to discuss how to perform the analysis. Indiana's DEM guidance, for example, instructs the analyst to estimate the number of small businesses and then estimate the average annual cost for a representative business (Appendix B).[110]

New York's Guidance (Appendix B) uses a readable narrative style that walks the respondent through the standard questions. The guidance adds a few elements, including cost, economic and technological feasibility, compliance schedule, and small-business participation.

Texas has the best all-round Guidelines (Appendix B). They go through the process in clear detail and provide guidance on how to think through the various steps of the analysis.[111] Texas is unique in that its guidance includes links to the Texas Workforce Commission website for employment data and a web page that provides data on numbers of businesses and small (by Texas statutory definition) businesses, by 4-digit NAICS code.[112]

4. Forms and Templates

Many states provide sample or mandatory forms for filing. Alternatively, they supply templates or summaries of information required. This is a type of guidance, albeit a passive one. In general, these forms ask for the information that the statute requires. Appendix B includes some of the most detailed forms, templates, and summaries found in the study.

The most basic forms literally quote or paraphrase the statute. Virginia is an example. Taking statutory requirements and phrasing them as a question also is a common practice illustrated by the Arkansas form and the Pennsylvania summary. South Dakota has a convenient check-box format and focuses on an individual representative business. Very few states have forms or templates that go beyond statutory requirements. Many states lack as much as Pennsylvania's concise summary of requirements, which was developed by the Independent Regulatory Review Commission as part of its "tool box." Other forms add various elements.

- Missouri's form calls for quantitative cost information as well as a very concise presentation of statutory requirements.

- The Ohio template emphasizes intent and development of rules but does not mention small business. This template was developed as part of broader regulatory reform the Common Sense Initiative rather than for regulatory flexibility analysis.
- California's Economic Impact Statement asks for costs of the rule and alternatives, but in a form so highly aggregated that the numbers are not analytically useful. With one exception (as a percent of total cost), it does not address small business impacts.
- Massachusetts uses a variation on the question format. The Yes / No / NA format makes it convenient for respondents when there is no information. The questions are phrased a bit better than most states' to provoke some thought. The information sought expands a little on the statutory requirements in the area of impacts.
- Michigan's form asks for more detail about costs than most forms. It is rare in that it introduces the concept of disproportionality, which is central to regulatory flexibility thinking. The Alternatives questions discard the standard checklist and encourage the respondent to think.

5. Training

Formal Classes

Some states provide training on development and writing of rules. States identified in this study include the following:

- The Arizona Governor's Regulatory Review Council conducts monthly seminars for state agency personnel to instruct and assist them with rulewriting and reporting requirements;[113]
- California's Office of Administrative Law has a "comprehensive" 3-day course on rulemaking.[114]
- Louisiana has rulemaking classes using PowerPoint presentations that are posted on the website of the Office of State Register;
- Missouri's Small Business Regulatory Fairness Board has developed a training package for staff of agencies doing regulation, which is available in an on-line slide show and on CD;[115]
- Montana's Professional Development Center offerings include a 12-hour class on *Writing Administrative Rules*;[116]
- The New Mexico Administrative Law Division provides two on-line courses on the rulemaking process for state employees;[117]
- The Rhode Island Office of Regulatory Reform conducts periodic training for agency Rules Coordinators;
- The Utah Division of Administrative Rules provides quarterly rulemaking training to state agencies.[118]

Five of these training courses are done by an administrative or training agency. They provide background and guidance on the overall rulemaking process but do not cover regulatory flexibility analysis. The other three courses are presented by small business regulatory review boards and an advocacy agency. They do cover regulatory flexibility.

Informal Training

To some extent, understanding of regulatory flexibility is a matter of institutional memory, which is transmitted orally and through practice. It is not a coincidence that state environmental agencies are consistently ahead of other agencies in their analysis and institutional infrastructure that supports regulatory flexibility analysis; they have the most practice. Small business advocates work with agencies on an ongoing basis, as does an ombudsman. Small business regulatory review commissions at least provide feedback and may provide considerable informal training. Offices with ongoing regulatory reform responsibility, such as Oregon's Office of Regulatory Streamlining (now part of the Economic Revitalization Team), are training all the time. Some of the recent regulatory reform efforts have included a committee that studied regulatory issues. These exercises raise consciousness and the committee – if kept in place – will continue to educate the agencies they work with. Training is not just a matter of teaching how to go through the mechanics; to be really effective it also requires explanations and persuasion that instill motivation.

B. Regulatory Flexibility Analysis

Most state guidance on rulemaking does not address regulatory flexibility analysis. Only occasionally does the agency that writes the book on rulemaking have regulatory flexibility as an explicit concern, and there is no reason to believe that most of those agencies would have any particular understanding beyond general procedures. The guidance on regulatory flexibility rarely goes much beyond the requirements of the statute.

SBA's model legislation provides a skeletal outline of the regulatory flexibility process, but guidance is needed to fill that out. SBA provided considerable guidance in the *State Guide to Regulatory Flexibility for Small Businesses*, but very little of that was absorbed by the states. The very rudimentary guidance provided by most states does not cover many of the techniques and thought processes that are part of regulatory flexibility analysis. Examples include the following:

- The concept of disproportionate impacts on small businesses is mentioned in only a few states, although identifying this should be a major focus of regulatory flexibility analysis and is the reason for analyzing costs of small and large businesses separately.
- Most guidance does not mention the statutory definition of "small." Moreover:
  - While many states have a definition suitable for regulatory flexibility analysis, the idea of looking at more than one class of "small" rarely appears,[119] and
  - Analyses rarely reach a level of quantitative detail that actually uses size classes.
- The requirement for "identification and estimate of the number of the small businesses" is almost never implemented with the sort of industry analysis described in the *State Guide*.[120]
- State guidance generally does not describe impacts in terms of "per-firm regulatory cost increase," although individual analyses much more often do. Guidance and forms often suggest only aggregate impact measures.[121]
- Guidance in a majority of states does not suggest quantifying or monetizing impacts.

- Only a minority of states recommend public participation prior to the NPRM as part of guidance.

Given the very basic level of guidance states need for rulemaking, there clearly needs to be much more detailed guidance on regulatory flexibility. Its omission is doubly important because this type of detail in analysis is a major source of insights about regulatory flexibility alternatives.

SBA's *State Guide to Regulatory Flexibility for Small Businesses* emphasizes the importance of "agency education in the law's provisions" and goes on to describe the SBA Office of Advocacy's role. Most states, however, do not have an office of advocacy. The model legislation relies on the "Department of Economic and Community Development or similar state department or council that exists to review regulations." In most states there is no such executive branch entity "that exists to review regulations," and the DECD may not have the understanding and/or the inclination to do the necessary agency education.

The sample of training classes cited above is instructive. States with a specialized regulatory flexibility office teach about regulatory flexibility; states without one do not. Regulatory flexibility analysis infrastructure – advocates, ombudsmen, review commissions, and the like – are necessary for providing good guidance on regulatory flexibility analysis.

IV. REGULATORY FLEXIBILITY INFRASTRUCTURE

Regulatory flexibility infrastructure has several components, including advocacy, an ombudsman, and regulatory reviewers. The first two are discussed here. Review is covered in later chapters.

A. Two Complementary Functions

There are two types of liaison between the small business community and regulatory agencies. Both involve extensive public outreach, but they deal with agencies in different contexts.[122]

- A small business advocate works with agencies developing regulations on behalf of the small business community to design the regulations to have as small an impact on small businesses as possible.
- A small business ombudsman works with regulatory agencies and individual businessmen to mediate and resolve issues that arise from the implementation of existing regulations.

Conceptually these are distinct. In practice, both functions may work closely together.

1. Advocates

Advocacy Offices

A few states have a formal office (or position) that has distinctive small business advocacy functions:

- Florida's Office of Small Business Advocate (OSBA), which was established by statute, has a mandate to:
  - Serve as principal advocate in the state on behalf of small businesses, including, but not limited to, advisory participation in the consideration of all legislation and administrative rules that affect small businesses,
  - Represent the views and interests of small businesses before agencies whose policies and activities may affect small businesses, and
  - Receive and respond to complaints from small businesses concerning the actions of agencies and the operative effects of state laws and regulations adversely affecting those businesses.
- Maine passed legislation in 2010 that established the Bureau of Special Advocate. The first Small Business Advocate was appointed on October 6, 2011.
- In Massachusetts an Assistant Secretary for Economic Development, appointed by the Governor, serves many advocate functions, including working with agencies, training, divising forms, outreach to the public, and related functions. She also reviews proposed rules for small-business impacts.
- The Rhode Island Economic Development Corporation (RIEDC) has the role of advising and assisting agencies in complying with regulatory flexibility legislation and providing written comments related to the economic impact and regulatory flexibility analysis. Subsequent rounds of legislation established the position of small business advocate, added the position of small business ombudsman, and then set up the Office of Regulatory Reform within RIDEC,[123] which now has a staff of three.
- Indiana's small business ombudsman has advocacy functions including responsibility to:
  - Review proposed rules,
  - Participate in rulemaking actions that affect small businesses,
  - Suggest alternatives to reduce the burden on small businesses of a proposed rule,
  - Coordinate with OMB to perform cost-benefit analyses, and
  - Assist in training agency coordinators that will be assigned to rules.[124]
- Illinois has an Office of Regulatory Flexibility, with one dedicated staff person that performs several advocacy-like functions, including:
  - Doing outreach to the business community to encourage their participation,
  - Facilitating and compiling comments on the proposed rules,
  - Working with agencies early in the rulemaking process to encourage them to hold hearings and explore ways to minimize impacts on small businesses, and
  - Compiling complaints about regulations for the next periodic review cycle.[125]

Review Commissions

Independent review and advisory commissions have the potential to play a significant advocacy role, depending on the timing of their review and mix of other activities. Indeed, there is considerable overlap between small business advocacy and small business review of regulations.

- The Arizona Governor's Regulatory Review Council (GCCR) reviews proposed rules with particular reference to analysis of small businesses impacts, and it has statutory authority to block rules that do not meet statutory criteria. Although the Council's formal review takes place after the comment period, the GCCR staff of four performs "courtesy reviews" and works with agency personnel to make changes and corrections to rules prior to submission for formal review.[126]
- Florida's Small Business Regulatory Advisory Council (SBRAC) was established by the same legislation as the OSBA, and they work closely together. SBRAC was assigned responsibility for monitoring and reviewing new agency rules and - at the request of small business owners - current rules and for studying their impacts on Florida's small business community.[127]
- Hawaii's Small Business Regulatory Review Board (SBRRB), which is appointed by the Governor, consists of small business representatives. The SBRRB consults with agencies and comments on rules that agencies have identified as having likely impacts on small business. The SBRRB has worked to set up positive lines of communication with agency contacts. Each member is assigned to one or more agencies to serve as a "discussion leader" and to do the preliminary review of rules from that agency. The SBRRB is the agency responsible for reviewing existing rules, which is done in response to complaints by small businesses. The SBRRB also disseminates information on proposed rules.[128]
- The Kentucky Commission on Small Business Advocacy "includes small business owners and advocates appointed by the governor." Its advocacy functions include:
  - "Create a process by which the small business community is consulted in the development of public policy," and
  - "Review administrative regulations and provide advisory opinions on potential impact to small business."[129]

  For the most part, however, its activities appear to be more associated with the ombudsman function.
- Missouri's Small Business Regulatory Fairness Board reviews and comments on rules and is otherwise proactive in the rulemaking process. The SBRFB:
  - Maintains a website (with extensive links) on proposed rules and related documents, which also enables the public to sign up for alerts on proposed rules,
  - Develops forms for agency filings (see Appendix B),
  - Provides training on rulemaking (discussed above), and
  - Works directly with agencies early in the process, which appears to be its preferred method of operating.[130]
- Pennsylvania's Independent Regulatory Review Commission (IRRC) is primarily a review body with some advocacy overtones.[131] IRRC review, however, has no particular focus on regulatory flexibility. The IRRC also provides guidance and instruction, acts as ombudsman in some circumstances, and provides broad liaison between agencies and the business community.
- Oklahoma's Small Business Advocacy Committee reviews and comments on rules during the comment period. The Committee spent much of its first two or three years

networking and building up relationships.[132] More recently, the Committee has taken on more of an ombudsman function, helping individual businesses work with agencies. The dynamic Committee Chairman[133] and the Economic Development Specialist assigned to the Committee, both of whom have been with the Committee since it was established ten years ago, perform most of the work with agencies.

- South Carolina's Small Business Regulatory Review Commission (SBRRC) reviews regulations as early as possible, using electronic notices on the Register and circulating them among industry representatives for further comment. The SBRRC has statutory authority to request an EIS/RFA, which is not otherwise mandatory.[134] The SBRRC also performs a number of liaison functions, including meeting with agency directors.[135]
- The Wisconsin Small Business Regulatory Review Board (SBRRB), by statute: □ "Shall determine whether there is a significant economic impact on a substantial number of small businesses"[136] that requires a regulatory flexibility analysis,
    - May conduct cost-benefit analysis in doing so,
    - Reviews proposed rules for compliance with analytical requirements, and
    - Notifies agencies of any failures to meet these requirements and may "ask" an agency to comply.[137]

  As originally constituted, the SBRRB consisted of representatives from nine agencies, six small business representatives, and chairs of the small business committees of both legislative branches. This format was conducive to interaction between agencies and the small business community.[138]

Executive Order Review

Several states have committees created (or tasked) by executive order to review existing rules on an ongoing basis and work to improve them. These organizations are to some extent advocates for regulatory flexibility and consideration of small business concerns. Examples include the following:

- New Jersey 's Red Tape Review Commission was established to review existing administrative rules and regulations, to analyze their impacts, and to make findings and recommendations on rules that are burdensome to the State's economy and ways to improve the regulatory processes of State government.[139]
- Oregon's Office of Regulatory Streamlining was established to oversee the development and implementation of an ongoing process of reviewing regulations and identifying opportunities to reduce regulatory burdens.[140]
- Washington's Office of Regulatory Assistance was charged with simplifying regulatory procedures and improving service to regulated businesses.[141]

Departmental Advocacy

The SBA model legislation has an implicit advocacy function for the agency providing advice and assistance, and statutes that use the model or a variant of it have incorporated this function to some extent.

- Connecticut's Department of Economic and Community Development has authority under its regulatory flexibility act to "advise and assist" agencies in complying with its provisions.[142]
- In Georgia, by Executive Order, the "Department of Economic Development through the Entrepreneur and Small Business Office Shall coordinate the ongoing Small Business Regulatory Reform activities," and "each state agency... shall identify at least one staff person to serve as their Small Business Liaison."[143]
- The Director of the Arkansas Economic Development Commission has the responsibility to review (or coordinate the review of) regulations and "provide detailed information in writing to the agency."[144]
- Alaska's pilot Small Business Regulations Program included a full-time regulatory coordinator position in the Department of Commerce, Community, and Economic Development.
- Michigan's Office of Regulatory Reform (ORR), by statute "shall review proposed rules, coordinate processing of rules by agencies, work with the agencies to streamline the rule-making process, and consider efforts designed to improve public access to the rule-making process.[145]
- Colorado's Office of Policy, Research, and Regulatory Reform (OPRRR) reviews regulations at a relatively late stage and does not appear to do much advocacy. The Department of Regulatory Agencies (DORA) - the umbrella agency over OPRRR and all regulatory agencies – has recently launched a *Cutting Red Tape Initiative* that appears to be having considerable effect, both as advocacy and as education.

The advocacy function, as defined above, is the heart of state regulatory flexibility programs. It is a common thread among many of the reasonably well functioning state programs. It seems to have been a major goal of the SBA model legislation's provision to designate an agency to "advise and assist" in regulatory flexibility. Advocacy is generally integrated with review and/or guidance and training, and advocacy embodies the attitude needed to make the whole package effective.

2. Ombudsmen

The function of an ombudsman is described in the mission statement of Arizona's ombudsman, whose office (with a staff of six) is relatively large:

> The mission of the Arizona Ombudsman – Citizens' Aide is to improve the effectiveness, efficiency, and responsiveness of state government by receiving public complaints, investigating the administrative acts of state agencies and, when warranted, recommending fair and appropriate remedy. In addition, the Arizona Ombudsman – Citizens' Aide promotes open government throughout the state, by providing assistance and education to state and local government officials and members of the public, resolving disputes, and investigating complaints in matters relating to public access laws.[146]

A number of the agencies described above under advocacy integrate the functions of advocate and ombudsman. Other states with an ombudsman include[147] the following:

- Florida's ombudsman, in the Executive Office of the Governor, has duties that focus on review of existing rules, including:
  - Reviewing state agency rules that adversely or disproportionately impact businesses, particularly those relating to small and minority businesses.
  - Making recommendations on any existing or proposed rules to alleviate unnecessary or disproportionate adverse effects to businesses.
  - Working with each state agency in identifying such rules.[148]
- Hawaii has a Regulatory Ombudsman with authority to investigate and attempt to resolve complaints about actions of executive branch agencies.
- Indiana's small business ombudsman, in the Economic Development Corporation's small business division, has responsibility to:
  - Work with state agencies to permit increased enforcement flexibility, seek ways to consolidate forms and eliminate the duplication of paperwork, and monitor any outdated, ineffective, or overly burdensome information requests from state agencies to small businesses, and
  - Investigate and mediate matters regarding compliance by a small business.[149]
- Maine passed legislation in 2010 that established the Business Ombudsman Program.
- New Mexico's new Office of Business Advocacy has a "mission... to advance New Mexico business and enterprise with expansion, retention, and growth by resolving challenging bureaucratic, intergovernmental, and public policy problems [and by] help[ing] small businesses break through regulatory roadblocks."[150]
- Washington's Office of Regulatory Assistance (ORA) assists businesses in dealing with regulations, particularly those related to permitting.

Some states require each individual department to appoint its own small business ombudsman:

- In Kentucky each cabinet secretary is required by statute to appoint a small business ombudsman, who "shall:
  - Respond to inquiries from small businesses on administrative regulations and other regulatory matters; and
  - Provide information regarding the procedure for submitting comments on administrative regulations."[151]
- A recent Ohio executive order requires "business-facing agencies" to designate "a Regulatory Ombudsman to act as a problem-solving liaison between the agency and those affected by its rules and processes."[152]

Environmental agencies generally have an ombudsman because of Clean Air Act Requirements. Pennsylvania's Department of Environmental Protection (DEP) provided a job description.[153] Health and social service agencies also are particularly likely to have an ombudsman.

The ombudsman function is not directly connected with rulemaking. Many rules-particularly environmental rules - are sufficiently complex to require guidance, and agencies provide this service. An ombudsman's role has a substantial educational component, and the ombudsman may function as a first responder.

Implementation of regulations is a major issue in in itself. Surveys done as part of state regulatory reform efforts have consistently reported substantial numbers of complaints that enforcement and other implementing staff are lacking in knowledge and/or treat businesses badly.[154] Regulations may be implemented in ways the framers did not intend. If nothing else, the less discretion people have because of their low status in a bureaucratic hierarchy, the more rigidly then tend to interpret rules. The ombudsman position was designed for dealing with implementation issues.

3. Coordination

The functions of advocate and ombudsman are highly complementary. Both are part of a larger context of assistance to small businesses. Consequently they tend to be put into the small business division of the state commerce and economic development department.

Synergy comes from the fact that the advocate and the ombudsman are looking at the same regulations from different perspectives. An ombudsman is a valuable source of information and feedback that an advocate can use in working with an agency. This is especially clear in review of existing regulations: The ombudsman identifies problems, and the advocate works with the agency to fix them.

The ombudsman and the advocate both need working contacts and there are economies of scale in developing contacts together or sharing them and making referrals. This is particularly true in the business community, but they can use each other's agency contacts as well.

There are several examples of one office integrating both functions. Rhode Island is a clear case in point, but Indiana, Kentucky, and Oklahoma's Small Business Advocacy Committee also provide examples. There are also states (e.g., Arizona) where different entities were assigned different roles and work closely together. Either way, collaboration strengthens both functions.

B. Support for Advocates

Advocacy is the heart of regulatory flexibility. Education and persuasion, as well as legal requirements, are required to get agencies to adopt regulatory flexibility practices. Many of the entities that perform advocacy were established by statute. Some were established by the Governor. Most are located in executive branch agencies, and the small business development office in the commerce and economic department is a natural environment. Complementarities between regulatory advocacy and small business development are similar to those between advocate and ombudsman. It is quite natural, for example, that Rhode Island considers its regulatory flexibility program to be part of the state's economic development strategy.

Regulatory flexibility and related advocacy, however, are distinct from other elements of small business assistance. They need to be understood and supported as such. Without adequate support, the regulatory flexibility infrastructure may wither and disappear.

One danger is that the advocate will be diverted to other activities. Alaska is a cautionary tale. A position for a full-time regulatory coordinator was funded in the Department of Commerce, Community, and Economic Development for the new Small Business Regulations Program.[155] The program met resistance in the affected regulatory agencies,[156] and the coordinator was shifted to other activities that the Department deemed more fruitful. After three years, a report to the legislature glowed with accomplishments – none of which was related to regulatory flexibility.[157] The three-year pilot program never had the support to become established, and when the three-year pilot was over there essentially was nothing to reauthorize.

Arkansas appears to be a partial example of administrative neglect. The legislature adopted Governor Huckabee's executive order as the regulatory flexibility statute in 2007 (shortly after a new governor took office). The Economic Development Commission was the designated point of contact, and its Small and Minority Business Development Division has a web page with regulatory flexibility information.[158] A 2009 statute (Act 809) added a Regulatory Review Committee, appointed by the EDC Director, to which the rules are to be sent for review. A search of the Arkansas state "Regulatory Review Committee" turned up nothing. When contacted, the person "designated as the point of contact for regulatory flexibility" could provide no information and sounded completely unaware of the Regulatory Review Committee.

Delaware's Regulatory Flexibility Act, enacted in 1983, was one of very first state Acts. The provisions are slightly more extensive than SBA model legislation Section 3. This statute is unusual in that there is no review by an oversight agency, the Governor, or any legislative review committee. Sending proposed rules to the standing legislative committees for comment concerning potential impacts on small business is the only requirement, and this has fallen into disuse.[159] The law has faded away – with one exception. Staff of the Department of Natural Resources and Environmental Control reportedly rediscovered the regulatory flexibility law while working on litigation on an entirely different matter. The Secretary, recognizing that noncompliance might be a legal liability in some future action, adopted and implemented that law as departmental policy.[160]

Georgia's regulatory flexibility legislation is a slightly simplified version of Section 4(a) of SBA's model legislation, with a charge to select the least burdensome alternative. There is no executive branch oversight. No written analysis or reports of any kind are required. Only the NPRM, with no supporting documentation, must be sent to the legislature, to be considered by the appropriate standing committees. The statutes contain no review criteria, and review by the standing committee appears optional, although there are statutory procedures "in the event a standing committee... files an objection." There is no trace of regulatory flexibility.[161]

Iowa's regulatory flexibility legislation consists of Section 3 and Section 4(a) of SBA's model legislation. A "regulatory analysis" is required only after the NPRM is published and if requested.[162] The Governor has a statutory right to "rescind an adopted rule by executive order within seventy days of the rule becoming effective," but otherwise there is no executive branch oversight of rulemaking. The Administrative Rules Review Committee's review is "selective," and existing rules are to be reviewed "as time permits." There is no filing requirement for a regulatory analysis. Although the Rule-Writing Style Guide states "a concise summary of the Regulatory Analysis must be published in the IAB 20 days prior to the adoption of the rule," searches of the issues of the IAB for "regulatory analysis" consistently resulted in "no matches were found."[163]

Louisiana adopted Section 3 and Section 4(a) of SBA's model legislation and required an agency to "notify the Department of Economic Development" if an adverse small-business impact was found.[164] Guidance (published by the Secretary of State) is limited to how to indicate that impacts are "negligible" (Appendix B), and the sample Notice of Intent in the *LAC Handbook* has no Small Business Impact Statement (SBIS).[165] There is no other executive branch review, and there is no requirement to send an SBIS to the legislature for review. A review of 46 NPRMs over a three-month period found one with an SBIS noting impacts on small business and taking steps to minimize them, 14 with an SBIS stating that there were no (or no significant) impacts, and 31 that had no SBIS (or statement that one was not needed) at all. Several of the "no impact" rules clearly had impacts, and a few of them were quite substantial.

New Mexico provides another illustration of the way lack of departmental support and leadership can undermine a fledgling program. The Small Business Regulatory Advisory Commission (SBRAC) was the heart of New Mexico's Small Business Regulatory Relief Act. The Commission's statutory mandate was that of an advocate.[166] It was "administratively attached to the economic development department" with staff provided by the department. It seemed to report to everyone and no-one,[167] and apparently nobody provided the direction and support to make the statutory mandate operational. The Commission was made up of small businessmen, who tend to be busy, and it foundered – a process described in a February 2011 blog posting.[168]

North Dakota's rulemaking process is administered entirely by the Legislative Council. The regulatory flexibility statute is essentially Section 3 and Section 4(a) of SBA's model legislation,[169] but there is no sign of executive branch involvement other than the Attorney General's legal review. The only assistance to small businesses on the Division of Economic Development and Finance website is a set of links to the SBA and USDA websites for their programs. Guidance (by the Legislative Council) is essentially limited to a recap of statutory provisions.[170] Agency analyses[171] are cursory, not very informative, and often so poorly done that it is not credible that they are being seriously reviewed or used for any purpose.[172]

V. Public Involvement

A. Notification

In most cases, the first public notification of a rulemaking is publication of a Notice of Proposed Rulemaking (NPRM). Statutes require that the NPRM (or notice of hearing) before the rule is adopted or a hearing is held. Usually this is 30 to 45 days before the rule is adopted, occasionally longer,[173] and always at least 20 days. In a few states[174] the statute requires a notice of an earlier period of rule development or drafting.

1. The Register and Its Publisher

Publication of notices varies in so many different dimensions that it is difficult to characterize anything other than individual aspects of publication.

- In 33 states notices are published in a hard-copy state *Register*,[175] and in 16 states notices are published only on line.[176]
- An executive branch agency (usually the Secretary of State) publishes the *Register* (in both formats) in about half the states, and the legislative branch publishes in most

of the rest of the states. In the two states the Register is published by a private firm,[177] and availability is limited because access to even the on-line edition requires a subscription fee of $100 or more.

- In some states, this *Register* contains only notices related to rulemaking. In others, it includes all sorts of public notices; in Kansas, the *Register* is referred to as the "Official State Newspaper."
- Formats vary widely. In many states they follow well-defined forms; in others they are more freeform. The layout and the style, quality, and clarity of writing also variy considerably among states.
- Organization varies. Some hard-copy *Registers* are organized by agency; others by type of notice – both types of regulatory notices (NPRM, Final Rule, etc.) and overall (e.g., regulatory notices or executive orders). Purely on-line registers are usually more free-form and organized to allow searches.

Any of these factors can affect the ease of access to information on rulemaking.

2. Use of the Internet

The *Register* on Line

Every *Register* is published on line. This is the most important factor in access, although it may be taken for granted.[178] The distinguishing feature is the extent to which each takes advantage of the internet.

The most basic use of the internet is to publish the hard-copy edition in a straight pdf format.[179] This largely solves the accessibility problem and can be quite readable, but navigation on a screen is can be more difficult than it is with hard copy.

Many states embed hyperlinks in the text, which can serve at least three purposes. Hyperlinks can be used to:

- Navigate around the document;
- Go to an agency's website;
- Facilitate contact with agency contacts (if the listed contact has an email address); and
- Gain access to documents such as the full Code of Administrative Regulations (CAR) or other rulemaking documents.

Most pdf *Registers* do not take adequate advantage of hyperlinks, and doing so may involve changing the information in the notice (e.g., adding email addresses). The ability to access documents has real significance. *Register* publishers face a decision whether or not to include the full proposed rule, which can be very cumbersome. Using a hyperlink greatly simplifies the notice itself,[180] but it requires that the rule be on line somewhere – and many agencies do not post their proposed rules on their websites.

Some states supplement the pdf edition with an html edition. This facilitates navigation by having a single table of contents with links to each notice on a separate page. It also introduces the possibility of search. A lot of html versions, however, have illegibly small print.

States that use a purely on-line format have much greater flexibility. When the volumeby-volume constraint of hard copy is abandoned, searching among documents becomes possible. Rulemakings can be arrayed chronologically, by agency, or by status, and all the notices for one rulemaking can be pulled together. This can be helpful. Fragmenting elements of notices to facilitate searches, however, can almost make it more difficult to follow a single rulemaking. Use of on-line capability is evolving; some entirely on-line *Registers* still reflect structural constraints of hard-copy publication.

Different state *Registers* have a wide range of combinations of internet capabilities. Statutes or executive orders of some states require electronic submission and publication of notices.[181] Other *Registers* are barely on line.

Agency Websites

Perhaps the only generalization that can be made about agency websites is that the websites of environmental agencies are unsurpassed for usefulness. Informative, user-friendly agency websites have fairly similar design elements:

- A tab on the home page, clearly labeled something like Laws/Regulations, leads to a page with a link for laws and a link for regulations.
- The link for regulations leads to a page with links for the published CAR for that agency (usually on a different web site entirely) and for newer regulations.
- The latter link lists regulations as proposed or recently adopted – sometimes with a third intermediate stage, depending on the rulemaking process.
- The links for individual rules can lead to anything up to the full cumulative docket, as well as the current status of the rulemaking.

Most agencies – even the ones that do have web pages on regulations – do not come close to this standard. Location of the right web page can be obscure.[182] Many agencies list only existing regulations in the CAR – not proposed rules. When there are pages for proposed rules, they often contain no more than the NPRM and the text of the rule.

Some states have tried to improve the situation with either statutory or administrative requirements.

- In Hawaii "Administrative Rules Proposed Changes" is a page on the Lt. Governor's website, which has a hyperlink to websites of agencies (and some divisions within agencies) under 17 Hawaii Administrative Code (HAC) Title. Each agency is supposed to post its own proposed rules. This was not entirely successful.[183]
- Colorado's Department of Regulatory Agencies has achieved a logical, useful format for accessing information on regulations that all agencies use,[184] but there is no consistency as to content.
- Washington statute states that "within existing resources, each state agency shall maintain a web site that contains the agency's rule-making information" and adds specific requirements.[185] Agencies tend to comply by using hyperlinks to the *Register* website.

The *Register* web site and the agency website should complement each other. One should be able to find out about a proposed rule starting on either website, travel between them easily, as appropriate, and find any information on one. That rarely occurs. The whole system is weakened by incompleteness of agency websites, which are natural sites for posting more detailed documents such as the full text of a proposed rule and impact statements,. NPRMs are available, but the sort of information one might want for commenting often is not.

3. Content and Format of NPRMs

Most state statutes require NPRMs to contain at least a fairly standard set of information, and many require additional elements as well. Such information includes:

- The name of the agency;
- Type of rule (regular, emergency, etc.) and intended action (adopt, amend, or repeal);
- Identifying information (Code of Administrative Rules (CAR) title and number);
- Reference to statutory authority and/or the portion of the Code being implemented;
- A description of the terms or substance of the intended action or a description of the subjects and issues involved;
- Public hearing information, including:
    - Whether a public hearing has been scheduled,
    - If so, the date, time, and place of the meetings,[186] or
    - If not, the actions necessary to require a hearing;
- Instructions for submitting written comments and the last day of the comment period;
- Contact information for a person at the agency who can provide more information, a copy of the proposed rule, and/or other documents; and
- Additional information, such as the following items that are required by at least a few states:
    - A summary or the full text of the proposed rule,
    - "How interested persons may review the text of the rule,"
    - A summary of the fiscal note (impacts on state and local governments),
    - The estimated cost to the agency for enforcement of the proposed regulation,
    - Results of a determination of whether small businesses will be affected,
    - An initial regulatory flexibility analysis or summary of the economic impact statement,
    - Estimates of other specific impacts (e.g., employment or housing),
    - The relationship to other regulations and justification of any overlap,
    - The relationship to federal laws and regulations,
    - The current status of the rule and projected future dates (e.g., adoption or effective date), and/or
    - An explicit and encouraging invitation for comments.

The key element in the NPRM is the "description of the terms or substance of the intended action or a description of the subjects and issues involved."[187] Ideally, this description would briefly summarize the purpose and need for the rule, what the rule will change (subject) and how (terms or substance), and consequences (effects) – both intended and collateral. In most of the simpler rules, this could be done in a paragraph consisting of a few sentences.

In some states this is accomplished reasonably well. In many of the states the description is incomplete, focusing mostly on the purpose, subject, or terms without filling out the whole picture. Many state statutes do not require a full picture. Ideally, the discussion of collateral effects (which is rarely included) should be enough to give the reader some idea of what to expect in an impact statement.

Attempts at standardized format do not necessarily help because rules can be quite different. In some cases the key description is reduced to little more than a topic sentence. This is adequate if there is a separate summary of the rule, but not very helpful if the only alternative is the full text (particularly when the full text is not published with the notice). Standardization should promote clarity, but sometimes it takes the form of boilerplate. Relatively simple information such as the date, time, and place for a hearing or instructions for written comments can be obscured by being embedded in a paragraph of turgid prose.[188]

Optimization of a pdf edition of a hard-copy *Register* entails full use of hyperlinks and separate linked availability of larger documents and other information (e.g., status of the rulemaking). Other ancillary changes would also be needed. Documents referenced in a notice must be on line for hyperlinks to work. Agency contacts' email addresses need to be included consistently, and urls (which can be copied from hard-copy) need to be added for referenced documents.[189] These relatively modest changes might be the occasion for rethinking format and making other editorial and stylistic improvements.

Leaving the hard-copy format is a far more substantial change. The benefits are less a matter of access to individual notices and the supporting materials as they are compiling the documents or chronology[190] for a single rulemaking and searching across rulemakings. Many states that have converted to electronic notices have also found an e-format efficient for sending the documents between executive departments or the legislative branch.

4. Documentation

In many states the small business impact statement or other impact statement is required to be completed at the time of the NPRM. Some statutes have no NPRM requirements about such documents; some require a summary; a few require inclusion of a full document. An alternative is to require that the document be sent to anyone who requests it. In some states impact statements are completed later and published with some other notice, in which case the same choices may arise. In some states impact analyses are not published but are required to be sent to a limited audience – usually the legislature or other review committee.

Large documents – particularly full texts of proposed rules and impact statements – do not fit well in NPRMs (or later notices), although summaries do. To the extent statutes allow discretion, publishers of hard-copy notices are faced with the choice of having concise notices or presenting complete information. Sometimes texts of proposed rules are included only if they do not exceed a certain length. Publishers usually default to the simplest choice; impact statements are included in notices by a relatively few states. Yet they rarely are found on line anywhere but in a notice.

5. Notification of Registered Persons

Sending a NPRM and other notices to persons who have "timely" requested such notices is an almost universal requirement of state statutes. Such notification is done far more efficiently electronically than on paper – as is the requesting. In many states an on-line registration is available, either on an agency website or a central one, such as the *Register* or the site of the agency (often the Secretary of State) that provides information about rulemaking to the public. Centralized registration allows requesting notices from multiple agencies. There are more advanced systems. Some states offer subscriptions to RSS (Rich Site Summary) feeds.[191] Hawaii has developed its own RegAlert system for comments.[192] On-line registration is a minimal best practice, but many states and agencies do not offer it.[193]

Many states also have requirements to notify the businesses affected by a proposed rule. This is phrased in various ways, such as notifying industry organizations or "interested persons"[194] and publication of notices in "appropriate trade, industry, or professional publications." In contrast to the "timely request" provision, this requirement has a pre-internet flavor and appears to presume that the agency needs to seek out such entities. Standing registration of trade groups is much simpler with the internet, and it is easy for an organization to forward notices – or send its own alerts – to its members.

6. Other Forms of Notification

Some states have developed additional forms of notification or publicity about rulemaking. Examples include the following:

- The Illinois Joint Committee on Administrative Rules publishes a weekly newsletter, *Illinois Regulation (The Flinn Report)*, which contains:
- Summaries of new regulations adopted by agencies in the past week;
- Summaries of regulations proposed by agencies in the past week, starting the 45- day First Notice comment period;
- A list of Second Notices, which start the JCAR review period; and
- Contact information for questions/requests for copies/comments on proposed rules.

There is a flag (r) designating rules of special interest to small entities.[195]

- The Ohio Business Gateway is a website that compiles information and links of potential interest to Ohio businesses. Its Regulatory Reform page features:
    - A sign-up for the E-Notification System,
    - Rule searches by criteria or rule number, and
    - Agency Tools for Rule Review (directives and forms).[196]

General paper notification is still required in some states. A few require publication in newspapers,[197] which may involve a short version of the NPRM. Nevada requires physical posting.[198]

7. Public Outreach

The *Register* and other statutory notification generally reach only those who are already somewhat familiar with the regulatory process. Some states require additional notice and or outreach with respect to individual rules prior to the NPRM (discussed further below). Many states provide background information for the public on a website or printed materials. These material often resemble, and sometimes overlap, background information about the rulemaking process provided to agency staff. Some of the more extensive efforts, which collectively include virtually all of the individual techniques used, are summarized below:

- The Colorado Department of Regulatory Agency's Office of Policy, Research and Regulatory Reform (OPRRR) has a website that includes:

   - A page on Colorado Regulatory Structure that includes a narrative and flowchart of the rulemaking process,
   - A page about the rule review process;
   - A FAQ page with information about regulations and receiving DORA regulatory notices,
   - Links for subscribing to agency notices,
   - A calendar of hearings,
   - A search facility for proposed rules and regulations, which leads to status information, detailed descriptions, hearing summaries, and other information,
   - Information about, and a comment line for, sunset reviews, and
   - Yet more links for subscribing to agency notices.[199]
- The Arizona Secretary of State's website has a number of other resources to encourage public participation in rulemaking, including:
   - An introduction to rulemaking, in a FAQ format,
   - A link to a page on Public Participation in the Rulemaking Process, which is also printed in the front material of each issue of the Register,
   - A list of notices published in the register (year-to-date),
   - A list of other filings (year-to-date), and
   - A list of public meetings (prospective).[200]

The Arizona Governor's Regulatory Review Council (GRRC) has an extensive website of its own, which focuses on public participation and provides:

   - Background information on rulemaking and the Council's role;
   - A list of rules received by the Council and awaiting review (during a 60-day period);
   - GRRC meeting agendas (including an archive); and
   - Five-year review reports.[201]
- The California Office of Administrative Law website includes a useful Public Participation page, which includes sections on:
   - Opportunities for participation in a rulemaking and
   - How to participate, including a link to a detailed, 25-page booklet, and
   - A link for subscribing for notices.[202]
- The Washington Governor's Office of Regulatory Assistance (ORA) website includes:
   - A narrative description of the rulemaking process and
   - A page of links to the rulemaking web pages of agencies that have them, which include notices, some additional status information, and regulatory agendas.[203]
- The Utah Division of Administrative Rules provides considerable additional information about rulemaking on its website, including:
   - The website has a page explaining administrative rules.
   - Another page walks through the rulemaking process and is supplemented by flow charts.
   - An Administrative Rule Hearings Calendar page includes links to the Notices of Proposed Rules.

    - A page on the Administrative Rules Review Committee provides minutes and agendas for meetings and review assignments of Committee members.
    - A Rulemaking FAQ page targets the public concerned about regulations.
    - RSS feeds – directly on the web site and by subscription - with several different emphases,[204] updated when the new issue of the Bulletin is published.[205]
- Virginia public outreach is part of an integrated system, which is discussed below.

8. An Integrated System: Virginia's Regulatory Town Hall

In many states the information is divided between agency websites, a *Register* website, and possibly other websites (e.g., a review agency or the Secretary of State). Virginia has integrated information about and access to the rulemaking process into one website, the Regulatory Town Hall. The home page of the Town Hall[206] presents the user with tabs or links for:

- Frequently asked questions about the rulemaking process;
- A comprehensive search tool;[207]
- Registration for an Email notification service;
- A comment forum where one can view and enter comments;[208]
- Additional resources, including a Town Hall User Manual;[209]
- A browser for regulations;[210]
- A browser for regulatory actions currently being created, amended, or repealed;[211]
- A list of all scheduled public meetings;[212]
- Guidance documents, by agency;[213]
- PowerPoint presentations for agency regulatory coordinator training, and guidance document training;
- Links (directly or indirectly) to other pages, such as the *Virginia Register of Regulations*.

The Town Hall User Manual provides a menu for accessing information on the website. It is organized into:

- Rulemaking in Virginia - A guide to the regulatory process;[214]
- irginia Regulatory Town Hall Website[215]
- Basic Functions[216]
- Working with Regulatory Actions *(details for state agency users)*[217]
- Advanced Functions *(details for state agency users)*[218]

The record for a current regulatory action includes a VAC citation, a one-sentence summary of the action, the stage where the action currently is and links to:

- Detailed information about stage,[219] including date submitted, date review was completed, and result for each stage that has been completed;
- Links to documents that have been completed;[220] and
- Complete contact information.

The Virginia Regulatory Town Hall is an informational tour de force that sets a standard unequaled in any other state.

B. Comments and Hearings

Statutory requirements of different states for comments and hearings on rules are similar in structure. Alabama's statute provides an exceedingly succinct summary:

> Prior to the adoption, amendment, or repeal of any rule, the agency shall... afford all interested persons reasonable opportunity to submit data, views, or arguments, orally or in writing. The agency shall consider fully all written and oral submissions respecting the proposed rule. Upon adoption of a rule, the agency, if conflicting views are submitted on the proposed rule, shall issue a concise statement of the principal reasons for and against its adoption, incorporating therein its reasons for overruling any considerations urged against its adoption.[221]

1. Written Comments and Comment Periods

Information on submitting written comments is a standard part of the NPRM. The notice itself provides background. The key information is where to submit the comments and the date the comment period ends. Most often it is 30 days; sometimes as little as 20 days; and sometimes longer. In some states the comment period ends with the hearing; in others it extends beyond, occasionally with the stated purpose of providing a rebuttal period (for agencies replying for the record as well as for the public). Most states only handle comments by mail. States with better developed websites[222] may offer on-line submission as an option.

While most states are terse and formal in invitations for comments, some states are more expansive in their requests. Oklahoma (among several others) asks for data. Florida's statute suggests fully developed regulatory alternatives.[223]

Written comments are submitted to the agency promulgating the rule. Some states also provide for submission to a review commission[224] as part of the rulemaking process. In a few instances, the commission may also hold its own hearings during the rulemaking process or as part of its review.

A number of states require each agency to designate a rules coordinator or liaison. At a minimum, this provides a point of contact with broader experience in rulemaking than the rule under consideration. Having a designated coordinator can also facilitate a working relationship between a small business advocate and the agency. A coordinator may also take a more active role in the commenting process. In Indiana, for example:

- The coordinator serves as a liaison to small businesses subject to the regulation, providing them with guidance on:
  - Requirements imposed by the rule,
  - How the agency determines or measures compliance,
  - Any penalties, sanctions, or fines for noncompliance, and
  - Any other questions or concerns of small businesses with respect to the rule; and
- The coordinator records all small business comments, questions, and complaints.

2. Hearings

Requirements for Holding Hearings

One of the basic decisions in a rulemaking is whether to hold a hearing or not. Many rules are so minor that a hearing would be a pointless waste of resources. For other rules a hearing is an essential part of the public comment and participation process. Statutes may require a hearing,[225] they may explicitly leave the decision to the agency,[226] or they may include a conditional requirement for a hearing.

A fairly common approach is to allow an agency to publish a NPRM without a scheduled hearing, but with notice that a hearing will be held if the agency receives a timely request for on from 25 persons or an association with at least 25 members.[227] In some states a hearing also must be held if such a request is made by a governmental subdivision; another state agency; a review committee such as the Small Business Regulatory Review Committee (executive branch) or the Administrative Rules Review Committee (legislative); or a committee of the legislature.

The Governor may also direct holding a hearing. Other provisions of various state statutes that address this issue of how to determine when to hold a hearing[228] include:

- Other minimum requirements for requesting a hearing;[229]
- A requirement that persons desiring to be heard at the hearing must notify the agency at least five working days before the scheduled hearing, with the proviso that the agency may cancel the meeting and proceed directly to written comments if it has received no notices;
- Characteristics of the proposed rule;[230]
- An exemption from hearings for certain types of rules, such as:
  - An emergency rule,
  - A rule dealing only with internal agency affairs, or
  - A rule where the agency has no discretion, as when the rule is directly required by a court order, statute, or federal rule.

Process

There is usually a minimum advanced notice for a hearing – typically 15 to 20 days. If the original NPRM did not include a notice of a hearing, a separate notice must be published. Specifics vary but typically include the following:

- The hearing is usually chaired by an agency head (or designee), by a hearing officer, or by an administrative law judge.
- An agency representative participates to make a presentation on the rulemaking and respond to questions and comments.
- Members of the public may comment and otherwise state their positions.[231]
- Other testimony may be presented.
- A record of the hearing is required, although whether it is published, otherwise released, or merely retained by the agency varies.

In addition to notice and outreach requirements, some states emphasize the importance of hearings as a means of public participation with statutory requirements that are more policy statements than operational directives. For example:

- Illinois requires that agencies utilize "special hearing or comment procedures to reduce the cost or complexity of participation in the rulemaking by small businesses, not for profit corporations, or small municipalities."
- Vermont requires, as part of filing a proposed rule, "an explanation of the strategy for maximizing public input on the proposed rule."

3. Reports

Hearing Report and Responses to Comments

Most states require a post- hearing report. Who files the report, who receives it, the form it takes, and its comments vary considerably.

State statutes require an agency to "consider" comments "fully" or "carefully." Most often it is the agency that prepares the report, which generally reflects these considerations. The report may be filed with a board that reviews regulations or with the legislature, it may be part of the order that the agency issues promulgating the regulation, or it may simply be "published" or retained. It does not appear to be intended to be grist for further general comment by the public and is not usually for public dissemination. An agency report usually contains:

- Summaries of comments received and agency responses to the comments;
- Other evidence and information received;
- A summary of the action taken (or ordered) by the agency; and
- A discussion of changes since the proposed rule,[232] including:
  - An explanation of changes that were made, and/or
  - An explanation of why suggested alternatives were not adopted.

Other elements that may be part of the report may include:

- All written materials submitted to the agency;
- A description of how the opinions or comments from affected small businesses were solicited; and/or
- Information on the numbers of people who attended and testified at the hearing.

A report written by hearing officer who conducted the hearing is sent to the agency. In New Jersey, the hearing officer "shall have the responsibility to make recommendations to the agency regarding the adoption, amendment or repeal of a rule," and the recommendations are made public.

The process is more formal if the hearing is conducted by an administrative law judge.[233] An administrative law judge makes findings concerning the need and reasonableness of proposed regulations. Other findings may include whether procedures have been followed and whether changes in the rule since its proposal have been "substantial." The administrative law judge will then advise the agency of any defects that need to be corrected. If the agency is not willing to make these changes, it must submit the unmodified regulation (with a copy of the written report) to the legislature for review, advice, and comment.

4. Changes in Draft Regulation

A substantial change in a draft rule after the NPRM raises the issue of how to allow public comment on the changed provisions. This is also a concern of legislative reviewers who have been supplied with the original proposed draft. Under such circumstances, statutes may:

- Require the agency to extend the comment period;[234]
- Require publication of a notice of revised rulemaking;[235] or
- Require the agency to re-propose the amended regulation.

Many states have a requirement for an agency to explain its decision. A summary of "the principal reasons for and against [the rule's] adoption" is a fairly common turn of phrase. Some states more explicitly require a summary of recommendations or objections about the proposed rule that were made in written or oral comments "together with an explanation of how the proposed action has been changed to accommodate each objection or recommendation, or the reasons for making no change."[236] Alternatively, the agency must explain the changes it has made. This statement is not part of the rule making. Most statutes specify that this is done after the rule has been adopted, although "at the time it adopts or amends a... regulation" is used once. In most cases this summary is provided at the request of an "interested" person, although in tow states it appears to be automatic.

5. Extent of Public Participation

It is difficult to assess the level of public participation through comments. Virginia is the only state that makes comments available in real time, and most hearing reports are not available. When comments were published (and in Virginia), they were meager. Except for environmental rules, very few rules had more than a handful of comments, and many had none. Where hearings were mandatory and a report was published, many hearings were reported as cancelled because nobody came.

C. Pre-Proposal Involvement

Comments and hearings are the core of the public participation process set forth in most Administrative Procedures Acts. Their timing, however, is not very suitable for public participation. A proposed rule is published essentially for review and approval purposes, and proposed rules are no longer very malleable. Development of the rule occurs before publication. There are inherent disincentives to an agency – and can be significant penalties – for making substantive changes at this point. Consideration of small-business issues, if not integrated into the rulemaking in the developmental stage, can result in substantive changes.

1. Statutory Provisions on Early Involvement

Some state statutes attempt to address this problem by suggesting and emphasizing earlier public involvement. California's statute states the objective:

> In order to increase public participation and improve the quality of regulations, state agencies proposing to adopt regulations shall, prior to publication of the notice [of proposed action] involve parties who would be subject to the proposed regulations in public discussions regarding those proposed regulations

Advance Notification

Eight states require agencies to publish a regulatory agenda. "The regulatory agenda must contain information for each rulemaking that the agency is considering proposing, but for which it has not published a notice of proposed rulemaking."[237] Regulatory agendas are published once or twice a year. Publication is usually in the *Register*, although individual agencies may publish the agenda on line (where it can be updated continually).

A few states open up the rulemaking prior to completion of a proposed rule by publishing an earlier notice.

- South Carolina has an initial drafting period. Agencies are required to publish a notice that includes a synopsis of what the agency plans to draft. Interested persons may submit written comments during this period before the rule is proposed.
- Florida agencies publish a notice of rule development. During the rule development period, an agency may hold regional workshops – and must do so if requested in writing by any affected person. Workshops may be facilitated or mediated by a neutral third person, or other dispute resolution alternatives may be used.
- Nevada also uses early workshops.
- Minnesota requires, and New Jersey allows, a pre-NPRM notice for comments.

Prescriptions for Public Participation

Pre-proposal public participation is generally described in several states:

> An agency may use informal conferences and consultations as means of obtaining the viewpoints and advice of interested persons with respect to contemplated rule-making. An agency may also appoint committees of experts or interested persons or representatives of the general public to advise it with respect to any contemplated rule-making.[238]

A Pennsylvania executive order emphasized that "regulations shall be drafted and promulgated with early and meaningful input from the regulated community" and provided pre-drafting and drafting guidelines.[239] Hawaii made the advisory committees more formal but also issued an open-ended directive.

> Each department may establish an administratively attached advisory committee on small business, whose members are appointed by the department. The members shall... have experience or knowledge of the effect of regulation by those departments on the formation, operation, or expansion of a small business... Each agency shall develop its own... creative procedures for the solicitation of comments from affected small businesses during the drafting or development of proposed rules.

Other state statutes have some similar provisions that use somewhat different language. None does more than authorize; the operative word is "may." "Shall" is used only for the directive to be creative in involving the public.

Several states require explanation of methods used to involve small businesses as part of the regulatory flexibility analysis.[240] Oregon puts the directive - "appoint an advisory council and obtain public input" – in its guidance and then requires a response – "How were small businesses involved in the development of this rule?" – on the form for Statement of Need and Fiscal Impact.

2. Negotiated/Consensus Rules

Several states[241] provide for negotiated rulemaking or consensus rules. A consensus rule is a process in which all interested parties and the agency seek consensus on the content of a rule. If a consensus is reached, most of the usual procedural and analytical requirements may be waived. New York seems to use this process to simplify development of relatively uncontroversial rules, and requirements are often waived. Other states have differing criteria.[242] Nebraska uses negotiated rulemaking as a "process to resolve controversial issues prior to the commencement of the formal rulemaking process," which "is not a substitute for the requirements of the Administrative Procedure Act but may be used as a supplemental procedure to permit the direct participation of affected interests in the development of new rules."

Nebraska has a rather structured process for negotiated rulemaking, which is prescribed by statute.

- The agency director first determines whether negotiated rulemaking is appropriate.[243]
- The agency then publishes a notice[244] and assesses the comments and applications to determine whether a committee can be formed that will adequately represent the interests of the persons that will be significantly affected by the rule.
- The negotiated rulemaking committee meets to "consider the matter proposed by the agency for consideration and... attempt to reach consensus concerning a proposed rule and any other matter the committee determines is relevant to the proposed rule."
- Negotiations may reach one of two outcomes:
  - If a committee achieves consensus, it sends the agency a report containing the proposed rule (which the agency is not required to accept).
  - If a committee does not reach a consensus, it sends the agency a report "specifying areas in which the committee reached consensus and the issues that remain unresolved," along with any other information, recommendations, or materials that the committee considers appropriate.

3. Informal Participation

The influence of these structured provisions is not clear. They have not been widely adopted, and they are not necessarily used with or for small businesses. To a considerable degree, getting in early on a rulemaking requires pre-existing contact with an agency and a relatively informal flow of information. This, in turn, means networking and building relationships. A standing small business advisory committee or a pool of business contacts on which an agency can (and will) draw can provide such relationships. Advocates and agency small business liaisons also can play vital roles as intermediaries.

VI. Regulatory Flexibility Analysis

A. Requirements For Analysis

Federal Requirements

For "any proposed regulation that may have an adverse impact on small businesses," SBA's model legislation requires an agency to scope out the impacts and describe "any less intrusive or less costly alternative methods of achieving the purpose of the proposed regulation" (Section 3). Then "the agency shall, where consistent with health, safety, environmental, and economic welfare... consider, without limitation... methods of reducing the impact of the proposed regulation on small businesses" (Section 4(a)). The description of regulatory flexibility analysis and most of the language are derived from the federal Regulatory Flexibility Act (RFA). The RFA, however, makes a distinction not found in legislation adopted by most states.

> Each initial regulatory flexibility analysis shall also contain a description of any significant alternatives to the proposed rule which accomplish the stated objectives of applicable statutes and *which minimize any significant economic impact* of the proposed rule on small entities. [emphasis added] § 603 (c)

The RFA divides regulatory impact analysis into an initial and a final stage. If an agency certifies that a rule will not have a significant impact on a substantial number of small entities, a final regulatory flexibility analysis is not required. State legislation does not have this checkpoint. Whatever the trigger for a regulatory flexibility analysis is, it applies to the whole process.

State Requirements

Many states[245] use either adopted SBA's language or an equivalent phrase – "affects small business" or has an "effect on small business" – as the trigger for regulatory flexibility analysis. An agency in any state that has adopted the SBA model provisions of Section 3 and Section 4(a) must consider – not just describe – regulatory flexibility alternatives whenever a small business is affected. Yet many – probably most – state regulations that affect small businesses do so only in relatively inconsequential ways.

Some states[246] at least specify that there must be "adverse" effects or "impacts" on small business for consideration of regulatory flexibility alternatives to be required. New York and New Jersey use peculiar wording that turns around the burden of proof.[247] Some states expand somewhat on the idea of impact.[248]

Other states introduce some sort of threshold for further action that goes beyond whether small businesses are affected or impacted. Some state[249] statutes introduce the idea of severity of the impact, and/or indicate that there must be an assessment process, which determines that further action is warranted. Some states specify an actual aggregate impact threshold as a trigger for regulatory flexibility analysis or some other action,[250] and three states set a threshold in terms of impact per entity.[251] In some states agencies develop their own terminology.[252] Three states[253] introduce the concept of disproportional impacts on small business as the trigger or purpose of the analysis. Washington uses a concept of a "significant rule."[254]

There are relatively few states in which there is any sort of clear indicator when (or that) a full regulatory flexibility analysis is not required. Missouri's $500 aggregate threshold illustrates the point. As a threshold, it seems absurdly low, but it would exempt many state regulations for which a regulatory flexibility analysis is pointless. In fact, this threshold comes from an executive order in which the governor was simply trying to define "economic impact on small business" in operational terms. Without some clear threshold (or some reasonable supervisory interpretation of the requirements), agency staff will go through the motions for every regulation. The danger is that regulatory flexibility requirements may come to be seen as the boy who cried "wolf."

California is the exception. The threshold for requiring a full regulatory flexibility analysis[255] is so high that it almost guarantees that one will not be done: It is required

> If a state agency... makes an initial determination that the action may have a significant, statewide adverse economic impact directly affecting business, including the ability of California businesses to compete with businesses in other states.[256]

B. Timing of Analysis

In most cases, the regulatory flexibility analysis, economic impact analysis, fiscal note, and other analytical documents must be complete and available (in some sense) by the time the NPRM is published. In a few states[257] a regulatory flexibility analysis may be required during the comment period, which is too late for effective analysis. Consideration of small business impacts should be part of a rulemaking at the outset for several fundamental reasons:

- Once aggregate data have been collected for analysis, it is not possible to break out small entities for analysis without going back and collecting new disaggregated data.
- Development of alternatives is easier before a rule has been semi-finalized for proposal.
- As the provisions of a regulation become more clearly defined, accommodate small business needs tends to require larger and more basic changes.

The 2011 report of a Colorado "Cutting Red Tape Initiative" summarizes the timing issues. Although written with respect to cost-benefit analysis (which may be ordered after the NPRM), it applies equally to regulatory flexibility analysis.

> Agencies should make the effort to determine the impact and cost implications on the regulated businesses and other stakeholders well before any proposed changes are formulated for implementation. Further, the process for a cost-benefit analysis should involve the affected businesses and stakeholder interests early on in the process of analysis, since these parties are in a good position to help project impacts and compliance costs. There seemed to be a consensus among the Roundtable groups that the current provisions for cost-benefit analysis under C.R.S. 12-4-103 are generally too little, too late. As presently structured, a cost-benefit analysis is not required until a rule has already been crafted, and proposed for implementation. Requiring a cost-benefit analysis effectively requires the agency to look well outside the scope of its proposal, including the consideration of viable alternatives. Unless the submitting agency has already

undertaken such an analysis, the practicality and utility of a cost-benefit analysis at this point in the rule making process is questionable, and its value often negligible.[258]

This statement highlights the importance of early public participation. Public participation usually occurs after the rule has been proposed and the regulatory flexibility analysis has been completed. That limits the potential for meaningful public input into the analysis.

Education and fostering of a suitable agency institutional culture also are critical for successful regulatory flexibility analysis. Advocates and review commissions that perform advocacy tend to spend the first couple of years building up contacts with agencies so that they can be involved early in the process. Without an institutional culture attuned to regulatory flexibility analysis, an agency is likely to put it off and/or do only a cursory job.

C. Agency Performance

Examples of agency analysis often were not available.[259] In most states where they were, they were available as part of notices published in the *Register.* For any such state, review covered all of the issues of the Register over a period of three to six months, which contained several dozen notices. In most cases a limit on the number of notices from any one was set, because the analyses tended to be quite similar.

Format

The actual small business impact statements usually do no more than follow whatever form has been prescribed (if there is one). The forms rarely do much more than cover the statutory requirements – often in question form or otherwise edited (see Appendix B). Requirements to do the analysis at all often depend (as discussed above) on some very broad condition, such as "small businesses are affected." The simplest response is often to state that there are no such effects – or costs. Wisconsin was unique in that it invoked the standard of no significant impact on a substantial number of small businesses.

Analysis

In most states, many - sometimes nearly all - rules reportedly have no real costs to consider. Sometimes an explanation is given;[260] sometimes not. In some states, where the form allows a yes/no response, the response is often just "no," or N/A, or a dash, or a blank. In some states there are patterns that suggest that very little thought is given to the question.[261] In other states, there is a pattern of skipping the analysis (or at least the reporting) entirely.[262] Among other things, this suggests a lack of substantive review or quality control.

Where compliance activities and costs are discussed, the depth of analysis varies widely. Often the conclusion is that there are no costs or that the costs are "minimal," and frequently this appeared probable.[263] In some cases costs were dismissed with a questionable analytical premise.[264] Costs are often described in terms such as "some impacts," "indeterminate," or "no basis for quantifying economic impacts." Occasionally this was explained by noting that costs would be highly variable. In some cases compliance activities are described without much sense of the scope of the burden.[265] In some cases compliance activities were described, but the analysis concluded with a statement that there were no costs.[266]

Some impact statements did include estimates of costs, but it is a general commentary on the lack of depth of analysis that use of the statutory definition of "small" was never observed. Estimated costs were usually no more than $150 per entity. Many of these costs were well-defined fees of a particular activity, such as taking an examination, filing for a permit, a fee for commercial use of natural resources, or professional licensure fees.[267] In a few instances, however, the impacts were much higher, but an analysis or explanation was not offered.[268] Some blind spots that were found in several states.

- In some states, out-of-state businesses are – by definition – not small.[269]
- Regulations on reimbursement for medical care were addressed in fiscal notes but not in small business impact analyses.[270]
- While costs of exams for certification or licensure were often estimated, costs of training, which could be much higher, were not.[271]

In a basic sense, the best performance meant simply providing all of the information required with adequate explanations. There was considerable variety within and among states.[272]

Environmental departments consistently did the most thorough analyses. The conscientiousness with which analysis is performed shows up most readily in the rules where analysis is not required.[273] It does not take much time or effort to write a sentence or two to provide a clear explanation of the reasons that an analysis is not needed, but many rule writers in most states did not even try.

Alternatives

The use of regulatory flexibility alternatives was spotty. Good examples were found. Two generalizations can be made:

- Alternatives were concentrated by state. In most states, they were rarely discussed and virtually never adopted; other states discussed and adopted them fairly routinely.
- When regulatory flexibility alternatives were used, they were not limited to cases where large impacts made them essential. They also were used to reduce burdens that would not necessarily exceed thresholds of "significance."[274]

Wisconsin provides an illustration of both points. Of 59 notices reviewed, 52 reportedly had no (or no significant) impact on small businesses. Six of the remaining seven included some kind of measure to reduce burdens on small businesses, most of which were tailored to meet specific concerns or issues.[275] One analysis noted that there could be significant impacts for some small businesses, but the rest were no more specific than "some impact."

A phase-in of requirements, delayed effective date, or grandfathering existing businesses was the measure most commonly used to reduce small-business impacts. Some sort of performance standard was sometimes used. Exemption was generally disfavored, although tiering of fees was observed.

In some instances no specific alternatives were mentioned, but there was a description of how the agency had worked with industry groups to minimize impacts. As the examples cited illustrate, alternatives tended to be fairly situation-specific.[276]

Some small-business impact statements included discussion of why regulatory alternatives were not adopted. With the exception of some very generic disclaimers, in most states such discussions were usually less frequent than actual adoption of alternatives. Usually the reason was one of a short list of explanations.[277] The statutes prescribe a fairly precise process of identifying and considering alternatives, and presumably these are then included in the small business impact statement. In practice, alternatives may have been developed more informally and either incorporated or discarded at an earlier stage. Small business impact statements are an imperfect indicator of this process, although it does appear that agencies that file complete and informative impact statements also are more likely than agencies that do not to develop alternatives informally.

A few states adopted an entirely different sort of measure to minimize impacts. As was discussed above, Minnesota has a statutory exemption provision based on impacts, and Hawaii and Washington have a first-offense waiver for minor infractions.

Comments

The vast majority of state regulations do not produce the sort of impacts that are amenable to regulatory flexibility. Most state regulatory flexibility statutes, however, apply to all regulations that have any kind of effect on small businesses. If an agency tries to follow through, the results can be absurd.[278] Guidance documents often provide a basic yes/no entry question but provide little guidance other than the statute beyond that, but many agencies in many states appear to respond by doing the minimum that will get by on all regulations.

In some states there is little or no quality control on small-business impact analysis. That is clear from the number of missing responses and documents. Agency reviewers let all kinds of things slip by[279] (and often it most likely really does not matter). Reviewers outside the agency usually are concerned with whether an analysis was done, not how it was done. There are exceptions where information is fairly complete and well presented, but these only highlight the lack of standards in most states (environmental agencies excepted).

Uniform requirements and lowered review standards make a poor environment for regulatory flexibility analysis. If it usually a pointless exercise, it will not receive priority and bad habits may set in.[280]

The danger lies in missing rules where regulatory flexibility analysis would make a difference and where there are opportunities for alternatives. Developing regulatory flexibility alternatives is something of a practiced skill, which is not enhanced by putting energies into rules where it cannot be used. Major impacts do not seem to be the problem; they probably will be identified. The concern is with rules that have lesser costs that are not identified or – if identified – are not explored.

Identifying rules with potential for regulatory flexibility improvement requires focus and prioritizing, and that (in turn) requires education and leadership. The best sources of education are advocates and the small business community. If they put a priority on assessment of small business impacts, reviewers have the potential to play a role, because they can provide feedback. Without leadership, regulatory flexibility can fade away entirely. The small business impact statements (and related documents) reviewed here suggest that the Cheshire Cat is active in many states.

VII. Review of New Rules

A. Introduction: Pre-Approval and Post-Approval Review

Prior to the NPRM, development of a rule is largely an internal agency. After the NPRM the proposed rule is available for general review, up until its publication and effective date – and even after in some cases. Final approval[281] by the agency, however, is a key milestone, at which the nature of review changes qualitatively. Distinguishing between review prior to and after agency approval is useful in understanding review by different entities.

- *Pre-approval review* occurs during the comment period and concerns the proposed rule. This is the last stage of rule development, and there is still significant scope modification. Review serves the purpose of providing input for making changes (or supporting the rule as is). Advocacy involvement and agency and commission review are pre-approval.
- *Post-approval review* occurs after the rule is in final form (at least as far as the agency is concerned).[282] Virtually by definition, a rule must be final before it can be definitively reviewed. The principal function of the review at this stage is to secure approval by an authority outside the agency. Approval is basically a yes/no decision, although it may be partial (only some sections approved). Review may entail changes that are necessary for approval, but these changes are more corrections than rule development. Legislative, gubernatorial, and technical review are usually post-approval.

B. Executive Branch Review

Depending on the state, several different parts of the executive branch may review new rules. The type of review varies with the reviewer, but it fundamentally is pre-approval review.

1. Oversight Agencies

Advice and Assistance

In some states[283] the regulatory flexibility legislation designated an agency to advise and assist in the regulatory flexibility process. These agencies have an oversight role throughout the rulemaking rather than an explicit review function.

Review Agencies

In some states an agency is designated to review regulations. The delegation may be by statute or administrative. In some cases, the review focuses on regulatory flexibility. In other states, it is primarily concerned with compliance with procedures and policies for rulemaking or with the fiscal note or general economic impact statement.

Arkansas' Economic Development Commission is designated by statute to review economic impact statements, including regulatory flexibility. Review functions are spelled out in the statute.[284] Legislation also established a Regulatory Review Committee "to assist the Director... in the review of proposed rules."[285]

California's Office of Administrative Law (OAL) reviews proposed regulations for fiscal impacts on local government and for compliance with the statutory requirement that an agency "shall assess the potential for adverse economic impact on California business enterprises and individuals, avoiding the imposition of unnecessary or unreasonable regulations or reporting, recordkeeping, or compliance requirements." This review potentially includes regulatory flexibility analysis, but the combination of a very high threshold requirement for regulatory flexibility and OAL's guidance tend to prevent such analyses.

Colorado's Department of Regulatory Agencies (DORA) is an umbrella agency over all regulatory agencies. DORA's Office of Policy, Research and Regulatory Reform (OPRRR) reviews all proposed rules and may order a cost-benefit analysis if it determines that the rule will have an impact on small business or economic competitiveness.[286] OPRRR also does extensive public outreach and conducts sunset reviews.

Illinois' Department of Commerce and Economic Opportunity has an Office of Regulatory Flexibility, within the Illinois Entrepreneurship Network Business Information Center. The Office reviews every rule that state agencies propose. Based on agency information, comments, and discussions with the business community, the Office then prepares an economic impact report for the JCAR.[287] A discussion of possible alternatives is based on summaries of testimony and other comments. The Office may comment on the suggestions or recommend specific changes.

Maine's Department of Secretary of State has a new Bureau of the Special Advocate. The Special Advocate reviews and comments on proposed rules and consults with agencies over business matters. The Office's primary function is ombudsman services.

Massachusetts' Department of Housing and Economic Development has an Assistant Secretary for Economic Development within the (HED), who reports to the Governor, reviews the prosed rule for small-business impacts and has the authority to reopen a rule. The Assistant Secretary also carries out other advocacy functions, including extensive work with agencies and outreach to the public.

Michigan's Office of Regulatory Reform (ORR) has a statutory mandate to "review proposed rules, coordinate processing of rules by agencies, work with the agencies to streamline the rule-making process, and consider efforts designed to improve public access to the rule-making process."[288] The review generally includes regulatory flexibility analysis. Agencies may not publish a hearing notice without ORR's approval. A more recent executive order renamed ORR (Office of Regulatory Reinvention), created Advisory Rules Committees to support ORR, and gave ORR a set of explicit review criteria.[289]

Rhode Island's Economic Development Corporation houses an Office of Regulatory Reform, which provides fairly comprehensive regulation related services, including advice and assistance to agencies,[290] advocacy for small businesses, and ombudsman services. ORR reviews proposed rules and provides recommendations to agencies on them.

Vermont's interagency committee on administrative rules was created "for assistance in the review, evaluation and coordination of programs and activities of state agencies, the development of strategies for maximizing public input, and the promotion of consistent measures among agencies for involving the public in the rulemaking process." The committee reviews proposed rules of agencies designated by the governor for style, consistency with the law, legislative intent and the policies of the governor.

Virginia's Department of Planning and Budget reviews proposed regulations and prepares an economic impact statement. The EIS uses data agencies using the report template for a Proposed Regulation Agency Background Document. The template resembles report forms found in other states, but follows the Virginia Code closely. (Appendix B)

Washington's Office of Regulatory Assistance (ORA) reviews "significant rules," which require cost-benefit and alternatives analysis to determine least burdensome alternatives. ORA prepares a report, *Impacts of Significant Legislative Rule-Making Requirement*, which draws on reports of the individual agencies covered by the law. ORA is primarily an ombudsman.[291]

2. Technical Review

Some states have post-approval review of legal and technical issues. The most common is a legal review by the Attorney General. The review results in an opinion as to whether the proposed regulation is legally sufficient; is it consistent with authorization in the statute and provisions of other laws and the state constitution? Sometimes the Attorney General also addresses the question of whether the rulemaking followed procedures properly. Usually this issue is narrowly defined in terms of actions taken, documents filed, persons notified, and adherence to schedules.[292] Style – whether the rule "is written in a manner that is not concise or easily understandable" - may also be an issue.

A few state statute require the Secretary of State to review the procedures as well.[293] This probably occurs because many statutes phrase their procedural requirements as actions that must be taken before the final rule can be filed (typically with the Secretary of State).

3. Governor's Review

Governors have broad oversight in the sense that agency heads report to them and they set policy. Governors usually are not involved in review, however. When they are it is usually in the role of making the final decision on adoption. Involvement may take several forms.

- Occasionally the Governor has an explicit role at an earlier stage.[294]
- In a handful of states the Governor's approval of the final rule is required by statute,[295] and this number has more than doubled as the result of recent executive orders that put the decision in the Governor's hands (discussed further below).
- In most cases, the Governor interacts in some way with the legislature's action on a proposed rule. There are several scenarios.
  - The Governor may veto a bill or a current resolution by the legislature to override a proposed rule, thus approving the rule. In most cases the Governor's decision is final; in Pennsylvania the legislature may override the veto (by a 2/3 margin).
  - Alternatively, an agency may appeal a legislative review committee's decision to the Governor, and he has the option to uphold the agency.
  - Similarly, the Governor may "disapprove" the action of a legislative committee or subcommittee.
  - In two states[296] the Governor has a slightly wider range of options:
    - Order the agency to withdraw the regulation,
    - Order the agency to modify the rule as the legislature deemed necessary, or
    - Approve the adoption of the rule as written.

    - In Oklahoma the Governor must approve a new rule, but the legislature can override the approval.
- Virginia has a more complicated process in which the Governor:
    - Reviews the rule to determine whether "substantial changes" have been made since the proposal (and may open a 30-day comment period if they have),
    - May file a formal objection to the rule, or
    - May (jointly with the legislature) suspend the rule, allowing an opportunity for:
        - The agency to modify the rule, and/or
        - The legislature to adopt a bill to nullify all or part of the rule.

Virginia is the only state where the Governor has any role other than an up-or-down decision on all or part of the rule and one of a very few where the Governor's decision is not dispositive.

C. Independent Commissions

1. Commissions

A dozen states have (or had) commissions, usually established by statute, to review regulations from a small-business point of view. In some cases they also perform a number of other functions. These commissions are independent in the sense that they are not part of the bureaucracy (although most of them receive staff support from an executive branch agency), and do not have other functions unrelated to regulations. Their review of regulations is pre-approval, and some of them get involved before the NPRM is published. Their composition, size, appointment, and reporting responsibilities vary from state to state.

Arizona

The Governor's Regulatory Review Council[297] reviews each rule, using a fairly extensive list that of criteria that starts with the completeness and accuracy of the economic, small business and consumer impact statements. The Council may meet with the agency or require an agency to attend a meeting and answer questions. The Council may also receive written comments and permit oral testimony at council meetings. The Council may return a rule to the agency "for further consideration" and "shall not approve the rule unless" the review criteria are satisfied. The Council hears appeals and has an integral role in periodic review. The Council also has extensive roles in facilitating public participation and training of agency staff. The Council's review function has been taken over by the Governor in a recent executive order.

Arkansas

The Regulatory Review Committee[298] was to be appointed by the Director of the Arkansas Economic Development Commission to assist in the review of proposed rules and to serve as liaison to small business organizations and associations who have "comments, objections, or opinions concerning the proposed rule." Statutory review criteria include completeness of the economic impact statement and sufficiency of "measures to balance the objectives of the proposed rule with the interests of the affected small businesses." The Committee apparently was never set up.

Florida

The Small Business Regulatory Advisory Council[299] reviews proposed rules "to determine whether a rule places an unnecessary burden on small business and make recommendations to the agency to mitigate the adverse effects." The Council also accepts requests by small business owners to review existing rules and conducts sunset reviews. The review functions have been substantially taken over by the Governor in a recent executive order.

Hawaii

The Small Business Regulatory Review Board[300] reviews and comments on proposed rules. The Board also, at the request of small businesses, reviews existing rules and makes recommendations for changes to the agency or the legislature. The Board files an annual report with the legislature.

Kentucky

The Commission on Small Business Advocacy[301] reviews administrative regulations that may impact small business, seeks input from interested parties, and may submit a written report during the public comment period. The report may include the Commission's own findings on small business compliance costs, as well as suggestions for reducing the regulatory burden on small businesses through the use of tiering or exemptions. The Commission also has extensive ombudsman functions and serves as liaison between the small business community and agencies.

Missouri

The Small Business Regulatory Fairness Board[302] reviews proposed rules, solicits input from small business owners, conducts hearings, and provides state agencies with input regarding rules that adversely affect small businesses. The Board also, the request of small business owners, reviews existing rules and submits an "evaluation report to the governor and the general assembly, including any recommendations and evaluations of state agencies regarding regulatory fairness."

New Mexico

The Small Business Regulatory Advisory Commission[303] had the same mission as the Missouri Small Business Regulatory Fairness Board. Lacking leadership or support, however, the Commission disintegrated.

New York

The Governor's Office of Regulatory Reform (GORR) reviewed proposed rules with an extensive set of criteria that explicitly included the statutory provisions relating to regulatory impact statement, regulatory flexibility analysis for small businesses and rural area flexibility analysis. If GORR concluded that the criteria were not met, it had the authority to make the agency to undertake additional analyses. GORR was also involved in the review of existing rules. GORR was established in 1995 by Governor Pataki's executive order.[304] In 2011 Governor Cuomo issued an executive order that repealed Governor Pataki's executive order and made reference to legislation that "discontinued" GORR.[305]

Oklahoma

The Small Business Regulatory Review Committee[306] reviews proposed rules that agencies have identified as having an adverse economic effect upon small business. The Committee provides agencies with input regarding those rules and makes recommendations to the agency and the legislature regarding the rule and the need for it.

Pennsylvania

The Independent Regulatory Review Commission (IRRC)[307] reviews each rule and may approve or disapprove a rule. The review criteria are fairly broad and include economic or fiscal impacts, but there is nothing explicitly about small business. During the comment period, the IRRC may submit comments, and the agency is required to respond. After the comment period closes, the IRRC considers the regulation at a public meeting, orders its approval or disapproval, and sends its order to the agency and the legislative committees. Disapproval bars the agency from promulgating the rule pending subsequent review.[308]

South Carolina

The Small Business Regulatory Review Committee[309] is responsible for determining if a proposed regulation has a significant adverse impact on small businesses.[310] The Committee may direct the promulgating agency to prepare a regulatory flexibility analysis and may request the Office of Research and Statistics of the Budget and Control Board to prepare a final assessment report of the impact of the regulation on small businesses. If the Committee determines that there is a significant adverse impact on small business, it advises the agency in writing.

Wisconsin

The Small Business Regulatory Review Board[311] reviews proposed rules (including regulatory flexibility analysis) that may have a significant impact on small businesses and determines whether it does have a significant economic impact on a substantial number of small businesses. The Board may perform further analysis. If the Board finds such impact, it may make suggestions on changing the rule to minimize the proposed rule's economic impact, and further regulatory flexibility analysis may be required.

2. Process and Outcomes

The independent review commissions hold meetings and review rules, but for most of them that does not seem to be their principal activity. Pennsylvania's IRRC has the most structured review process, and it is the one independent commission without a specific small business mission. Many commissions, their members, and their staff, as well as other advocates, spend a lot of time working directly with agencies – providing guidance and education (formal and otherwise) and discussing specific rules. Many of the commissions also do considerable public outreach and education, since part of their mission is to facilitate public involvement. Published materials and reports of the commissions and contacts with them indicate a preference for informal action early rather than formal action later. Much of their activity and impact does not leave much of a paper trail.

Most members of commissions are from the private sector – usually current or former business owners. The value of this small business perspective for rulemaking cannot be overstated, but there are significant limitations. Time is a serious constraint; business people are busy, and meetings can easily become inefficient. Geography is a constraint; branches of government are mostly in the same place; commission members likely are not. Liaison with agencies is important, and business people may need orientation as well.[312] Most of the commissions that provide a history through minutes or reports speak of taking the first two years or so just building up contacts. Support is important, both in the sense of solid staff and in the sense of having a strong advocate for the commission's function in the bureaucracy – the division director, cabinet secretary, or governor. An energetic commission can build its own reputation over time, but the authority is necessary to get established.

Each commission has to develop its own method of functioning. Oklahoma provides an interesting example. The chairman is dynamic and recognized in the business community. He has been in this position for the 10-year life of the Committee. The staff is small, but the Economic Development Specialist has been there for 10 years as well. Between them, they do much of the liaison work the agencies. The Committee receives proposed rules and rule impact statements as soon as they are available. The Committee's Counsel reviews regulations, summarizes them,[313] and distributes them to Committee members as appears appropriate. Committee members interested in the rule respond with their comments, which are forwarded to the agency. Communications are almost entirely by email. This system minimize burdens on Committee members, makes it easier to review rules in the short 30-day comment period, and allows formal meetings to be kept to a maximum of four a year.

The Hawaii Small Business Regulatory Review Board (SBRRB) takes a different approach. It has been meeting monthly since 1999 to consider rules. Minutes show agency representatives present to explain and discuss the rules. Most rules are considered before the public meeting; some after. Earlier consideration makes it easier to modify the rule to meet objections. After consideration, the SBRRB votes whether to recommend that the Governor send the rule to a public hearing or, as appropriate, to adopt it. The SBRRB is selective in its review; it considers only rules that the agencies have identified as having likely impacts on small business. The SBRRB has made considerable effort to set up positive lines of communication with agency contacts, using a division-of-labor approach. Each member is assigned to one or more agencies to serve as a "discussion leader" and to do the preliminary review of rules from that agency. Hawaii has no legislative review; the Board is the only reviewer of regulations. Although it has significant staff,[314] the Board's plate is very full, as indicated by a recommendation of a recent Working Group that it be enlarged.

Missouri's Small Business Regulatory Fairness Board (SBRFB) is proactive in the rulemaking process. Its statutory review, commenting, and reporting activities are broader than most commissions.[315] The SBRFB has built on this authorization to develop outreach (including an web site with extensive information about proposed rules and a place to subscribe for alerts), mobilize the public, create forms (including a Small Business Impact Statement), provide training on regulatory flexibility analysis, and work with agencies on the rulemaking process and individual rules. All of these activities provide additional leverage for working with agencies early in the process, which appears to be SBRFB's preferred method of operating. This is an example of a Board that has created its own sort of authority over time.

The make-up of commissions vary. Some are entirely business people; some have several cabinet department representatives or even legislators. There are trade-offs. A mixed commission can provide education and entre into agencies and project as a collaborative effort. A commission with only business members may focus on issues better, but may seem more adversarial. Implementation is important; continued contact with agencies can build up collegiality with any commission structure.

Commissions also vary by appointment. Some are appointed by the governor; some roughly half (each) by the governor and the legislature. There is an inherent trade-off. Split appointment can achieve buy-in and ownership of both branches, but the risk is that neither really provides the authoritative backing necessary. A governor-appointed committee may have more authority in the executive branch but less recognition in the legislature. Leadership is important.

There is a certain fragility to these commissions. Of the 12 summarized above, four have lost major functions or gone out of existence. In Arizona and Florida, executive orders have stripped the commissions of at least their review functions. New Mexico's disintegrated, although apparently it may be reconstituted. New York's GORR has been eliminated by legislation and executive order. In some states (e.g., New Jersey) formation of new commissions is in progress. These changes underscore the importance of gubernatorial support for the regulatory flexibility process.

D. Legislative Review

Most states, including those without a regulatory flexibility statute, have legislative review of regulations. Very little - usually nothing - has changed about the process because of regulatory flexibility requirements.

1. Overview

The Actors

Almost all aspects of legislative review are performed by a few legislative entities, whose names and exact assignment of roles changes from state to state.

- The Legislative Council is a committee of legislators that generally make policy and set procedures for the legislature. The Council rarely actually performs review bit may have an oversight or organizing role.
- The Legislative Reference Service[316] is a staff office that (among other things) supports the Legislative Council. The LRS may also do research for legislators, publish the *Register*, provide rulemaking guidance, or prepare rules and laws for publication – or (in any given state) it may not. In rule review the LRS may serve as a conduit for rule dockets or prepare them for review.
- The Joint Committee on Administrative Rules (JCAR) most often is the actual reviewer of rules that makes findings and recommendation. It meets periodically to review rules – its principal function.
- The standing committees of both houses have subject matter jurisdiction over regulations and get involved only when they are appropriate for a given rule. Sometimes they perform the primary review and sometimes a secondary review after the JCAR. The house and senate committees usually work in parallel; occasionally jointly. They are likely to be involved in a bill or resolution that results from review.

Timing

Most legislative review is post-approval review. Legislators really want to check out the final version. Even if the legislature initially receives documents at the time of the NPRM, the review may wait until the rule is final. Then there is the added review factor of whether – and how – the rule may have been changed since proposal.

In a few states, legislative review is pre-approval. It follows the normal comment procedures, but with a bit more authority than most commenters. There is a trade-off between the two times. Pre-approval review is more likely to have influence over a wider range of topics, but it gives up control over the final version.

2. Forms of the Process

Most legislative reviews follow the same basic structure of several steps with some choices after each one.

- Initially the JCAR receives and considers the text of the rule and the accompanying documents, including the economic impact statement and/or small business impact statement, if one has been done. It has the choice of:
  - Approving the rule (or doing nothing, which usually eventually defaults to approval);
  - Disapproving the rule; or
  - Approving parts of the rule and disapproving parts of the rule.[317]

  The JCAR sends its objections and an explanation (including modifications that would make the rule acceptable) to the agency.
- The agency then has the choice of:
  - Making the recommended corrective amendments and resubmitting the rule;
  - Withdrawing the rule (possibly revising it and proposing a different version later); or
  - Refusing to make the changes (or enough of them to satisfy the JCAR).
- If the agency refuses to make changes, the state statute prescribes one (or more) of several scenarios:
  - The JCAR may file its objection in the *Register*, which then becomes an annotation in the administrative code. This action puts the burden of proof on the agency in any litigation to show that the JCAR's objection was not valid.[318] As a system, filing an objection implicitly assumes that grounds are something that a court would recognize as a legal issue that it could rule on. This is consistent with relatively narrow, legal review criteria. It is also interesting to not that an objection may have considerable threat value against an agency that wishes not to get bogged down in litigation.[319]
  - The JCAR may send its objection to the Governor for disposition (or the agency may appeal to the governor).
  - The JCAR may send its objection to the General Assembly for action. The usual action is a concurrent resolution, to ratify the JCAR's recommendation and nullify the regulation (or separable parts thereof). Often, as a preliminary step, each standing committee must separately approve the JCAR's disapproval of the rule. In some states the Governor may then veto such a resolution.

There are numerous variations on this basic review structure, depending on the particulars of each state's statute.

- The LRC may perform an initial review to set up the issue for the JCAR. This may result in a report. The LRC review can extend up to the point of making findings or recommendations for the JCAR to approve.
- The JCAR may require an agency representative to make a presentation and answer questions at a meeting.
- The JCAR may order up new analysis.
- The JCAR may hold hearings and/or provide its own opportunity for public comment.
- There may be multiple iterations of agency revision and resubmission of the rule.
- The agency may have to revise the rule until the JCAR accepts the revisions, which happens only in states with particularly narrow and technical criteria.[320]
- Standing committees (as assigned by the Legislative Council or the leaders of each chamber) or their subcommittees may perform the review, rather than the JCAR.
- The review committee may send the rule back to any prior state in the rulemaking process to correct what it considers to be a deficiency.
- The legislature may act in response to a decision of an independent regulatory review committee.[321]
- A rule may be formally suspended to allow time for legislative action.[322]
- Rule review may be performed by an interim committee.[323]
- The Legislative Council may review an objection – either by its own subcommittee or by a standing committee (on appeal).
- The standing committees may consider "corrective legislation"[324] instead of or in addition to a resolution to object to the rule.
- The JCAR may be selective in the rules that it reviews, either rule by rule or by class of rules (e.g., only major substantive rules).

3. Criteria for Objection

In many states, the statute states criteria for review. The phraseology can vary from restricting review to certain issues to prohibiting the review committee from approving the rule unless certain criteria are met.

Regulation is an extension or implementation of legislation. Thus the natural question for a legislature to ask is "did the agency do what we meant them to do (and no more)." As a result, a short set of issues is found on almost every list of review criteria:

- Is there statutory authority for the rule?
- Is the rule consistent with legislative intent?
- Does the rule conflict with the state constitution or other statutes?[325]
- Were proper procedures followed in the rulemaking?[326]

A number of states include general criteria related to the overall quality of the regulation. These may include:

- Could the rule be made, less complex, clearer, and/or more easily understandable?
- Is the rule reasonable and necessary for its objective?
- Is the rule arbitrary?

A few states include review criteria that pertain to economic impacts or consideration of alternatives, but these apply generally to business, not specifically to small business. For example:

- New York (and Utah, using identical language) require examination and determination of

  "(iii) impact on the economy and on the government operations of the state and its local governments, and

  (iv) impact on affected parties."[327]
- Illinois has a statutory review criterion of "whether the agency has considered alternatives to the rule that are consistent with the stated objectives of both the applicable statutes and regulations."[328]
- Ohio, in a very recent statute, makes it grounds for invalidating a rule:

  That the rule-making agency has failed to demonstrate through the business impact analysis, recommendations from the common sense initiative office, and the memorandum of response the agency has filed... that the regulatory intent of the proposed rule, amendment, or rescission **justifies** its adverse impact on businesses in this state.[329]

Legislative review criteria may include – as part of the review of procedures – whether an economic impact analysis or small business impact analysis was done, but few require consideration of the substance of the analysis. Most of those are concerned with impacts on business in general – or fiscal impacts on state and local jurisdictions. There are very few examples of review criteria that explicitly address small business issues, such as:

- "Whether the rule is designed to minimize economic impact on small businesses"[330] or
- "The agency did not adhere to the strategy for maximizing public input prescribed by the interagency committee on administrative rules."[331]

4. Process and Outcomes

Minutes of JCAR meetings and Register notices that reflected JCAR decisions were reviewed wherever possible to obtain a picture of review proceedings. The JCARs generally met monthly or quarterly – occasionally more often or twice a year. Meetings frequently dealt with a dozen or more regulations – allowing an average of 15 to 20 minutes per regulation. It was clear that initial review, pre-screening, and extensive preparation of materials had been done by staff. In some cases agency and/or industry representatives were present and involved. In a few cases an agency representative made a presentation and/or submitted a prepared statement. Discussions on individual rules could become fairly extensive, but often there did not seem to be much controversy.

Most rules did not come to the point of filing an objection or disapproval. Where the type of objection was given, it was almost always a legal or technical point. Where the subject matter was described, it very rarely involved anything remotely related to impacts on businesses.[332]

Demonstrating the absence of something is a tedious process, but this review found very little in the way of consideration of small business impacts. Only six rules were found that could be construed as relating to business impacts. One affected large businesses,[333] and three applied to circumstances sufficiently where regulatory flexibility does not seem particularly applicable.[334]

Two rules involved impacts on small businesses:

- The Illinois JCAR objected to one rule on cemeteries:
  because licensure fees, indemnification costs and continuing education requirements, as well as cemetery maintenance standards that are not differentiated based on the size and financial strength of the cemetery as is required by the statute, will create a serious financial hardship for some cemeteries.
- An Ohio Livestock Care Standards Board rule on the size of pens for livestock would – so industry representatives argued – seriously affects small farmers, including Amish. Steps were taken to mitigate such impacts.[335]

The Illinois objection was pure regulatory flexibility reasoning, and Illinois is virtually the only state to make minimization of economic impact on small business a criterion of legislative review.[336] In the Ohio case, it is not really clear why the rule would have a proportionately greater impact on small farmers than on large veal producers (who could face more serious space constraints). If the veal industry really was representing small farmers, it seems curious that then Ohio Farm Bureau considered the regulation appropriate. Still, an appropriate mitigating action was taken.

These two examples notwithstanding, there is no indication that legislative review plays any role in holding agencies accountable for regulatory flexibility analysis or otherwise implementing or enforcing regulatory flexibility statutes.

E. Observations

Small business impacts of regulation and regulatory flexibility are not a significant concern to most parties involved in the regulatory process. This is clear in the review part of the process. At this stage, the governor is involved only in a big-picture way, if at all. Some executive branch entities that review rules are looking only for legal or technical defects. Outside of the small business office in the department of commerce and/or economic development, other agencies are being reviewed, not reviewing. For legislative reviewers in almost all states, a small business impact statement is a procedural matter whose existence may be of concern but whose substance is not.

That basically leaves the independent review commissions and the advocates within the Small Business Office as the only active agents of oversight of the regulatory flexibility process. The best of them do advocacy, education, and review, but the majority of state regulatory flexibility programs do not have this. SBA's model legislation assumed that the "Department of Economic and Community Development or similar state department or council that exists to review regulations" would naturally be concerned with small business impacts, but did not include a provision for such focused review, or for advocacy.

VIII. Periodic Review

A. Systems for Reviewing Existing Rules

1. Overview

Review of existing rules is not unique to regulatory flexibility analysis. Many states already had review procedures in place before enacting a regulatory flexibility statute, and they kept those procedures in place. Although they are not mutually exclusive and there is some overlap and blurring, there are fundamentally three ways of structuring such a review.

- **Periodic or Scheduled Review.** All rules are reviewed, or scheduled for review, on a fixed cycle of (depending on the state) five to 12 years.
- **Review on Demand.** Rules are reviewed in response to complaints or issues raised by the business community, legislators, or an executive branch agency.
- **Automatic Expiration.** Rules expire, or "sunset" after a fixed number of years and must be readopted or reauthorized.

2. Periodic and Scheduled Review

SBA Model

SBA's model legislation includes review by the agency of all existing regulations at set time intervals (five years is suggested). For new rules, the first cycle begins with promulgation. There is also a provision for reviewing rules existing at the time the regulatory flexibility legislation is passed, which subsequently come under the periodic review cycle. The model legislation includes a useful set of consideration for review.[337]

Several states[338] have adopted SBA's model legislation in its entirety. This provides a highly structured time frame, as well as criteria for review. In these states, no procedure for review or amendment is specified.

Several other states[339] require agency review of rules on a regular cycle of four, five, or ten years. The simplest way of stating the purpose of the review is "to determine whether any rule should be repealed, amended or a new rule adopted."[340] Various other purposes and criteria are given in specific states.[341] Some of these states specify that original rulemaking procedures or a somewhat simplified procedure must be used to change a rule.

Scheduling and Pre-Screening

Some states require announcement of a schedule for rule review - in effect a regulatory agenda. In several states[342] the statute requires the preparation of a review schedule on an annual, biennial, or (in Georgia) unspecified basis. This allows significantly more flexibility. Only some rules need to be reviewed in detail – "those that create an undue burden on small businesses and that have an opportunity to be streamlined" (Georgia) or those that are "obsolete, unnecessary, or duplicative." (Minnesota) In some states the process involves more than the agency making a schedule.

- New York requires that every January an agency post rules to be reviewed that year, with a request for comments. After review, an assessment of comments and a justification for continuing the rule or not must be published.
- Arizona requires submission of a report to the Governor's Regulatory Review Council.
- Hawaii agencies must review rules identified by the Small Business Review Board and report back to the Board on the results.
- Nevada requires submission of a report to the Legislative Counsel, describing any rules that must be amended or repealed as a result of the review.
- Florida agencies must file a biennial evaluation report with the legislature.

Rule Modifications

The potential actions following a review of rules are commonly stated as: retain, amend, or repeal. In most states, aspects of a periodic review other than time frames are left in the agency's hands. If there is agency review, the first – and principal – question is whether to make and change and (if so) what to change and how. Other than possible oversight by the Governor and occasional reports to the legislature or an independent review commission, there really are no controls or accountability. No documentation of this internal agency decision is available. To judge from the relatively high proportion of rulemakings that make only minor changes, however, a fair amount of review does occur.

Amendments to a rule proposed by an agency typically require a new rulemaking. This is a disincentive to an agency. It also raises some practical and conceptual issues. If changes are minor, the full rulemaking process is overkill. Most states do not seem to distinguish between major and minor rules beyond the terms "substantive" or "significant." Most states do not have a Fast Track, although there generally is discretion whether to have a hearing or not, and the absence of comments simplifies matters considerably. The problem of getting bogged down and losing focus analyzing minor rule amendments (discussed above) is likely to be present.

On the other hand, rule revisions following review are not necessarily minor. If the process is expedited simply because the rule is being reviewed, important aspects of the change may be missed. This danger is compounded by conceptual issues related to impact analysis. The triggers for analysis – and the acceptability of the rule after reviewing the analysis – are defined in terms of impacts on small business. A rule under review after several years, however, is its own baseline, so that enquiry about the adverse impacts is the wrong question. The issue is how much the rule amendment will or can reduce impacts on small business, and that is an issue that the small business impact guidance and forms are not designed to address.

Review Beyond the Agency

The outside review process is be fairly similar to that for a new rule. Independent review commissions typically review both proposed and existing rules. The legislative review statutes that refer to concurrent regulations that may be introduced after JCAR review often use parallel language (e.g., "repeal, amend, or withdraw") that refers both to action on a proposed rule and action on an existing rule under review. Any rule that reduces burdens is likely to undergo little scrutiny.

3. Review on Demand

Selecting rules for review because there has been a complaint or a request for review is a "squeaky wheel gets the oil" strategy. The "squeak" can be detected in a number of ways. There also typically is discretion on whether and how far to pursue a review in response to such initiation. In some states[343] the JCAR, the independent small business review commission, the Governor, or all of them can direct an agency to review a given rule. The process plays out in a number of ways in different states.

Legislative Initiative

In some states[344] the JCAR conducts reviews of rules "as time permits," "at its own initiative," or systematically. The rule may involve hearings. In Vermont and Wisconsin (which have the same statutory language), if the rule has remained unchanged for six years, the JCAR may then notify the agency that the rule will expire in one year, allowing/ forcing the agency to readopt the rule.

Business Initiative

A few states allow an affected person to petition an agency for revision. Arizona provides an example, which focuses expressly on the impact statement.[345] In some respects, the two-year limit makes the petition an extension of the review process. A petition, however, is based on actual experience, rather than projections of impacts. While the burden of proof is on the petitioner, in this case the agency must publish notice of then petition, allow 30 days for comments, publish a summary of comments, reevaluate the rule and its economic impacts, and make a decision whether to amend or repeal the rule.

Hawaii, Missouri, and Oklahoma allow a petition on almost identical grounds,[346] but without the two-year time limit. The agency must respond in writing, and if it rejects the petition, the petitioner may take the matter to the review commission. The Oklahoma SBRRC may send an evaluation report and the agency's response to the legislature for potential action.

Independent Review Commissions

Most the independent review commissions also serve as a liaison to the business community. A majority have statutory authority to consider complaints about regulations and requests for reviewing them – and most of the rest probably do this informally. In several states this process is institutionalized:

- The Missouri Small Business Regulatory Fairness Board provides each agency with a list of any rules adopted by the agency that affect small business and have generated complaints or concerns. The agency is required to "submit a written... response [and] state whether the agency has considered the continued need for the rules and the degree to which technology, economic conditions, and other relevant factors may have diminished or eliminated the need for maintaining the rules."[347]
- The Hawaii Small Business Regulatory Review Board also submits lists of rules that have generated complaints, to which agencies must at least respond.
- The South Carolina Small Business Regulatory Review Committee may initiate its own recommendation that an agency review a rule, based on the criteria used for a petition by business (described above).

Other Channels

Ombudsmen routinely deal with problem regulations and sometimes formally report on them. They can be effective – particularly in cooperation with a small business advocate – in persuading an agency to reexamine a rule.

The legislature generally receives any reports prepared by independent review commissions, advocates, and ombudsmen. Individual legislators also hear from constituents. Although there is no formal mechanism for requiring review of any specific rule, legislators can initiate requests for review or introduce legislation to address an issue.

Recent Initiatives

Several regulatory reform initiatives have called for the public to provide examples of regulations that were burdensome or defied common sense. This may lead to amendment of the regulation.[348] Even if this does not occur, publication of such examples can have a salutary consciousness-raising effect on the public and on agencies.

Several recently elected Republican governors have required sweeping reviews of regulations. These moves appear to be intended to reduce regulatory burdens across the board, with no particular focus on small business. Repeal of a regulation does not take much review when the Governor requires it.[349] When a governor keeps score in terms of the number of regulations rescinded and the number of pages by which Administrative Code is reduced, however, the quality of the underlying analysis comes into question.

4. Automatic Expiration

The idea of forcing regulations to be reviewed under threat of expiration is appealing. A sunset provision in a law is a standard way of guaranteeing that the law will revisited (assuming its continuation is desired). Two general types of automatic expiration of rules are found:

- Traditional sunsetting, after up to ten years; and
- Short-term expiration after less than two years.

Sunset

Four states[350] have sunset provisions for regulations after four to ten years. The agency may readopt the same rule or a modified one. The procedures used for readoption are the same as those for adopting a new rule.

Such a sunset provision functions much like a periodic review requirement, but with teeth in the requirement to review.[351] Review is subject to the same inherent limitations discussed above under periodic review.

Short-Cycle Expiration

Three states have adopted statutory provisions that make every regulation[352] expire one legislative session after it was promulgated. When applied to all regulations in this manner a sunset provision creates overwhelming practical problems. Some action must be taken or regulations may expire and the whole regulatory structure potentially may collapse. Because so many regulations are involved, states usually renew them in an omnibus bill.[353] If a legislator wants a particular rule reviewed, he can amend the omnibus bill to remove it. How this plays out depends on the state.

- In Colorado, "the General Assembly, in its discretion, may postpone such expiration, in which case" the rule is subject to review by the General Assembly.
- In Utah the JCAR sends the Governor an explanation why the committee believes the rule should not be authorized, the agency may petition the Governor for an extension, and the Governor can publish a notice declaring it extended.
- In Tennessee, the rule must at least go through the standard legislative review, in which case the standing committee may vote to allow a rule to expire.

B. Observations

There are trade-offs in the methods of requiring review of existing rules. Mandatory review of all rules provides coverage, but may reduce scrutiny by making the process too routine and lacking in priority. Short-cycle expiration is an extreme example of this. Review on demand is better suited to focusing on real problems, but it is incomplete. Some sort of triage or pre-review screening would be helpful for mandatory periodic review, and some states appear implicitly to use this approach. Prioritization based on experience benefits review, and inclusion of complaints and comments among the SBA criteria, for example, is helpful.

Review of rules should be a matter of rebalancing benefits and burdens that may have shifted over time. Something of a different perspective is needed for periodic review. Conventional screening rules for adverse impacts may not be very helpful when the question is how – and by how much – burdens can be reduced. Some type of benefit-cost calculus is appropriate.

In the real world, a lot of burdens seem to come from implementation, interpretation, and unintended side-effects. Complaints about "customer service" are not necessarily addressed by changing the rule. Unintended side-effects may be a matter of wording rather than substance, which is not addressed by asking whether there is a continued need for the rule.

The recent reform initiatives indicate that current review of existing rules is only partially effective. Whether the reform is an improvement depends on its implementation. New Jersey's "common sense" approach – and calls for examples of unnecessarily burdensome rules in general – has a focus that leads to practical improvements. Tallying numbers on regulatory reduction, on the other hand, is a measure of success that largely disregards balanced, rational review criteria.

Based on the performance in reviewing new rules, there is no reason to believe that legislative review – or initiation of review – is an effective way of addressing burdens on small business. The short-cycle expiration seems especially prone to arbitrary and erratic selection of rules for review by individuals. Agencies probably have a better understanding about what to look for, but amending existing rules to reduce burdens may not be a priority.

The most fruitful single approach appears to be review by demand by independent commissions and/or based on complaints funneled through them, as well as other channels such as ombudsmen. Combining periodic and on-demand review is more effective than any single approach.

IX. EXECUTIVE ORDERS AND RECENT INITIATIVES

Executive orders and initiatives on regulatory reform have played a significant role in the development of regulatory impact analysis and regulatory flexibility. a majority of states with regulatory flexibility legislation have such executive orders or initiatives with studies. Some date from the earliest days of state regulatory flexibility, but there is a concentration in the last two years. They are reviewed below in roughly chronological order of the state's first order.

A. Actions

1. Utah: Executive Orders

Executive Orders

Two early executive orders by Governor Bangerter[354] ordered and followed up on a rather massive regulatory review that reduced the volume of the Utah Administrative Code by a reported 61 percent. The latter executive order spelled out a rulemaking checklist,[355] ordered agency heads to develop their own procedures, and generally ordered compliance with the statutes.

Governor Herbert issued an executive order[356] to supplement procedures in the Utah Administrative Rulemaking Act. E.O. 013-2011:

- Laid out some extremely basic guidelines for rulemaking;[357]
- Provided some additional detail for the statutorily required analysis of costs;
- Directed agency heads to designate a rules coordinator, whose responsibilities were specified; and
- Gave the Office of Planning and Budget responsibility for regulatory review, coordination, and legislative liaison.

E.O. 013-2011 basically was a tweaking of the system with a goal of improving it.[358]

2. New York: Executive Orders

Governor Pataki issued an executive order,[359] which established a system of executive branch review of proposed state agency regulations by the Governor's Office of Regulatory Reform (GORR). New York has one of the most detailed and complete regulatory flexibility statutes of any state. GORR had a broad scope for review, which was described in the front matter of the New York State Register.[360]

Governor Cuomo recently issued an executive order that "repealed, cancelled and revoked [E.O. # 20] in its entirety."[361] Governor Cuomo made reference to legislation that "discontinued" GORR, and he cited the Spending and Government Efficiency Commission's recommendation to discontinue the Position of State Director of Regulatory Reform.

3. Pennsylvania: Executive Order

Executive Order

Governor Ridge issued **an** executive order to address the "increasing volume and burden of regulations [which] remain an appropriate and necessary means of protecting the public health and safety" but "has grown at an alarming rate in recent years."[362] Requirements of E.O. 1996-1 included:

- General requirements for drafting new regulations and reviewing existing regulations;
- Involvement of the public in pre-drafting and drafting activities;
- Review by Governor's office and related analysis;
- Non-regulatory guidance documents;
- Periodic review; and
- Publication of a regulatory agenda.

Pennsylvania's Regulatory Review Act, which provided the statutory framework for review was already in place.[363] It included a two-tier review of proposed rules - first by the Independent Regulatory Review Commission (IRRC) and then by the legislature – in which the executive branch played no part. E.O. 1996-1 somewhat redressed this balance, but primarily addressed the rulemaking process prior to review. E.O. 1996-1 is unusually detailed in its guidance and its emphasis on involvement of the public. It does not mention small business or regulatory flexibility analysis.

Effects

There is nothing about E.O. 1996-1 that would not easily fit into any well designed regulatory analysis program, but much of it augmented existing statutory requirements. The regulatory agenda and direction on public involvement still rise to the level of best practices.

Much of the guidance appears still to be in effect. The IRRC seems to have adopted elements of it and is well positioned to keep intact any provisions of E.O. 1996-1 that it sees value in. For the most part, this complementarity with the statutory program appears to have enabled much of E.O. 1996-1 to become established practice.

Pennsylvania still has no regulatory flexibility provisions, however, except for one passing statutory reference to general provisions for special needs of certain groups.[364]

4. Massachusetts: Executive Orders

Executive Orders

Governor Weld issued an executive order,[365] which set general review standards for all rulemaking.[366]

Governor Romney issued an executive order 453,[367] which (among other requirements):

- Required a Small Business Impact Statement;
- Required each agency to designate a small business liaison;
- Required the Secretary of Economic Development to designate a Small Business Advocate; and

- Gave the Department of Administration and Finance authority to determine whether an agency satisfactorily considered and accommodated the interests of small businesses.

Governor Patrick issued an executive order,[368] which superseded E.O. 384 on the grounds that it "imposed requirements that were unduly burdensome and complex for state agencies." E.O. 485

- Required review by the Department of Administration and Finance; and
- Required each agency to appoint a senior official to be the contact person for all reviews.

Effects

It is not clear what became of Governor Romney's executive order. The legislature enacted its own regulatory flexibility statute. Governor Patrick appointed an Assistant Secretary for Economic Development in the Department of Housing and Economic Development, who does most of the functions assigned to the Small Business Advocate – and more. There may not have been much left of E.O. 453.

The claim that Governor Weld's requirements were unduly burdensome and complex is intriguing. They are all valid criteria. Yet conscientiously documenting that all of them were met *would* be unduly burdensome for a large number of new or amended state rules. Governor Patrick apparently chose to pursue a more informal approach.

The new Assistant Secretary combines the roles of regulatory advocate, reviewer, liaison, and educator. She has Governor Patrick's active support and the authority to send a rule back for more work if necessary. Massachusetts, however, is as good an example as any of the impermanence of any arrangement based solely on gubernatorial authority.

5. Missouri: Executive Order

Governor Carnahan issued an executive order[369] 96-18 in reaction to recent legislation that required fiscal notes for proposed legislation to state whether such legislation will have an economic impact on small businesses. He considered that the impact of rules and regulations was of as much concern as that of legislation and simply ordered agencies to determine whether there would be an economic impact on small businesses.[370]

Governor Holden issued an executive order[371] to expand that determination into a more detailed analysis. E.O. 03-15 had two principal elements:

- Regulatory flexibility analysis criteria, which build on SBA's model but appear to have been developed separately;[372] and
- Creation of the Small Business Regulatory Fairness Board.

Within a year, the Missouri legislature enacted legislation that incorporated E.O. 03-15.

6. Oregon: Executive Orders

Executive Orders

Governor Kulongoski an executive order "to create a stable climate for investment and a secure environment for business."[373] E.O. 03-01 sought to streamline regulation.

- E.O. 03-01 directed agencies that regulate business activities in Oregon to:
  - Review their regulations to identify opportunities to reduce burdens,
  - Review and evaluate their delivery of customer service and customer satisfaction,
    and
  - Make regulatory streamlining efforts a priority.
- E.O. 03-01 established an Office of Regulatory Streamlining to:
  - Oversee the development and execution of regulatory streamlining actions, and
  - Obtain input from regulated entities and other stakeholders about the impact of regulatory processes.

The Office of Regulatory Streamlining was closed at the end of the 07-09 biennium due to budgetary shortfalls.

Governor Kulongoski then issued Executive Order[374] to give some of the oversight functions of the former Office of Regulatory Streamlining to the Economic Revitalization Team (ERT) in the Governor's office.

Effects

According to an ERT report,[375] the Office of Regulatory Streamlining had:

- Helped facilitate more than 300 state agency streamlining projects; and
- Helped to "instill the importance of regulatory streamlining into the mindset of state agencies" and to "focus on customer service."

7. West Virginia: Executive Order

Governor Wise issued an executive order[376] to establish a regulatory flexibility program. E.O. 20-03:

- Adopted Section 3 of SBA's model legislation;
- Required an analysis to be reported;
- Required initial and ongoing review of existing regulations; and
- Gave the Director of the Small Business Development Center of the West Virginia Development Office authority to implement and manage appropriate procedures.

Eight years and two governors later, no signs of this program were found.

8. Washington: Executive Orders

Executive Orders

Governor Gregoire issued an executive order "to make it easy to do business in the state of Washington."[377] E.O. 06-02 was addressed to regulatory, taxing, licensing, and permitting agencies and programs. It directed them to improve and simplify their processes and set specific management goals.[378] The Office of Regulatory Assistance was given the task of helping agencies work toward these goals.

Governor Gregoire also issued an executive order,[379] which suspended non-critical rulemaking until January 1, 2012. The preamble described E.O. 10-06 as a measure to provide relief for small business. The Office of Financial Management was directed "to publish guidelines identifying circumstances in which rule making may proceed."

Effect

The OFM guidelines defined critical rules in terms that were conventional for a rulemaking freeze. OFM required review of all rules but allowed 13 months to do so.[380] The principal requirement for resuming rulemaking was small-business friendly:

> If an agency decides to proceed with a rule that has a small business impact or an impact to local government, the agency must consult with small businesses and/or governments on how the impact can be mitigated.

9. Arkansas: Executive Order

Governor Huckabee issued an executive order,[381] which required agencies to determine whether a proposed rule would affect small businesses and (if so) to prepare an economic impact statement detailing the impact of the proposed rule on small businesses. The wording of the requirements for the impact statement are very similar to Missouri's and probably were copied from there. The Attorney General provided interpretive opinions to guide implementation E.O. 05-04.

In 2007, shortly after Governor Beebe took office, the legislature adopted the provisions of E.O. 05-04 as a statute.[382] The SBA Office of Advocacy (among others) testified in favor of this legislation. The new law was referred to as "formerly Executive Order 05-04." Forms and procedures were carried over from the executive order.

10. Tennessee: Executive Order and Jobs4TN Review

Executive Order

Governor Bredesen issued an executive order[383] to require state agencies to assess the effect of new regulations on small businesses. E.O. No. 38 resembles part of Section 3 of SBA's model legislation.[384]

About a year later, the Tennessee legislature adopted the Regulatory Flexibility Act of 2007.[385] This legislation more closely and completely resembled SBA's model legislation (although it reversed Section 3 and Section 4) but also the included elements of E.O. No. 38 not found in SBA's model. There was no executive branch role or support for regulatory flexibility analysis. The analyses reviewed were of poor quality.[386]

Jobs4TN Review

In early 2011, the Department of Economic and Community Development (ECD) undertook a regulatory review as part of Governor Haslam's Jobs4TN plan.[387] The goal of this review was "to make improvements to our state government's regulatory system as well as the way it conducts business." The review process involved three steps:

- ECD distribute a survey of businesses to identify unnecessarily burdensome laws, regulations, practices, and policies.
- Working with local chambers of commerce, ECD held a series of about 25 roundtables and discussions across the state regarding business interaction with the state.
- Each state department was asked to self-assess regulations that they feel are unnecessary, unduly burdensome or come at excessive cost to businesses.

The resulting report was published in January 2012.[388] The findings of the report included many concerns about regulations, such as:

- Uneven interpretation of regulations and lack of transparency of such interpretation;
- Inconsistent and inefficient enforcement of regulations;
- A perceived lack of accountability in regards to state inspectors;
- A lack of transparency in the regulatory process that makes monitoring difficult; and
- A lack of "customer service" by agencies.[389]

Recommendations addressing rulemaking and implementation of regulations included:

- Implement a process that assesses all regulations prior to becoming final.
- Require regulatory enforcement entities to make efforts to work with constituents to help them comply with regulations and to help them understand inspector expectations.
- Assess the benefits of providing customer service training to employees and developing customer service standards; assess reforming aspects of the state employment process.
- Direct each department to begin the process of eliminating or modifying the regulations provided during the departmental review of this process.
- Conduct an annual survey of businesses tracking problematic federal regulations.
- Review all procedures or processes that are performed by more than one department to assess whether these procedures and processes can be streamlined.
- Search for legislative or regulatory opportunities to address business concerns regarding certain laws such as worker's compensation or unemployment laws.
- Require that every department enforcing regulations create uniform regulatory guidance, where applicable, in order to promote regulatory certainty and oversight within this process.
- Develop an interactive, "one stop" website for information about regulations.
- Assess the necessity of each board and commission.

These recommendations were very broad, which may have reflected of the wide variety of comments (provided in more detail in appendices). It was not clear how results of the study would be used. It is interesting to note that there were two recommendations about rulemaking and review and four about implementation.

11. Georgia: Executive Order and Red Tape Watch

The Executive Order

Governor Perdue launched the Governor's Small Business Regulatory Reform Initiative, whose mission was "to identify and develop a process that will help reduce any unique burdens that small businesses have in complying with state-level rules and regulations." [390] It included a framework and general directives but little in the way of specifics.[391] Specific provisions included the following:

- "The Georgia Technology Authority... shall develop a Georgia Rules and Regulations website that... indexes all State Agency rules and regulations including proposed regulatory changes and is kept current by the relevant agency."
- "The Georgia Department of Economic Development through the Entrepreneur and Small Business Office shall coordinate the ongoing Small Business Regulatory Reform activities."
- "Each state agency... shall identify at least one staff person to serve as their Small Business Liaison."
- "The Georgia Department of Economic Development and the Agency Liaisons shall... develop an annual progress report on regulatory reform for submission to the Governor."

Effects

One objective was achieved. Georgia is one of the very few states with a website instead of a published *Register*. Otherwise the Initiative has been discontinued. "Ongoing Small Business Regulatory Reform activities" that the Entrepreneur and Small Business Office might coordinate were never developed. A website for the Initiative was created, but (as of April 2012) it was moribund[392] and scheduled to sunset on June 30, 2012.

Red Tape Watch

On January 25, 2012, the Speaker of the House charged the Special Committee on Small Business Development and Job Creation[393] with reviewing and evaluating Georgia's regulatory environment. As part of this "Red Tape Watch," small businesses were invited to testify, and a web page containing a form was set up for this purpose. As a member of the Committee explained, "the special committee will meet periodically throughout the 2012 legislative session to hear directly from small business owners about burdensome or onerous state regulations that constrain economic development, business growth and job creation in Georgia."[394]

There is no indication that anything ever came of this effort. Aside from the comment form, the latest related web page found was a press release in mid February. The archive of the Committee's web page shows no activity after the initial organizational meeting.[395]

12. Virginia: Government and Regulatory Reform Task Force

Attorney General McDonnell's Government and Regulatory Reform Task Force was announced in June of 2006. The task force was set up to conduct a systematic review of state regulations to improve or remove them so as to eliminate redundancy and undue or unnecessary burdens on business and taxpayers.[396] The Task Force was methodically organized for an extended review that took about two years. The effort included Working Groups on Agriculture, Small Business, Healthcare, and the Environment.

Individual recommendations came out of the working groups, which addressed specific issues. One recommendation that was adopted, which affected rulemaking in general was the Fast Track process for "rules that are expected to be noncontroversial." It allows the first stage (Notice of Intended Regulatory Action) to be skipped – subject to the approval of the Governor and legislature and in the absence of 10 objecting comments from the public.

13.Ohio: Executive Orders

Executive Orders

Governor Strickland issued an executive order,[397] which focused on the process of rulemaking and the characteristics that rules should have in areas including:

- Development of rulemaking;[398]
- Administration of rules;[399]
- Establishment of a departmental regulatory ombudsman; and
- Review of existing rules and regulatory processes.[400]

Governor Kaisch issued an executive order,[401] which provided an institutional framework and focused more explicitly on small business. E.O. 2011-01K established a Common Sense Initiative Office under the Lt. Governor, with responsibilities to

- Develop processes for assessing impacts of regulation on small businesses that would "proactively seek the input of stakeholder groups during the development of the rules";
- Review proposed rules and existing rules; and
- Serve as a point of contact for small businesses to voice concerns about regulations; and
- Established a Small Business Advisory Council to provide a business perspective. E.O. 2011-01K also
- Directed "business-facing agencies" to designate a Regulatory Ombudsman;
- Emphasized electronic communication and the Ohio Gateway website; and
- Generally restated the principles of E.O. 2008-04S (which it did not rescind or supersede), but with more of an emphasis on small business.

Effects

E.O. 2011-01K had a certain amount of rhetoric about doing something new and different, but on the whole built on the foundation of E.O. 2008-04S, which was strong on good principles but light on implementation. Ohio statutes had very sketchy requirements for economic impact analysis[402] and relied largely on public comments and review by the

JCARR.[403] These two executive orders really created Ohio's regulatory impact analysis process. E.O. 2008-04S emphasized "common sense... appropriate flexibility, and a reasonable balance between the underlying regulatory objectives and the burdens imposed by the regulatory activity" (concepts later embraced by Governor Christie in New Jersey). E.O. 2011-01K emphasized disproportional impacts on small business and instituted regulatory flexibility analysis process – giving it the authority of the Lt. Governor and leaving it open-ended enough for development. In January 2012 the legislature enacted legislation that the CSI had developed.

14. Hawaii: Working Group

Working Group

The Small Business Regulatory Review Board established a working group pursuant to a 2008 statute, Act 230. The working group was tasked with reviewing the rulemaking process and procedures under the Small Business Regulatory Flexibility Act.[404] The Working Group summarized its findings in its January 2009 report:

(1) **Whether the current statutes are adequate to meet the concerns of small business**. The Current statutes are not adequate to meet the concerns of small business. The Working Group is proposing a remedial bill that includes a new section, §201M-10 Small Business Bill of Rights, as well as additional changes as submitted.

(2) **What concerns have been raised by small businesses, the small business regulatory review board, or government agencies in implementing the statutes**.

A. **Concerns raised by small business**. Hawaii small businesses are still not fully aware of the SBRRB's purview and its processes; particularly, §201M-6 Petition for Regulatory Review.

B. **Concerns raised by the Small Business Regulatory Review Board**. The SBRRB is limited in its authority as it is only advisory and lacks the capacity to enforce recommendations.

C. **Concerns raised by government agencies**. Government agencies have expressed concern and questioned the necessity of the SBRRB's post-public hearing reporting process when there are either no changes or no substantive changes made to the rule during the public hearing process pursuant to §201M-3 Small business statement after public hearing.

(3) **The level of difficulty in adequately meeting the requirements of the statutes**. Government agencies have expressed the need for flexibility and explicit guidance as to the information the SBRRB is requesting from them. Therefore, proposed changes to the statute are expected to improve communication and flexibility of internal procedures and processes.

(4) **Any other issues that may arise during the review**. Other issues that arose during the review process include the adequacy of the number of existing board members. An increase in the number of SBRRB members from eleven to thirteen is proposed under §201M-5 Small business regulatory review board powers, in order to meet the SBRRB's added responsibilities.[405]

Effect

Administrative Directive No. 09-01 (a routine directive concerning procedures under the law) was issued nine months after this report.[406] Several of its provisions addressed concerns raised by the working group. In particular, A.D. 09-01 loaned gubernatorial authority to the SBRRB on regulations affecting small business. It also placed extra emphasis on consideration of small business alternatives, with SBRRB as a reviewer. The Small Business Bill of Rights was not enacted.

15. Florida: OSBA/SBRAC FY 2009-2010 Report and Executive Orders

OSBA/SBRAC Report

Florida's Small Business Regulatory Relief Act, adopted in 2008, established the Office of Small Business Advocate (OSBA) and the Small Business Regulatory Advisory Council (SBRAC).[407] Their joint annual report provides a picture of the first years of an advocacy office. A great deal of this report was devoted to introducing the OSBA and SBRAC. The text gave a lot of background on what they were supposed to do, as well as what they had done. Both have spent considerable time doing outreach and identifying small business concerns.[408]

OSBA conducted 15 Small Business Issues Forums state-wide, as well as an on-line Small Business Issues Survey.[409] Onerous State Regulations ranked fifth on the list of concerns. OSBA summarized the findings:

> Until FY 2009-2010, state agencies on average proposed 500 new rules or rule modifications affecting small businesses yearly. Most of these rules included adverse impacts, including increased fees, fines and administrative expenses.[410]

In its review and training role,[411] SBRAC devoted a lot of effort to building up contacts and relationships with agencies. Among other things, "JAPC [the Joint Administrative Procedures Committee] has supported SBRAC's recommendations and has worked with the agencies in these cases to resolve concerns." The report contains a number of success stories. It also indicates that there is a lot of work to be done. For example:

> Much of SBRAC's initial interactions with agencies involved requests that each proposed rule that will have an impact on small business include a SERC [statement of estimated regulatory costs] that contains enough fiscal analysis for SBRAC to determine the nature and extent of such impact... One of the future goals of SBRAC is to increase agency awareness of the importance of considering Florida's SMEs during initial stages of rulemaking in order to better craft rules that will meet the agency's goal while still providing protection to these businesses.
>
> For a few agencies the change has been difficult. One example is a rule package promulgated by the Department of Environmental Protection (DEP). The proposed rule changes would have a very significant adverse impact on small businesses. The Office of Small Business Advocate requested a public hearing and the agency scheduled one. When OSBA and SBRAC staff expressed grave concerns regarding the fiscal impacts of the rule, the agency was not open to any modification. However, other DEP departments have worked with SBRAC and staff when promulgating rules.[412]

Executive Orders

The day he took office, Governor Scott issued an executive order,[413] which created the Office of Fiscal Accountability and Regulatory Reform within the Executive Office of the Governor. E.O. 11-01 gave OFARR sweeping responsibility for review of regulations, as well as other program oversight.[414] E.O. 11-01 also:

- Temporarily suspended all rulemaking;
- Required all proposed rules to be submitted to, and approved by, OFARR prior to publication; and
- Directed agency heads to determine whether existing rules were duplicative or unnecessarily burdensome and to repeal any that were.

E.O. 11-01 was superseded by a further executive order,[415] which continued provisions of E.O. 11-01 and required that:

- Agency heads must prepare an annual regulatory agenda (new);
- Agency heads must prepare a statement of regulatory costs analyzing the economic impact of agency rules (already required by statute), and
- Agency heads may not publish a NPRM without prior permission of OFARR (new).

Governor Scott's executive orders changing the system were explicitly political. They were accompanied by press releases trumpeting his fulfillment of campaign promises to hold government accountable. From the rhetoric, one might reasonable assume that Florida had no prior controls on regulation. In fact, E.O. 11-01 and E.O. 11-72 pre-empted an existing, developing regulatory review process and SBRAC's role in it.

Effects

OFARR embarked on a zealous review of regulations. In the first three months of its existence, according to Governor Scott, OFARR

- Reviewed over 11,000 existing rules and regulations;
- Helped agencies identify 1,035 unnecessary rules and regulations for repeal;
- Reviewed 334 agency rules for requested development, amendment, or repeal; and
- Reviewed and approved hundreds of agency requests to move forward.[416]

"OFARR's review process," Governor Scott added, "has thus far been successful in ensuring efficient and effective performance by State government." It is not credible that a new and newly staffed agency could review 170 regulations per working day in any meaningful way.

The regulatory reform has not gone smoothly. On August 16, 2011, the Florida Supreme Court held that the Governor may not, pursuant to Executive Order 11-72, require agencies to obtain formal approval from the Office of Fiscal Accountability and Regulatory Reform prior to publishing rulemaking notices.[417] Governor Scott responded with an executive order, in which he criticized the Supreme Court's reasoning and – citing "the Governor's inherent constitutional powers" - restatered OFARR's review role but softened the requirement with the phrase "to the extent permitted by law."[418]

Governor Scott's reforms are a broadside against all regulation. There is no indication of any particular interest in small business. The only mention of small business in the executive orders is a directive for OFARR to "work with" SBRAC, OSBA, and the Rules Ombudsman "to identify rules and regulations that adversely or disproportionately impact businesses, particularly those relating to small business." That is an excellent approach, but there is no indication that it is being implemented. The overall emphasis on tallying numbers and the lack of visible presence of SBRAC and OSBA suggest that it is not. A review of 92 proposed rules found none that identified impacts on small businesses, with agencies almost always excusing themselves from doing a Statement of Estimated Regulatory Cost. That – contrary to Governor Scott's claims of "efficient and effective performance" – appears to be a step backwards.

16. Arizona: Moratorium on Rulemaking

Moratorium on Rulemaking

As soon as she took office (January 22, 2009), Governor Brewer issued a memorandum to all state agencies[419] ordering them not to send any rule to the Secretary of State for publication, to withdraw any proposed rules that had been submitted, and to postpone further action on rules that had been finalized but not published. An exception would be granted for a rule (if the agency identified it in writing) that "impacts critical public peace, health, and safety functions of the agency or that are needed to address the state budget deficit." The memorandum announced a "regulatory review [that] will be implemented by the Governor's Office" and required agencies to provide the Governor's office with a brief summary on each rule making activity. The moratorium was extended through the present with a series of gubernatorial notices, legislative bills, and executive orders - each one seemingly temporary – that added some details, particularly with respect to exemptions.[420]

Effects of the Executive Orders

The cumulative effect of these memoranda, bills, and executive orders was to give the Governor's Office complete control over rulemaking. Every notice published in the *Register* is prefaced by an editorial note:

> Editor's Note: The following notice of Proposed [or Final] Rulemaking was reviewed per Executive Order 2011-05 as issued by Governor Brewer. (See the text of the executive order on page [number][421].) The Governor's Office authorized the notice to proceed through the rulemaking process on [date].[422]

The first 13 issues of the Arizona Administrative Register in 2012 contained 15 notices of proposed rulemaking and seven notices of final rule – an unusually small number in any state. Nine of the notices claimed some type of exemption from the Moratorium;[423] three others emphasized that the agency was protecting the health, safety, and welfare of the public. In citing the statutory authority, only a handful said something like "this legislation allows the Department to... adopt rules." In the section on justifying the regulation, most of the non-exempt notices indicated some type of statutory compulsion: The "rulemaking will amend the rules [to] ensure compliance with" the statute or 'to be consistent with... statutory authority;"

"The Board is required to make rules to implement the statute;" or simply, "the statute requires..." Such an emphasis is not common among states.

What started out as a fairly conventional, temporary moratorium with a design that was not very detailed evolved into a seizure of control of the rulemaking process by the Governor. The delays could be pointlessly disruptive to routine administrative processes.[424] There already was a functioning periodic review process in place.[425] It is one thing to claim that excessively burdensome regulations need to be reined in. It is something quite different to state, in extending a moratorium for a third year:

> **WHEREAS**, the current regulatory review and moratorium expires on June 30, 2011; and
> **WHEREAS**, the expiration of the current regulatory review and moratorium could result in a regulatory explosion detrimental to job creation and retention in this State...[426]

The moratorium did not appear to benefit small businesses in a regulatory flexibility sense. Arizona had one of the best developed systems for regulatory flexibility analysis and review of any state. The rulemaking process was announced and open earlier in rule development than in most states, and there were numerous opportunities for public participation. The GRRC is well conceived and implemented. It had a mission to review impact analyses, the authority to send regulations back for reworking, a membership that has a useful mix of perspectives, and a reasonable sized staff that is active in educating and working with agencies. A decade ago, MRP found Arizona to be exemplary,[427] and the passage of time probably has only added to the continuity, experience, depth of connections, and visibility of the GRRC to the public. The GRRC continues to exercise its non-review functions. The irony is that the Moratorium has taken an open, functioning review process focused on small business and inserted a screening step that is performed by a small, probably non-expert, bureaucratic office whose processes are opaque, whose concern with small business is not evident, and which lacks public input.

17. New Jersey: Executive Orders and Red Tape Review Group

The Executive Orders

One of Governor Christie's first actions upon taking office was to issue three executive orders on regulatory reform (January 20, 2010).

- Executive Order No. 1 froze (with some exceptions) proposed and pending regulations for a 90-day review period, and ordered executive agencies to review their regulations.
- Executive Order No. 2 spelled out a strategy for a reformed regulatory process.
- Executive Order No. 3 established a Red Tape Review Group, which included both legislative representatives and executive department heads.

The executive orders were thoughtful and pragmatic. In freezing proposed and pending regulations, for example, Governor Christie identified 154 regulations that could be "frozen without compromising the public health, safety or welfare," and gave not just criteria for exceptions from the freeze, but lists of regulations that would be frozen and not. The rhetoric was not anti-regulation but rather a call for "regulations that are reasonable, comprehensible, consistent, predictable and responsive."

The mantra invoked was "common sense." The strategic steps spelled out in E.O. No. 2 (and grouped as immediate, intermediate, and long-term) were described as common sense. They also incorporate many principles of good regulatory analysis.[428] The executive orders projected a sense of balancing, recognition that there were tradeoffs, and interest in doing it right.

Red Tape Review Group

Governor Christie's Executive Order No. 3 established a Red Tape Review Group, which included both legislative representatives and executive department heads and was chaired by the Lt. Governor. The Group's mandate was to "review pending and proposed rules and regulations, as well as all operative Executive Orders from previous administrations, in order to assess their effects on New Jersey's economy and to determine whether their burdens on business and workers outweigh their intended benefits." It went on to "chronicle a number of other legislative, regulatory and policy issues... that address a number of long-range policy issues relating to reform of the regulatory system."

Staff actually started work during the gubernatorial transition period, so that its work provided background for the executive orders. This included numerous discussions with state and local government officials and members of the public, as well as a review of regulatory reform efforts in four other states. The Group held three major public meetings, as well as meetings with legislative committees, conducted an intensive review of the regulatory process and previous regulatory reform efforts in New Jersey, and examined the results of the regulatory reviews that had been ordered. After three months, it issued a report that (considering the short time frame) was impressively thorough.[429] The report included legislative,[430] regulatory,[431] and other policy[432] recommendations. The report was filled with illustrative examples of specific regulations.

The executive orders and work of the Red Tape Review Group reflected a policy philosophy that was balanced, rather than simply being politically anti-regulation.[433] As the report's Executive Summary put it:

> The central thesis of this report is simple and clear: the state must achieve a better balance between protecting the public and nurturing free enterprise... The overarching theme of what the Group heard, as reflected in the recommendations, is that there is a great need for the application of common sense in rule-making and rule enforcement and that State Government must learn to operate in a user-friendly manner.[434]

"Common Sense Principles" was a recurring theme that echoed Executive Order No. 2.

Executive Order 41

Among the policy recommendations of the Red Tap Review Group was establishment a similar rule review group on an ongoing basis. Executive Order 41 (September 23, 2010) reconstituted the Red Tape Review Group as the Red Tape Review Commission[435] with a three-year mandate[436] to review rules and rulemaking.[437]

Effect

The practical effects of these executive orders on rulemaking practice in the time frame of this study are not clear. New Jersey was already producing some of the most complete and clear analyses of any state. New Jersey's statute is taken directly from the SBA model legislation, and both the spirit and the "common sense principles" of these executive orders seem complementary to these requirements.

The Red Tape Review Commission's first report was published in February 2012.[438] The number and specificity of modifications of regulations that were recommended by the Commission or proposed by agencies is striking. The follow-up process of ferreting out examples of nonsensical regulations and holding them up to ridicule was cleverly used as a tactic to raise consciousness and encourage people to go out and find some examples of their own. Including legislation in the Commission's scope (two dozen legislative efforts were listed) also addressed an important part of the regulatory problem.[439] Follow-up of previous recommendations is also a significant element. It is clear that the Commission is settling in to become an ongoing review process for new and existing regulations.[440]

These New Jersey executive orders were one of the best examples of positive leadership fund in the study.

18. New Mexico: Executive Order and Small Business-Friendly Task Force

As soon as she took office, Governor Martinez issued am executive order,[441] which had three principal elements. E.O. 2011-001:

- Suspended all proposed and pending regulations, which included suspending them (with exceptions for safety, health, judicial orders, essential functions, and federal funding) for a 90-day review period;
- Ordered agencies to review existing regulations within 30 days and "identify... each rule or regulation, the rescinding or revision of which could significantly enhance the business environment in New Mexico through economic development and employment growth;" and
- Established a "Small Business-Friendly Task Force with a vaguely defined mandate to review rules, apparently using input provided by the agencies, and report back in 90 days (discussed further below).

In its opening section, E.O. 2001-001 borrowed heavily from the language of New Jersey Governor Christie's E.O. No. 1. It did not mention "common sense" after the second "whereas" clause, however, and went straight rule review. After stating that 90 days was "a reasonable time" to review proposed and pending rules, E.O. 2001-001 directed agencies to review existing rules in 30 days. There was none of Governor Christie's balance, nuance, planning, or analysis. E.O. 2001-001 was only about rescinding regulations and revising them in favor of business.[442] In a subsequent action (January 10, 2010), Governor Martinez established the Office of Business Advocacy. The Office, which has a staff of three, serves an ombudsman function.[443]

Small Business-Friendly Task Force

Governor Martinez's E.O. 2011-001 established a "Small Business-Friendly Task Force." Agencies were ordered to review rules and regulations "with a view to enhancing the purpose of this task force" and were required to report the results of their reviews to the Secretary of Economic Development, who chaired the Task Force. The Task Force also was authorized "to make specific legislative and regulatory recommendations to achieve economic growth and stability in New Mexico." Its report was due in 90 days.

The Task Force report[444] received reports of agencies and considered their own experience[445] in formulating recommendations. The Task Force made several general recommendations:

- State rules and regulations should not be more stringent than federal standards.
- Revive the Small Business Regulatory Advisory Commission (SBRAC).[446]
- Enhance utilization of the new Office of Business Advocacy and its ombudsman function.
- Deal with employees in agencies and the permitting and licensing process.[447]

The Task Force made more specific recommendations concerning specific agencies or industries.[448] Some of these recommendations promoted simplification and rationalization.[449] Some concerned implementation, rather than regulations as such.[450] Many recommendations called for further review, sometimes quite comprehensive.[451] There was a certain superficiality and lack of discrimination to some recommendations; most seemed to deal with unnecessary burdens, but some simply failed to recognize the real purpose.[452] In several instances, the summary prescription was to roll regulations back to 2001 levels.

The Task Force singled out 11 environmental regulations by NMAC number and called for revision or rescission of five air quality standards – three of them greenhouse gas standards. These recommendations are more specific than those in any other area; the subject is too complex for a 90-day review by non-experts to produce a rescission recommendation; and stationary sources of greenhouse gasses are not typically small businesses. The Task Force also called for reducing involvement in the Western Climate Initiative from participant to observer status. In this area, the Task Force went beyond regulatory reform into the area of policy.

On the whole, the Task Force report probably presented a reasonable demonstration of what can be accomplished in a 90-day review. It usefully pointed out some directions, but it did not have the depth to resolve any specific issues. The general recommendations concerning the Small Business Regulatory Advisory Commission and the Office of Business Advocacy addressed the importance of institutions for regulatory flexibility analysis. No other elements of the Task Force's work advanced the process of regulatory review.

19. Nevada: Executive Order

Governor Sandoval issued an executive order[453] on his first day in office. E.O. 2011-01 nominally froze all regulations for one year, with some exceptions. Each agency was required to review its regulations and make recommendations for rescission. After 90 days, new regulations were allowed to go forward, subject to justification and approval by the governor. The same evaluative criteria, which included reference to business size, were established for both existing and new rules.[454]

20. Maine: Executive Orders

Executive Orders

Within a week of entering office, Governor LePage issued an executive order ,[455] which required review and approval by the Governor of any proposed rule both prior to publication of a NPRM and after the comment period. E.O. 09 FY 11/12 also set a moratorium of sorts by extending the comment period of any rule in that stage for 90 days. This executive order was effective for six months, in expectation of adoption of the Regulatory Fairness and Reform Act (which was signed on June 13, 2011). **A subsequent** executive order[456] renewed the requirements for review and approval by the Governor and required that an agency - before drafting a new regulation - must take a set of considerations[457] into account.

Effect

The executive orders were part of a general overhaul of rulemaking procedures, most of which were contained in the Regulatory Fairness and Reform Act. The extent of gubernatorial review is a bit unusual, but the considerations for rulemaking are quite standard. The executive orders do not address the issue of small businesses, but the Act did – among other things setting up the Office of Special Advocate and establishing an ombudsman.

21. Kansas: Executive Order

Governor Brownback issued an executive order[458] establishing the Office of Repealer, who has responsibility to:

- Investigate to determine instances in which those laws, regulations, or other governing instruments are unreasonable, unduly burdensome, duplicative, onerous, or in conflict;
- Recommend outright repeal or for modification of such law or regulation;
- Implement a tracking system to follow the action taken by any originating body on any recommendation; and
- Create a system for receiving public comment suggesting various laws, regulations, and other governing instruments to be considered for possible repeal.

E.O. 2011-01 did not order a regulatory freeze or an immediate review of all rules. It established a standing review mechanism, which is much more of a system reform – and probably more useful. Kansas statutes include one passing reference to small business. This executive order did not explicitly address regulatory flexibility issues, but the public comment mechanism could be helpful.

22. Michigan: Executive Orders

Executive Orders

Governor Snyder issued two executive orders that affected rulemaking.[459] E.O. 2011-4 extensively reorganized the executive branch, including reconstituted the Department of Energy, Labor, and Economic Growth as the Department of Licensing and Regulatory Affairs (LARA). E.O. 2011-5 created the Office of Regulatory Reinvention (ORR) and located it in LARA. ORR was directed to “review and evaluate all promulgated and proposed rules,” considering “without limitation” certain factors.[460] E.O. 2011-5 also described some best regulatory management practices.[461]

Effects

Despite the reshuffling, there was a good deal of continuity in the executive orders. The Office of Regulatory Reinvention, for example, has all of the functions of the former Office of Regulatory Reform (ORR). Overall, there was little emphasis on small businesses (Michigan already had a regulatory flexibility statute), but the executive orders led to a number of improvements.

- There had been no periodic review; ORR got the job of reviewing existing rules.[462]
- Analytical requirements for the regulatory impact statement were strengthened.[463]
- ORR is responsible for the forms in Appendix B (which include the seldom seen concept of disproportionate impacts).

Oversight of the rulemaking process is concentrated in ORR to an unusual degree, which is likely to be beneficial. There are excellent opportunities for education, for example, when the same entity creates the form and guidance and also reviews the results – as ORR does. ORR is clearly pro-active and appears quite well organized and thorough.

These executive orders are an emphatic statement of policy priority. E.O. 2011-5 had rhetoric about getting rid of regulations; there was an initial push to review regulations that seems overly ambitious; and ORR does keep score.[464] On the whole, however, the rejuvenation of the rulemaking process appears thoughtfully and well designed.

23. Colorado: Cutting Red Tape Initiative

In 2011, the Department of Regulatory Agencies (DORA)[465] organized a series of six “pits and peeves” roundtables throughout the state. Participants included Executive Directors and senior staff of a dozen state agencies and a broad and diverse group of representatives totaling approximately 100 business organizations, local governments, advocacy and community groups. As noted in the cover letter to the report:

> The principal objective of the Initiative was to provide a forum for senior government officials to listen to the problems and experiences of businesses and the community at large with respect to governmental red tape, and to understand, as fully as possible, what we heard.

The roundtable results were compiled in a report to the governor.[466] Issues were grouped into a set of “broad themes”:

- Need for change in government culture to focus on customer service;
- Regulatory inefficiencies and delays in issuing permits and licenses;
- Need for greater coordination among state agencies;
- Need for better coordination between Federal and local agencies on regulations;
- Need for periodic review of agency rules and regulations to evaluate continued need and effectiveness;
- Need for better use of new technology for communication and customer service;

- Need for a "go to" person in each agency to help the customer;
- Need to pay greater attention to economic/unintended adverse impacts of proposed regulations, requirements and procedures;
- Need to pay more attention to ensuring that new regulations reflect legislative intent.

The discussions, as reflected in the report, were incisive and insightful. The Roundtable participants offered a broad and varied range of suggestions, which DORA grouped into the following recommendations:

- Changes in Personnel Practices;
- Greater Interagency Coordination;
- Improved Communications;
- More Transparent Administrative Rulemaking;
- Greater Use of Public/Private Collaboration and Partnerships; and
- Better Utilization of Technology.

Specific Red Tape Reports were sent to the appropriate agencies after each roundtable. DORA reported that agency representatives found the roundtables to be a positive experience that provided helpful information. In the months between the roundtables and publication of the report, a number of agencies began reviewing their regulations or other initiatives. A number of these were reflected in "Red Tape" report. DORA has continued the review process with a Regulatory Help Line on its website for the dual purpose of reporting instances of red tape and seeking assistance in resolving problems.

The report concluded by identifying "four key Roundtable suggestions [that] deserve thoughtful consideration for action

- Designate an agency concierge or "go to" person in each department who acts as a clearinghouse, and source of information and direction for the public
- Establish "Regulatory Facilitation Teams," aligned around the industry clusters to be identified pursuant to Blueprint Colorado, to provide support and guidance to businesses in each respective cluster
- Issue an Executive Order that requires periodic rule review by each State agency to evaluate and determine the continued need and effectiveness of existing rules and regulations[467]
- Reconvene the original Roundtable participants and others to assess the progress of the Administration's efforts to cut red tape, and continue the dialogue on longer-term efforts to streamline State government in Colorado."

If the report had a single conclusion it was that, "while we believe that the 'Pits and Peeves' Roundtables Initiative has been successful in its mission, it is only part of a larger process that must be continued."

24. Wisconsin: Executive Order

Executive Order

Governor Walker issued an executive order[468] shortly after the legislature revised Chapter 227 of the Wisconsin Code (Administrative Procedure and Review).[469] E.O. # 50 set out requirements for statements of scope, economic impact analyses, and draft final rules. The procedures closely track the statutory requirements. E.O. # 50 frequently directs agencies to follow the statutory requirements and cites them often. E.O. # 50 even cites its own basis in statute: "the Governor, by executive order, may prescribe guidelines to ensure that rules are promulgated in compliance" with statutory requirements. "Guidelines" appears to be an apt description of E.O. # 50.

Effects

E.O. # 50 pulled together in compact form requirements that are scattered throughout Chapter 227. It filled out the statutory language with procedural details[470] and expanded on the statutory language.[471] Like the statutes, it stressed participation in rulemaking by the business community and local governments. E.O. # 50 (along with 2011 Wisconsin Act 46) also changed the structure of the Small Business Regulatory Review Board, removing all executive branch members.[472]

E.O. # 50 (and the new legislation) made changes that were more incremental than revolutionary. E.O. # 50 was thought through much more thoroughly than executive orders of governors who issued the order in their first week in office. E.O. # 50 is a clear statement of policy priority. What the effects are remains to be seen.

B. Observations

1. Patterns

Twenty-three states with executive orders on regulation were identified,[473] as well as six initiatives that included some kind of study of regulatory burdens.[474] There are patterns in the executive orders and initiative studies; most of them fit into a few categories.

- Six executive orders were issued to initiate regulatory flexibility analysis. Of these:
    - Three[475] were adopted as statute within two years or coincided with legislation, and
    - Three[476] subsequently disappeared.
- Two[477] were adjunct to existing or newly adopted regulatory flexibility legislation.
- Seven[478] were designed to overhaul and/or improve the rulemaking and review process.
- Four[479] were focused principally on long-term review and burden reduction.
- Five[480] froze ongoing rulemaking as part of an intensive short-term effort to reduce regulation.
- Initiative studies[481] were undertaken to gain background information.

Regulatory flexibility programs initiated by executive order are perishable. They rely on the Governor, and will fade away if the next Governor is not interested. Regulatory flexibility needs to become established and supported by infrastructure, such as guidance and education, advocacy, review commissions, and procedures. An executive order is usually not enough. Being adopted as legislation gives more staying power.[482] Executive orders that are adopted alongside existing legislation and make lesser changes do not appear as vulnerable.

The executive orders characterized as overhauls made substantial changes to existing rulemaking and review systems. Governors wanted to put their stamp on regulatory flexibility; this was part of a political agenda. These executive orders were designed to shake up and revitalize the system, and some involved extensive reorganization and/or renaming. They generally utilized or added to the existing rulemaking and review infrastructure, sometimes (e.g., Ohio) explicitly making it more responsive to small business. These executive orders were intended to reduce regulation, but these efforts were based on an understanding of the purpose of regulation and the need for balance with business interests, as reflected in the mantra "commonsense regulation."

The executive orders that focused on regulatory review also had burden-reduction goals. They approached this goal by seeking to improve the rule-review infrastructure by assigning specific tasks to an office or (Virginia) establishing a long-term Task Force.

The executive orders freezing rulemaking – particularly those of Arizona, Florida, and new Mexico – had a different character. The objective was to eliminate regulation. The rhetoric (e.g., "unnecessarily burdensome") seemed to be treated as if it were self-evident without much background study.[483] The three leading practitioners of regulatory freezes moved review and decision-making into the Office of the Governor. Arizona and Florida had some of the best rulemaking and review infrastructure of any state, but this was pushed aside.

The initiative studies took the opposite approach. They generally were designed to provide background on how regulation affects business, with a view to improving rulemaking, review, and implementation. The initiative came from different sources – legislative (Hawaii), gubernatorial (Tennessee), and departmental (Colorado). The Hawaii initiative focused on rulemaking; others were much broader. Some (especially Colorado) served to build bridges between agencies and the small business community. A consistent report was that businesses were not treated well by agency staff who implement and enforce regulations – a lack of "customer service." This suggests the value of an ombudsman and the importance of an ombudsman's feedback to rulemaking. Findings were consistent enough that it appeared that each initiative was re-inventing the wheel – but it was a wheel that each state took ownership of.

2. Small Business and Regulatory Flexibility

The executive orders involved regulatory flexibility to different degrees. Some were completely about regulatory flexibility. Some included regulatory provisions, among others. Some dealt with regulatory burdens on business in general with little or no reference to regulatory flexibility.

In the six states they initiated regulatory flexibility, the executive orders dated from the earlier stages of SBA's Regulatory Flexibility Initiative – 2003 through 2006.[484] Four of these adopted SBA's model legislation. Initiative subsequently shifted to the legislatures.

The executive orders described as "adjunct" were not about regulatory flexibility as such. Pennsylvania's executive order added executive branch review of regulations with no more than passing reference. Maine's was issued in conjunction with new regulatory flexibility legislation, which it complemented but did not affect.

Most of the executive orders described as overhauling or improving the rulemaking process are recent. Five were issued in 2011, and only New York's (1995) is more than three years old. Most of these did not regularly address regulatory flexibility as such, although their provisions likely benefitted small businesses generally:

- Ohio's executive order made significant improvements in the regulatory flexibility infrastructure;
- Hawaii's executive order implemented some recommendations of the Small Business Regulatory Review Board's Working Group;
- Utah's order listed small business among the groups whose costs must be estimated.
- New York's and Wisconsin's executive orders covered regulatory flexibility by cross-referencing the legislation but made no changes; and
- The others did not address regulatory flexibility, although New Jersey's order spawned a study that did.

Most of the executive orders that focused on reduction of regulatory burdens did not address regulatory flexibility as such. Washington is an exception. A second executive order temporarily froze rulemaking but provided that an agency could move forward if any impacted small entities were consulted on how to mitigate the impacts.

Most of the executive orders that froze ongoing rulemaking did nothing to further regulation. Two paid lip service to regulatory flexibility.[485] New Mexico's order is the exception; it created a task force,[486] which recommended reviving the defunct Small Business Regulatory Advisory Commission. Other task force recommendations pertained to small business but not generally to regulatory flexibility.[487] Arizona's and Florida's executive orders did substantial damage to the regulatory flexibility infrastructure.

All of the initiative studies identified and addressed small business issues. Hawaii and Florida focused on small business. New Jersey's report had a section on small business concerns. In Colorado and Tennessee, small business concerns were sprinkled through the report. In New Mexico restoration of small business infrastructure was recommended.

Almost all of the executive orders prior to 2007were concerned with regulatory flexibility and building up the infrastructure. Very few of the executive orders since had this focus, although many of the reforms addressed concerns of small business. Particularly considering Arizona and Florida, this is not a positive trend. The initiatives involving studies probably are more helpful to small business than most recent executive orders.

X. Observations on Best Practices

Effective practice of regulatory flexibility in rulemaking requires an infrastructure. In states that have adopted regulatory flexibility legislation (or executive order) on without creating the infrastructure, regulatory flexibility has not become effective or has faded away. In addition to economic and regulatory flexibility analyses, reasonably complete infrastructure would include:

- A clearly defined statutory basis for the major elements of infrastructure;
- Available and complete public information on rulemakings;
- Mechanisms for involvement of business and other stakeholders - early and often;
- An small business regulatory advocate;
- Review of rules proposed rules from a small-business perspective;
- Education, guidance, and advice on regulatory flexibility for agencies;
- Channels (e.g., an ombudsman) for feedback about implementation and outcomes of rules; and
- Administrative (gubernatorial and departmental) support for regulatory flexibility as a distinct component of small business assistance.

Most states have some elements; few, if any, have a complete system.

A. Statutory Foundation

Executive Orders have their uses. They can set the stage for regulatory flexibility legislation. They can fill in procedures and other details. Executive orders establishing regulatory flexibility, however, do not have the staying power of a statute. They appear to be much more effective and durable when used to improve on existing statutory requirements.

Inclusion

A statutory basis is a common feature of most of the effective institutional elements of regulatory flexibility infrastructure:

- Advocates, review commissions, and ombudsmen (and often their location within the executive branch) are usually established by statute.
- Process and reporting requirements for analysis of small business impacts and regulatory flexibility alternatives are statutory.
- Procedures for public notification and comment, post-approval review of proposed rules, and periodic or ongoing review of existing rules are part of state Administrative Procedures Acts.
- Many of the useful processes for public involvement - pre-NPRM notifications, departmental small business advisory committees, negotiated rulemaking, and post-approval appeals based on inadequate small business impact analysis – are statutory.

The best practice is simply to include all these elements; many states do not.

Imperative

Wording of statutory provisions that cover a range of circumstances is an issue. In general, “shall, where possible” – the approach taken in SBA’s model legislation - is much more effective than “may.” In the case of involvement of the public during pre-NPRM rule development, such an imperative can be buttressed with a requirement in the small business impact statement to explain what steps were taken to involve the public.

The issue is less clear when the question is whether a step is necessary and appropriate. Hearings provide an example. Allowing the public a voice is important, but if a rule amendment is minor and non-controversial, a hearing is likely to be a waste of time and other resources. The best practice here is a procedure for a no-hearing notice that will allow expeditious adoption, with mechanism that that requires a hearing if the original notice meets a certain level of objection. Emergency rules also are an expedited process, although for different purposes.

The requirement for a regulatory flexibility analysis is a more subtle issue of this type. The standard language, "affects small business," is far too broad because – in the absence of a subsequent checkpoint to indicate that no more analysis is required – this standard literally requires a full analysis of many rules that have minimal impacts. Needlessly burdensome requirements for analysis can (paradoxically) result in little or no analysis even where it is warranted. Aggregate impact thresholds tend to divert focus from the impacts on individual businesses, which may be significant for some businesses. Missouri's $500 aggregate threshold – originally designed to make the concept of affecting small businesses operational - is attractive for its clarity as a preliminary screen. It requires some consideration of cost numbers, terminates analysis where it clearly is not warranted, and otherwise provides a signal to proceed. An even better practice would be to combine this with an additional checkpoint based on impacts on an individual business,[488] which implicitly would require some further analysis to establish.

Preamble Rationale for Regulatory Flexibility

The preamble to SBA's model legislation contains a very clear statement of the issue of disproportionate impacts on small businesses, which is the basis for regulatory flexibility analysis. Washington is the only state whose statute contains such launguage. Most legislation says nothing. Most executive orders contain generalities about burdensome regulations and adverse impacts on employment and business development, which focus attention on aggregate impacts rather than disproportionate impacts on small business. A clear statement of the issue of disproportionate impacts – preferably in the statute – provides guidance for the analysis, takes much of the ideology out of the subject, and provides a common ground with which rational regulatory analysts can agree.

Statutory Detail

Statutes are usually reasonably thorough in spelling out details of responsibilities, requirements for issues to be addressed in analysis, contents of filings, review criteria, and grounds for appeal. Authority of advocates, review committees, and ombudsmen is particularly important, because it may have to be invoked. Even where such an entity does not have the authority to compel (which it usually does not), it is helpful to include requirements for agency response and explanation, which is often absent. Requiring agency staff to think and articulate – particularly when dealing with advocates – can have beneficial consequences for dialogue and education.

Some of the details in the SBA model legislation on how to do an economic impact statement are not specific enough to serve as guidance. This lack of clarity has carried over into state legislation. SBA's Section 3 outlines the analysis in aggregate terms and requires only descriptions. The phrase "the likely per-firm regulatory cost increase" (found in SBA's *State Guide*) is missing. This brief phrase includes both the idea of estimating costs and assessing impacts on representative businesses – both of which are typically missing from state analyses. It would also be helpful if the legislation specified that different types of businesses may be affected in different ways, and that these need to be considered separately. Such matters could be addressed in guidance, but in many states the guidance does no more than repeat the statute.

Limitations of Models

SBA's model legislation served a very useful purpose in getting states to address regulatory flexibility. Models and examples (which SBA's *State Guide* provides in quantity) help prime the pump.

Adopting a model, however, is only a first step – necessary, perhaps, but not sufficient. Too many states have done little more than adopt a model. This shows up in the tendency to quote statute as guidance and in the number of state programs that have withered or died for lack of additional infrastructure.

A comparison of New Mexico's Small Business Regulatory Advisory Commission (SBRAC) and Missouri's Small Business Regulatory Fairness Board (SBRFB) provides a striking example.

New Mexico copied Missouri's statute almost verbatim, but the SBRAC withered away while the SBRFB flourished. There are two discernible differences. Missouri's statute was adopted after two years of operation with strong gubernatorial support under an executive order, and the SBRFB's membership includes the chair of the minority business advocacy commission, which had been in operation for many years. The SBRAC, on the other hand, was established *de novo*, with no context, no experience, and no leadership.

B. Public Information

Public information includes background information on rulemaking, information on individual proposed rules, and opportunities to receive notification and make comments. Best practice means taking advantage of the internet to inform the public in these ways. The details have changed very little from those described by SBA in the *State Guide* five years ago.

Background

Background information is generally provided on the website of the Secretary of State or some other agency that publishes the *Register* or oversees parts of the rulemaking process. The objective is to give the public both information to understand the process and initial access to means of participation. Information on a well-designed site should include:

- Background information on regulations;
- Background information on the rulemaking and rule review process;
- Information on participating in the rulemaking process (opportunities and procedures);
- A calendar of public hearings;
- A link (or links) for subscribing to notices or RSS feeds; and
- Links to sources of information on proposed rules, such as:
    - The *Register*,
    - Regulatory agendas (if any),
    - Agency contacts,

- Rulemaking web pages of agencies that have them,
- Other pages providing lists of rules, dockets or status information, and/or
- Search engines for proposed rules.

Notices and the Register

Notices in state Registers generally provide the necessary standard information. Access to other information can problematic. The notification process should both flag attention and provide resources for further study before commenting.

While electronic publication is more cutting-edge, a pdf publication of a printed register can be effective if it has adequate electronic backup. The same links are needed in notices sent by email. Printed editions are limited to volume-by-volume presentation, but initial notices are not too difficult to find in that format.[489] A clean layout and readable text are helpful. Hyperlinks are essential. They should include links within the *Register* from the table of contents to notices, links to any contact persons and/or the agency website, and links to documents available at the time the notice was published – either individually or on a collected web page.

The summary of rulemaking is the heart of a notice. It should give the reader a clear idea of whether a rule is of interest and worth looking into more deeply. A best-practice notice should have a summary that includes:

- A brief summary of the purpose and need for the rule;
- A brief explanation of what the rule will change and how it will be changed; and
- A brief description of effects known at the time. Most state notice summaries contain only part of this explanation.

Other Documentation

A notice (*Register* or electronic) should be linked to documents that have been developed. The text of the proposed rule (in mark-up form) is the key document, but any impact statements, summaries of comments, or other written materials should also be available. In states where the statute requires publication of these documents or (given space considerations) a summary, links could actually be a simplification.

Best practice is to have web pages that present all notices, documents, and status information (milestones passed, schedules, etc.) for every rule. Such a presentation enhances access to the rulemaking, and it mitigates most of the practical shortcomings of pdf publication of a print *Register*. Preferably, this information should be on the agency website, with clear drill-down access from the home page. This information can also be assembled centrally (e.g., Virginia) and accessed by links from the agency website.

It is best practice for an agency to have its own website on the regulations that it promulgates.[490] Environmental agencies typically have such a website; many agencies do not. A website provides an overview of the agency's regulatory activity as a whole, and for agencies with a lot of regulations this is a very useful feature.

Communication

Virtually all states require sending notices to persons who have "timely" requested them. Some statutes authorize electronic notices; others don't say. Many, but far from all, states have an opportunity to subscribe on line for such notices or for other notification systems, such as RSS. Best practice requires this. Given the ease of linking, access to a subscription page should be found on the agency website, the website that provides general public information, and the *Register* website.

It should also be possible to submit comments electronically. At a minimum, this requires providing an email address in notices. Some states or individual agencies have comment pages. Virginia puts all comments on a rule on line as a thread.

C. Stakeholder Involvement

Informal, early public participation does not leave much of a paper trail, and so this study has not been able to observe activities of this nature. Statutes suggest several methods, which can be pursued even without statutory authority. Negotiated rulemaking provides a blueprint for stakeholder discussions. Even if a consensus is not reached, the process helps clarify issues on a complex rule. Similarly, consultation of interested parties or experts can be fruitful whether or not they constitute and advisory committee. If an agency makes a number of rules in the same area and consults the same people, however, it would probably facilitate the process to formalize a committee. Early notice of intent need not be confined to published notices in the *Register*. There are milestones between a regulatory agenda (itself a best practice) and an NPRM where some type of notice and request for comments could be appropriate.[491]

The list of electronic notice subscribers is a valuable resource for early public involvement. It makes it easy to provide pre-NPRM notices. A little analysis of the list would probably produce useful and fairly representative contacts for consultation. Email makes it easy for an organization to forward notices to its members for comment. Discretion, however, may be advisable. Email forwarding also has the potential to let a request for helpful comment morph into a campaign against the regulation.

Early public participation is particularly important for regulatory flexibility. For rules that impact small businesses, business representatives are likely to have a much better sense than agency staff for the practicalities of how something will play out. Additional eyes from a different perspective may be valuable in spotting wording or provisions that have unintended consequences. It is easier to incorporate regulatory flexibility elements early in development than later.

D. Small Business Regulatory Advocate

An advocate is the personification of regulatory flexibility. This function, if not the title, probably is the most important element of a regulatory flexibility program (aside from the statute itself), in part because advocacy supports other elements. Only half a dozen states have an advocate or advocacy office, although most independent review commissions also perform advocacy functions.

An advocate works with agency staff to inculcate regulatory flexibility principles and practices. A knowledgeable advocate may well have a better understanding of regulatory flexibility than anyone else is involved in rulemaking. An advocate can provide guidance and classroom training on regulatory flexibility as well, but this on-the-job training is demonstration. An advocate builds relationships and persuades and motivates agency staff. This function is perhaps best illustrated in a comment that the Oregon Office of Regulatory Streamlining helped "instill the importance of regulatory streamlining into the mindset of state agencies."

As that comment illustrates, advocacy is valuable in reviewing and revising existing rules as well as proposed rules. An advocate can also be an important link in public participation. An active advocate will work with the business community as well as agencies. Public outreach is an activity shared with an ombudsman, and it can be strengthened when both work together.

Regulatory flexibility needs to have its own identity, distinct from both Regulatory Reform and small business assistance. The focus on disproportionate impacts can be lost in the tide of regulatory reform, as in Arizona and Florida. The focus on rulemaking can be lost in the varied assistance provided to small businesses, as in Alaska. An advocate helps anchor regulatory flexibility, and probably would have filled the void of executive branch leadership in a number of states with weak programs.

An office of small business regulatory flexibility advocate, with a well-qualified advocate and some staff, is a best practice.

E. Small Business Regulatory Review Commission

Legislatures in most states review proposed and existing rules. Except in Illinois, however, they have no discernible interest in impacts on small business. Only a few states have executive branch agencies that (in the absence of an advocate or independent commission) do substantive review of rules.[492]

Concern with small business and regulatory flexibility is the mission of small business regulatory review committees. Statutes generally do not give review committees real authority[493] but generally do require agencies to respond meaningfully to their comments. In a few states, the Governor essentially delegated his authority to the commission. The quality of analysis appears to be relatively good where a commission is active.

States have various ways of organizing periodic review of existing rules. Except for short-cycle expiration of rules, any can be effective – depending on the care of the reviewer. Periodic review is a best practice, but review is strengthened by on-demand review that a regulatory review commission can provide.

Review commissions are usually made up of, or dominated by, small businessmen. That gives them a valuable practical perspective, but it means that their time is usually limited. Most of the review is nominally done after the rule is approved, but many of these commissions seem to encroach on earlier stages.

Established commissions have enough interaction with agencies to assume an advocacy role and something of a teaching role. The most active of the commissions prepare guidance materials and provide training as well. How much they are able to accomplish appears to depend on their organization, leadership, and staffing.

Review commissions have certain elements in common with advocates. They build up relationships with agencies, do advocacy, educate, and seek to foster public participation. They are essentially complementary, although there is some degree of substitutability. Only two states – Florida and (recently) Maine – have established both an advocate and a review commission, and both states did this in the same legislative package.

Establishing a small business regulatory review commission that has a dozen or so business members and several staffers, with authority to do the actions outlined above is a best practice. Arizona, Hawaii, and Missouri appear to be leading models.

F. Guidance

Guidance should pick up where the statute leaves off, but in most states it does not. Most states do little more than repeat the statute. In this context, best practice is phrasing the requirements in the form of a question that makes one think and respond (Massachusetts –

Appendix B). It is uncommon to find guidance that improves on the statutory language,[494] or that begin to indicate the sort of information the analysis should yield.[495] The lack of guidance materials is reflected in the fact that the best guidance was actually on templates and forms.

Regulatory flexibility guidance for state agencies should be expanded in three basic directions.

- Background on what regulatory flexibility is about is needed. The first two paragraphs in the *Forward* of SBA's *State Guide* provide a better orientation than anything found in state guidance.
- The mechanics of estimating cost impacts need to be explained, including such basics as:
  - Count and analyze separately small businesses that are in different industries and/or are differently affected by the rule,
  - Develop cost estimates for different size classes of business, and
  - Estimate savings in costs from regulatory alternatives considered.
- Illustrative examples, particularly for regulatory flexibility alternatives and criteria for revising rules on periodic review, are most helpful for understanding.

One reason that the advocacy role is so important is that example, demonstration, and practice provide effective guidance that cumulatively develops understanding. It takes time to instill the importance and practice of regulatory flexibility into "the mindset of state agencies."

G. Feedback

The value of public input does not end with the promulgation of a rule. Conditions change, and rules have unintended and/or unforeseen consequences. Changes are a major reason for periodic review. The nature of complaints or comments received from the public is an important factor in performing – and possibly initiating – review. Mechanisms for feedback are part of the regulatory flexibility infrastructure.

Regulatory review commissions usually have a role in review of existing rules as well as new rules. The role can include reviewing and forwarding public complaints to an agency and initiating requests for review on its own. Both of these are valuable functions. In some states the commission may also be involved (either as a channel or as a reviewer) in an appeal of a rule by an affected person on the grounds of an incomplete or defective small business impact statement. A procedure for such an appeal also is a best practice. It is the most explicit form of quality control on small business impact statements found, and it is based on actual outcomes rather than projections.

An ombudsman may deal real with actual impacts of a rule or with misinterpreted implementation. In either case, the information gained is useful – either to be compiled for the next rule review or for an agency to use in working with its own staff. Environmental agencies have ombudsmen. Ohio has instituted regulatory ombudsmen for "business-facing" agencies. A somewhat similar role may be played by an agency regulatory coordinator – required in some states – who can collect feedback as well as dispense information. A few agencies (e.g., Colorado's DORA) have set up on-line complaint pages.

The initiatives reviewed have collected extensive feedback through surveys, focus groups, roundtables, and other meetings. This feedback has not been regulation-specific, but it does provide information for policy and administrative purposes. The insight that poor "customer service" contributes to what is broadly understood as "burden" of regulations indicates that the issues extend beyond regulatory development and the rulemaking process.

All of these channels are really best practices, although initiatives are not routine practices. States that initiate them have a better regulatory infrastructure than states that do not.

H. Leadership and Support

Executive branch support for regulatory flexibility is essential. States where the legislature has a monopoly on the rulemaking process have relatively high mortality and morbidity rates for regulatory flexibility. There are a few states in which an advocate or independent commission reports to the legislature. Aside from Illinois' public outreach, however, legislative branches do not provide significant support for the regulatory flexibility infrastructure other than publishing the *Register* and reviewing rules. Support must come from the executive branch, and it is important at two levels.

Regulatory flexibility needs gubernatorial support. At a minimum, regulatory flexibility must be regarded as a legitimate activity in its own right. It should be a policy priority. In some states (e.g., Hawaii and Massachusetts) a governor has strengthened small business regulatory review by delegating his own review authority to the review commission or advocate. Rhode Island is an excellent example of integrating regulatory flexibility into its economic development strategy and using it as part of a campaign to attract small businesses to the state.

Ironically, regulatory flexibility is vulnerable to a "regulatory reform" campaign. Regulatory flexibility is a relatively nuanced matter of leveling the regulatory playing field for small businesses. Reform that seeks only to eliminate regulation and its burdens is not interested in this sort of nuance. The contrast between Michigan, New Jersey, and Ohio (on the one hand) and Arizona and Florida (on the other) is stark. Ohio put substantial emphasis on regulatory flexibility in its recent reforms. Michigan and New Jersey were rather neutral on regulatory flexibility, but they made serious attempts to reform the rulemaking process in ways that seem to benefit small businesses. Arizona and Florida, by comparison, went about rescinding and reducing regulations as quickly as possible. The Governors opted for gubernatorial control of rulemaking, as opposed to established functioning process. By taking the review powers into their own offices, they pushed aside two of the best designed regulatory flexibility infrastructures in any state.

At the departmental level, regulatory flexibility must be recognized as a distinct activity and given support. Advocates are generally located within agencies. Review commissions are independent but their staff comes from agencies. The issue here is a matter of dedication of resources to regulatory flexibility activities.

I. Conclusion

There are many potential elements of regulatory flexibility infrastructure, and states have different mixes of them. There are also many different configurations and ways of performing functions. Best practice is not so much a matter of how these functions are carried out as how thoroughly. Information and guidance, for example are subject to a performance standard: How accessible and complete is the information?

While there are a number of specific techniques and features that enhance regulatory flexibility, best practices would seem to be defined in broad, basic terms:

- Keep the focus on regulatory flexibility – mitigation of disproportionate regulatory burdens on small business.
- Give elements of the regulatory infrastructure a solid, durable, preferably statutory, foundation with clear authorization to act.
- Build a complete and well-coordinated regulatory flexibility infrastructure.
- Find creative, dedicated people who understand the mission.
- Make regulatory flexibility a policy priority, and provide adequate resources.
- Recognize and prepare for the fact that this is a long-term endeavor.

REFERENCES

General References

National Conference of Commissioners on Uniform State Laws, *Model State Administrative Procedure Act*, 1981.

National Conference of Commissioners on Uniform State Laws, *Revised Model State Administrative Procedures Act*, 2010.

Public Law 96-354 – Sept. 19, 1980, *Regulatory Flexibility Act of 1980.*

Public Law 104-121 – March 29, 1996, *Small Business Regulatory Enforcement Fairness Act.*

Small Business Administration, Office of Advocacy, *Small Business Regulatory Flexibility Model Legislation Initiative*, September 2005.

Small Business Administration, Office of Advocacy, *State Guide to Regulatory Flexibility for Small Businesses*, March 2007.

State References (by State)

Alabama

Code of Alabama

Title 41 (State Government), Chapter 22 (Administrative Procedure): §41-22-5, §41-22-6, §41-22-10, §41-22-22, and §41-22-23.

Legislative Reference Service, Administrative Procedure Division, *Alabama Administrative Monthly,* http://www.alabamaadministrativecode.state.al.us/monthly.html.

Legislative Reference Service, Administrative Procedure Division, *Instruction Manual and Drafting Style Manual*, Revised: July 27, 2004.

Alaska

Alaska Statutes

Title 24 (Legislature), Chapter 20 (Agencies of the Legislature): §24.20.410, §24.20.445, and §24.20.460.

Title 44 (State Government), Chapter 62 (Administrative Procedure Act): §44.62.040, §44.62.060, §44.62.125, §44.62.190, §44.62.195, §44.62.200, §44.62.210, §44.62.215, §44.62.218, §44.62.300, and §44.62.320.

Department of Law, *Drafting Manual for Administrative Regulations*, 19th Edition (August 2011).

Department of Commerce, Community, and Economic Development - Office of Economic Development, *AS 44.62.218. Regulations Affecting Small Businesses, 2005: A Program Report*, April 2, 2008.

Office of the Lieutenant Governor, *Online Public Notices*,
http://aws.state

Arizona

Arizona Revised Statutes

Title 41 (State Government), Chapter 6 (Administrative Procedure):

Article 1 (General Provisions): §41-1001.

Article 3 (Rule Making): §41-1021, §41-1022, §41-1023, §41-1034, and §41-1035.

Article 4 (Attorney General Review of Rule Making): §41-1044.

Article 4.1 (Administrative Rules Oversight Committee): §41-1046, §41-1047, and §41-1048.

Article 5 (Governor's Regulatory Review Council): §41-1051, §41-1052, §41-1053, §41-1055, §41-1056, §41-1056.01, and §41-1057.

Title 41 (State Government), Chapter 8 (Agencies of the Legislative Department):

Article 5 (Office of Ombudsman-Citizens Aide): §41-1376 and §41-1377.

Arizona Governor's Regulatory Review Council website,
http://www.grrc.state

Arizona Ombudsman – Citizens' Aide website, About Us web page,
http://www.azleg.gov/ombudsman/about.asp.

Brewer, Janice K., Memorandum, The Governor's Regulatory Review Plan, January 22, 2009.

Brewer, Janice K., Executive Order 2010-04, Establishing the Commission on Privatization and Efficiency, January 21, 2010.

Brewer, Janice K., Executive Order 2010-13, Continuation of the Moratorium on Proposed Rulemaking, June 30, 2010.
Brewer, Janice K., Executive Order 2011-05, State Regulatory Rule Making Review and Moratorium To Promote Job Creation and Retention, June 30, 2011.
Office of the Secretary of State, Public Services Division, Arizona Administrative Register Online, http://www.azsos.gov/public_services
Office of the Secretary of State website, http://www.azsos.gov/Info/Office.htm.
Office of the Secretary of State and the Rulewriters' Consortium, Arizona Rulemaking Manual, September 2011.

Arkansas

Arkansas Code
Title 25 (State Government), Chapter 15 (Administrative Procedures):
Subchapter 2 (Administrative Procedure Act): §25-15-204, §25-15-207, §25-15-215, and §25-15-216.
Subchapter 3 (Administrative Rules That Impact Small Businesses): §25-15-301, §25-15-302, §25-15-303, and §25-15-304.
Arkansas Economic Development Commission, Small and Minority Business Development Division regulatory flexibility website, http://arkansasedc.com/entrepreneurs
Department of Environmental Quality regulations website, http://www.adeq.state
Huckabee, Mike, Executive Order 05-04, February 1, 2005.
Secretary of State *Arkansas Register* (monthly), print and published online at http://www.sos.arkansas.gov/rulesRegs/Pages/ArkansasRegister.aspx.
Secretary of State website, http://www.sos.arkansas.gov/Pages/default.aspx.

California

California Code
Title 2 (Government of the State of California), Division 3 (Executive Department), Chapter 3.5 (Administrative Regulations and Rulemaking):
Article 2 (Definitions): §11342.610
Article 5 (Public Participation: Procedure for Adoption of Regulations: §11346.2, §11346.3, §11346.4, §11346.45, §11346.5, §11346.6, §11346.8, and §11346.9.
Article 6 (Review of Proposed Regulations: §11349.1, §11349.3, §11349.4, and §11349.5.
Article 7 (Review of Existing Regulations §11349.7 and §11349.8.
Article 8 (Judicial Review): §11350.
Governor's Office of Business and Economic Development website, http://business.ca.gov.
Office of Administrative Law, *The California Regulatory Notice Register Online*, http://www.oal.ca.gov/California_Regulatory_Notice_Online.htm.
Office of Administrative Law, *California Rulemaking Law Handbook*, 2011.
Department of Finance *Economic Impact Statement* (STD. 399), http://www.fgc.ca.gov/regulations
Office of Administrative Law, *How to Participate in the Rulemaking Process*, April 2006.
Office of Administrative Law, *OAL Checklist Notice Review*, http://www.oal.ca.gov/res/docs/pdf/checklist/NoticeReviewChecklist.PDF.
Office of Administrative Law, P:ublic Participation web page,

http://www.oal.ca.gov/Public_Participation.htm.
Office of Administrative Law, *Rulemaking Course Under California's APA: Course Agenda*, http://www.oal.ca.gov/res/docs/pdf/3-DayCourseAgenda.pdf
Office of Administrative Law website, http://www.oal.ca.gov/Default.htm.

Colorado

Colorado Revised Statutes
Title 24 (Government – State):
Article 4 (Rulemaking and Licensing Procedures by State Agencies: §24-4-102, §24-4-103, §24-4-106, and §24-4-108.
Article 34 (Department of Regulatory Agencies): §24-34-101 and §24-34-104.
Department of Regulatory Agencies, *Annual Report on Colorado's Regulatory Environment: FY 2008-2009.*
Department of Regulatory Agencies, *Cutting Red Tape in Colorado State Government*, Omnibus Report to the Governor on the "Pits and Peeves" Roundtable Initiative, December 2011.
Department of Regulatory Agencies website, http://www.colorado.gov/cs/Satellite?c=Page&childpagename=DORA%2FDORALayout&cid=1249686120221&pagename=CBONWrapper.
Department of Regulatory Agencies, Office of Policy, Research & Regulatory Reform website, http://www.colorado.gov/cs/Satellite/DORA-OPRRR/CBON/DORA/1251614750683
Secretary of State, Administrative Rules Program, *Code of Colorado Regulations: Rules Styling Manual*, July 2010.
Secretary of State, *Colorado Online Register*, http://www.sos.state

Connecticut

Connecticut General Statutes
Title 4 (Management of State Agencies), Chapter 54 (Uniform Administrative Procedure Act): §4-166, §4-168, §4-168a, §4-168b, §4-169, §4-170, §4-170a, §4-170b, §4-171, §4-172, §4-175 and §4-183.

Commission on Official Legal Publications, *Connecticut Law Journal*

The Legislative Commissioners' Office, *Manual for Drafting Regulations*, Revised: December 2009. Legislative Regulation Review Committee website, http://www.cga.ct.gov/rr.
Legislative Regulation Review Committee, *A Practical Guide for Adoption of a Regulation in Accordance with the Connecticut Uniform Administrative Procedure Act and the Rules of the Legislative Regulation Review Committee,* Revised: February, 2012.
Office of Legislative Research website, http://www.cga.ct.gov/olr.

Delaware

Delaware Code
Title 29 (State Government):
Chapter 101 (Administrative Procedures):

Subchapter II (Agency Regulations): §10115, §10117, and §10118.
Subchapter V (Judicial Review): §10141
Chapter 104 (Regulatory Flexibility Act): §10402, §10403, §10404, §10405, §10406, and §10407.
Delaware General Assembly, Division of Research, *Drafting and Style Manual*, September 2009.
Delaware General Assembly, Division of Research website, http://legis.delaware.gov/legislature.nsf/Lookup/Division_Research?open&nav=divisions
Delaware General Assembly, Legislative Council, Office of the Registrar of Regulations, *Delaware Register of Regulations*, http://regulations
Department of Natural Resources & Environmental Control, Delaware Small Business, Secretary's Order No. 2007-F-0004, *Re: Application of Regulatory Flexibility Act to Regulation 3215, Horseshoe Crab Harvest Moratorium*, February 5, 2007.

Florida

Florida Statutes
Title X (Public Officers, Employees, and Records), Chapter 120 (Administrative Procedure Act): §120.52, §120.54, §120.541, §120.545, and §120.74.
Title XIX (Public Business), Chapter 288 (Commercial Development and Capital Improvements), Part IV (Small and Minority Business): §288.7001, §288.7002, and §288.70015.
Department of State, *Florida Administrative Register & Florida Administrative Code*, https://www.flrules.org/default.asp
The Florida Legislature Joint Administrative Procedures Committee website, https://www.flrules.org/notice/QuickResult.asp?P0=Stat_Comm_All&P1=0.
Office of Fiscal Accountability and Regulatory Reform website, http://www.floridahasarighttoknow.com/office_fiscal_accountability
Office of Small Business Advocate, *Report on Small Business Issues and Recommendations*, September 2010.
Office of Small Business Advocate & Small Business Regulatory Advisory Council, *FY 2009-10 Annual Report*.
Scott, Rick, Executive Order 11-01, *Suspending Rulemaking and Establishing the Office of Fiscal Accountability and Regulatory Reform*, January 4, 2011.
Scott, Rick, Executive Order 11-72, *Office of Fiscal Accountability and Regulatory Reform*, April 8, 2011.
Scott, Rick, Executive Order 11-211, Superseding Executive Order 11-72; *Office of Fiscal Accountability and Regulatory Reform*, October 19, 2011.
Florida Supreme Court, *Whiley v. Scott*, No. SC11-592, August 16, 2011.

Georgia

Official Code of Georgia Annotated
Title 50 (State Government), Chapter 13 (Administrative Procedure): §50-13-2, §50-13-3, §50-13-4, and §50-13-10.

Atwood, Alex, Session Update, *Rep. Alex Atwood Requesting Input from Business Community*, February 6, 2012, http://www.alexatwoodstaterep.com/update feb6 2012.html.

Georgia Republican Party (GAGOP), House Speaker David Ralston Charges Small Business Committee with Red Tape Watch Initiative, January 30, 2012, http://www.gagop.org/house-speaker-david-ralston-charges-small-business-committee-with-red-tape-watch-initiative.

Perdue, Sonny, Executive Order, *Small Business Regulatory Reform Initiative*, March 6, 2006. "Red Tape Watch" website, www.house.ga.gov/redtapewatch. Secretary of State website, http://www.sos.georgia.gov.

Hawaii

Hawaii Revised Statutes

Division I (Government):

Title 8 (Public Proceedings and Records), Chapter 91 (Administrative Procedure): §91-2, §91-2.6, §91-3, and §91-7.

Title 13 (Planning and Economic Development), Chapter 201M (Small Business Regulatory Flexibility Act): §201M-2, §201M-3, §201M-4, §201M-5, §201M-6, and §201M-7.

Department of Business, Economic Development and Tourism, RegAlert Description, http://hawaii.gov/dbedt/programs/sbrrb/regalert/FOLDERNOTE.2008-07-11.2333/view?searchterm=RegAlert.

Hawaii Small Business Regulatory Review Board, *Periodic Review – Evaluation Report In Compliance with Regulatory Flexibility Act Section 201M –7, Hawaii Revised Statutes*, December 2010.

Hawaii Small Business Regulatory Review Board, *Annual Report Summary - Review of Administrative Rules, Legislation And Rules Requested by Small Business In Compliance with Chapter 201M Hawaii Revised Statutes, January 2011 - December 2011.*

Hawaii Small Business Regulatory Review Board Working Group, *Report Findings and Recommendations*, January 2009.

Hawaii Small Business Regulatory Review Board website, http://hawaii.gov/dbedt/programs/sbrrb.

Office of the Lieutenant Governor, *Administrative Rules Proposed Changes*, http://ltgov.hawaii.gov/the-office/administrative-rules

Lingle, Linda, Administrative Directive No. 09-01, *Policy and Procedure for the Adoption, Amendment, or Repeal of Administrative Rules*, October 29, 2009.

Office of the Ombudsman, *State of Hawaii, Fiscal Year 2010-2011 Report No. 42*, December 2011.

Idaho

Idaho Statutes

Title 67 (State Government and State Affairs):

Chapter 4 (Legislature): §67.454

Chapter 52 (Idaho Administrative Procedure Act): §67.5202, §67.5220, §67.5221, §67.5223, §67.5224, §67.5278, and §67.5291.

Office of the Administrative Rules Coordinator, *Idaho Administrative Bulletin*, http://adminrules.idaho.gov/bulletin/index.html.
Office of the Administrative Rules Coordinator, *The Idaho Rule Writer's Manual*,
Legislative Services Office website, http://legislature.idaho.gov/lso/lso.htm.

Illinois

Illinois Compiled Statutes
Government, Chapter 5 (Administrative Procedures Act):
Article 1 (Title And General Provisions): §100/1-5.
Article 5 (Rulemaking Provisions): §100/5-30, §100/5-40, §100/5-75, §100/5-100, §100/5-110, and §100/5-115.
Article 10 (Administrative Hearings): §100/10
Health and Safety, Chapter 415 (Environmental Safety): Article 5 (Environmental Protection Act), Title VII (Regulations): §415/5-27 and §415/5-28.
Joint Committee on Administrative Rules, *Illinois Regulation (The Flinn Report)*, weekly.
Joint Committee on Administrative Rules website, http://www.ilga.gov/commission/jcar.
Office of Regulatory Flexibility website, http://www.ildceo.net/dceo/Bureaus/Entrepreneurship+and+Small+Business/Regulatory+Compliance+Assistance/RegFlex.htm.
Secretary of State, *Illinois Register*, http://www.cyberdriveillinois.com/departments/index/register.
Secretary of State, *Style Manual: Illinois Administrative Code and Illinois Register*, June 2004.

Indiana

Indiana Code
Title 2 (General Assembly), Article 5 (Legislative Agencies and Study Committees): §2-5-18-8.
Title 4 (State Offices and Administration), Article 22 (Administrative Rules and Procedures):
Chapter 2 (Adoption of Administrative Rules): §4-22-2-23, §4-22-2-24, §4-22-2-28, §4-22-2-28.1, §4-22-2-32, §4-22-2-34, and §4-22-2-46.
Chapter 2.1 (Rules Affecting Small Businesses): §4-22-2.1-5, §22-2.1-6, and §4-22-2.1-8.
Chapter 2.5 (Expiration and Readoption of Administrative Rules): §4-22-2.5. Title 5 (State and Local Administration), Article 28: Indiana Economic Development Corporation):
Chapter 2 (Definitions): §5-28-2-6.
Chapter 17 (Small Business Development): §5-28-17-5.
Title 13 (Environment), Article 14 (Powers and Duties of Department of Environmental Management and Boards), Chapter 9 (Rulemaking Procedures): §13-14-9.
Department of Environmental Management rules web page, http://www.in.gov/idem/4087.htm. Legislative Services Agency, *Indiana Register*, http://www.in.gov/legislative/register/irtoc.htm.
Legislative Services Agency, Indiana Register and Administrative Code Division, *Administrative Rules Drafting Manual*, May 2008.

Legislative Services Agency website, http://www.in.gov/legislative/2547.htm.
Office of Management and Budget, *Fiscal Management Circular #2010-4*, November 1, 2010.
Indiana Economic Development Corporation, Regulatory Ombudsman web page, http://iedc.in.gov/programs-initiatives/regulatory-ombudsman.

Iowa

Iowa Code
Title 1 (State Sovereignty and Management), Subtitle 6 (Administrative Procedure), Chapter 17A (Administrative Procedure Act): §17A.3, §17A.4, §17A.4A, §17A.8, §17A.19, and §17A.33.
Iowa Legislature Administrative Rules Review Committee website, https://www.legis.iowa.gov/Schedules/committee.aspx?GA=85&CID=53.
Iowa Legislature, Iowa Administrative Rules website, https://www.legis.iowa.gov/IowaLaw/AdminCode/adminLaw.aspx.
Legislative Services Agency, *Iowa Administrative Bulletin & Code Supplement*, https://www.legis.iowa.gov/Help/Iowa Law & Rules/Administrative Rules/Iowa Administrative_Rules/Iowa_Administrative_Bulletin.htm.
Legislative Services Agency, *Rule-Writing Style*, 2006.

Kansas

Kansas Statutes
Chapter 77. (Statutes; Administrative Rules and Regulations and Procedure)
Article 4. (Rules and Regulations): §77-415, §77-416, §77-420, §77-421, §77-423, §77-424, §77-426, and §77-436.
Article 6. (Kansas Judicial Review Act): §77-607 and§77-611.
Brownback, Sam, Executive Order 11-01, *Office of the Repealer*, April 10, 2012.
Department of Administration, *Policy and Procedure Manual for the Filing of Kansas Administrative Regulations*, Revised: January 2010.
Joint Committee on Administrative Rules and Regulations website, http://www.kslegislature.org/li 2012/b2011 12/committees/ctte jt rules regs 1.
Legislative Research Department, *Kansas Legislator Briefing Book, 2012: Administrative Rules and Regulations.*
Secretary of State, *Kansas Register*, http://www.kssos.org/pubs/pubs_kansas_register.asp.

Kentucky

Kentucky Revised Statutes
Title III (Executive Branch):
Chapter 11 (The Governor): §11.175, §11.200, and §11.202.
Chapter 13A (Administrative Regulations): §13A.010, §13A.030, §13A.040, §13A.080, §13A.160, §13A.210, §13A.230, §13A.240, §13A.245, §13A.250, §13A.255, §13A.270, §13A.290, §13A.320, §13A.330, §13A.331, and §13A.337.
Commission on Small Business Advocacy, *2009-2010 Annual Report*
Commission on Small Business Advocacy website, http://www.thinkkentucky.com/advocacy
Kentucky Legislature, Kentucky Administrative Regulations website, http://www.lrc.ky.gov/kar/frntpage.htm.

Legislative Research Commission, *Administrative Register of Kentucky*, http://www.lrc.ky.gov/kar/contents/2013/04register.htm.

Legislative Research Commission, *Kentucky Administrative Regulation*, Informational Bulletin 118, June 2003.

Louisiana

Louisiana Revised Statutes

Title 49 (State Administration): §49:953, §49:963, §49:965.3, §49:965.4, §49:965.5, §49:965.6, §49:965.8, and §49:968.

Office of the State Register, *Louisiana Register*, http://doa.louisiana.gov/osr/reg/register.htm.

Office of the State Register, *LAC Handbook*, October 2011.

Office of the State Register website, http://doa.louisiana.gov/OSR/osr.htm.

Maine

Maine Revised Statutes

Title 5 (Administrative Procedures and Services):

Chapter 5 (Secretary of State):

Subchapter 2 (Special Advocate): §90-N, §90-Q, §90-R, §90-S, and §90-T.

Chapter 375 (Maine Administrative Procedures Act):

Subchapter 2 (Rulemaking): §8051-A, §8052, §8053, §8056-A, §8057-A, §8058, §8062, and §8063.

Subchapter 2-A (Rulemaking Procedures Governing Rules Authorized and Adopted After January 1, 1996): §8071 and §8072.

Lepage, Paul R., Executive Order 09 FY 11/12, *An Order to Improve Review of the Rule Making Process*, January 10, 2011.

Lepage, Paul R., Executive Order 20 FY 11/12, *An Order Establishing Comprehensive Rulemaking Oversight*, August 24, 2011.

Maine Legislature website, http://maine.gov/legis/.

Secretary of State, *Guide to Rule Making.*

Secretary of State's website, http://www.maine.gov/sos.

Maryland

Annotated Code of Maryland

State Government, Title 10 (Governmental Procedures), Subtitle 1 - Administrative Procedure Act – Regulations

Part III (Proposal and Adoption): §10-110, §10-111, §10-112, and §10-113. Part IV (Limited Provisions): §10-124 and §10-125.

PART VI (Regulatory Review and Evaluation Act): §10-132, §10-132.1, §10-133, §10-134, §10-135, §10-136, §10-137, and §10-138.

Secretary of State, *Maryland Register Online*, http://www.dsd.state

Massachusetts

General Laws of Massachusetts

Part I (Administration of the Government), Title III (Laws Relating to State Offices), Chapter 30A (State Administrative Procedures): 30A §1, 30A §2, 30A §5A, 30A §5A, 30A §6B, and 30A §7.

Office of Housing and Economic Development, Regulation Reform website, http://www.mass

Office of Housing and Economic Development, *Small Business Impact Statement Overview and Guidelines*, http://www.mfbo.org/news%20&%20events/2012%20proposals/SBIS-%202012%20Intl%20Ener%20Cons%20Code%20-%20Commercial%20(item%208).pdf.

Patrick, Deval L., Executive Order No. 485, *Coordinating Agency Regulations*, May 25, 2007.

Romney, Mitt, Executive Order No. 453 (03-11), *Promoting the Consideration of Small Businesses in Agency Rulemaking*, September 25, 2003.

Secretary of the Commonwealth, *Massachusetts Register* subscription information http://www.sec.state

Secretary of the Commonwealth, *The Regulations Manual*, September 2008.

Weld, William, Executive Order No. 384, *To Reduce Unnecessary Regulatory Burden*, February 9, 1996.

Michigan

Michigan Compiled Laws

Chapter 24 (Printing and State Documents), Act 306 of 1969 (Administrative Procedures Act of 1969)

Chapter 1 (General Provisions): §24-207 and §24-208.

Chapter 3 (Procedures for Processing and Publishing Rules): §24-234, §24-235, §24-236, §24-239a, §24-240, §24-241, §24-242, §24-245, and §24-245a. Chapter 6 (Judicial Review): §24-301.

Joint Committee on Administrative Rules web page, http://council.legislature.mi.gov/jcar.html.

Legislative Service Bureau, *Administrative Rules in Michigan: A Manual of Style and Procedures*, June 2003.

Legislative Service Bureau website, http://council.legislature.mi.gov/lsb.html.

Office of Regulatory Reinvention, *Michigan Register*, http://www.michigan.gov/lara/0,4601,7-154-35738 40280---,00.html.

Office of Regulatory Reinvention, Administrative Rules Process Summary web page, http://www.michigan.gov/documents/lara/Admin_Rules_Process_353271_7.pdf.

Office of Regulatory Reinvention, Regulatory Impact Statement and Cost Benefit Analysis web page, http://www.michigan.gov/documents/lara/Regulatory_Impact_Statement_401371_7.doc.

Office of Regulatory Reinvention website, http://www.michigan.gov/lara/0,4601,7-154-35738---,00.html.

Snyder, Richard D., Executive Order 2011-4, *Executive Reorganization*, February 23, 2011.

Snyder, Richard D., Executive Order 2011-5, *Executive Reorganization*, February 23, 2011.

Minnesota

Minnesota Statutes

Chapter 3 (Legislature): §3.305 and §3.842

Chapter 14 (Administrative Procedures):§14.05, §14.055, §14.07, §14.14, §14.15, §14.22, §14.25, §14.26, §14.44, §14.101, §14.116, §14.126, §14.127, and §14.131.
Department of Administration, *State Register*, http://www.comm.media
Minnesota Administrative Rules, 1400.2100.
Office of the Revisor of Statutes, *MINNESOTA RULES: Drafting Manual with Styles and Forms*, 1997.
Office of the Revisor of Statutes website, https://www.revisor.leg.state.

Mississippi
Mississippi Code
Title 25 (Public Officers and Employees; Public Records), Chapter 43 (Administrative Procedures), Article 3 (Rule-Making Adoption and Effectiveness of Rules): § 25-43-3.102,
§ 25-43-3.103, § 25-43-3.104, § 25-43-3.105, § 25-43-3.110, and § 25-43-3.114.
Administrative Procedures Act Rules, Title 1: Secretary of State, Part 1 Chapter 4: Rule Making Procedures.
Secretary of State, Administrative Procedures Frequently Asked Questions web page, http://www.sos.ms.gov/regulation_and_enforcement
Secretary of State, *Mississippi Administrative Bulletin*, http://www.sos.state
Secretary of State, Regulation and Enforcement Home Page, http://www.sos.ms.gov/regulation and enforcement.aspx.

Missouri
Missouri Revised Statutes
Title XXXVI (Statutory Actions and Torts), Chapter 536 (Administrative Procedure and Review):§536.015, §536.021, §536.024, §536.025, §536.026, §536.028, §536.037, §536.200, §536.300, §536.303, §536.305, §536.310, §536.315, §536.323, and §536.328.
Carnahan, Mel, Executive Order 96-18, October 17, 1996.
Holden, Bob, Executive Order 3-15, August 25, 2003.
Secretary of State, *Missouri Register*, http://www.sos.mo.gov/adrules/moreg/moreg.asp.
Secretary of State, *Rulemaking 1-2-3: Drafting and Style Manual.*
Secretary of State website, http://www.sos.mo.gov.
Small Business Regulatory Fairness Board, Small Business Impact Statement Form web page, http://www.sbrfb.ded.mo.gov/pdf/ImpactSt.doc.
Small Business Regulatory Fairness Board website, http://www.sbrfb.ded.mo.gov.

Montana
Montana Statutes
Title 2 (Government Structure and Administration), Chapter 4 Administrative Procedure Act): Part 3 (Adoption and Publication of Rules): §2-4-302, §2-4-304, §2-4-305, and §2-4-314.
Part 4 (Legislative Review of Rules): §2-4-402, §2-4-405, §2-4-406, and §2-4-412. Part 5 (Judicial Notice and Declaratory Rulings): §2-4-506.
Legislative Services Division web page,

http://leg.mt.gov/css/Services%20Division/default.asp.
Montana Legislature, Montana Legislative Committees web page, http://leg.mt.gov/css/Committees/default.asp.
Professional Development Center, Writing Administrative Rules, http://pdc.mt.gov/default.mcpx Secretary of State, *Montana Administrative Register*, http://sos.mt.gov/arm/register.
Secretary of State web page, Administrative Rules of Montana, http://sos.mt.gov/ARM

Nebraska

Nebraska Revised Statutes
Chapter 84 (State Offices): §84-907, §84-911, §84-922, §84-924, §84-926, and §84-927.
Secretary of State, Rules and Regulations website, http://www.sos.ne.gov/dyindex.html#boxingName.

Nevada

Nevada Revised Statutes
Title 18 (State Executive Department), Chapter 233B (Nevada Administrative Procedure Act), Administrative Regulations: §233B.0382, §233B.050, §233B.060, §233B.0603, §233B.0607, §233B.061, §233B.063, §233B.064, §233B.066, §233B.067, §233B.0675, §233B.0608, §233B.0609, §233B.105, and §233B.110.
Attorney General, *Administrative Rulemaking: A Procedural Guide*, 6th ed., 2007.
Legislative Counsel Bureau, Register of Administrative Regulations, http://www.leg.state
Sandoval, Brian, Executive Order 2011-01, *Establishing a Freeze on Regulations*, January 3, 2011.

New Hampshire

New Hampshire Revised Statutes
Title LV (Proceedings in Special Cases), Chapter 541-A (Administrative Procedure Act): §541-A:2, §541-A:5, §541-A:6, §541-A:11, §541-A:13, and §541-A:24.
Joint Legislative Committee on Administrative Rules website, http://www.gencourt.state.nh.us/Rules/about rules/about rules.htm.
Office of Legislative Services, New Hampshire Drafting and Procedure Manual for Administrative Rules, Last Amended Effective September 2011.
Office of Legislative Services, New Hampshire Rulemaking Register, http://en.io.gov.mo/Links/record/415.aspx.

New Jersey

New Jersey Statutes
Title 52 (State Government, Departments and Offices), Chapter 14B (Administrative Procedure Act):§52:14B-3, §52:14B-4, §52:14B-4.1, §52:14B-4.3, §52:14B-5.1, §52:14B-17, §52:14B-18, §52:14B-20, §52:14B-21, §52:14B-22, §52:14B-23, and §52:14B-25.
Office of Administrative Law, Division of Administrative Rules, *New Jersey Register*, http://www.lexisnexis.com/njoal.

Christie, Chris, Executive Order No. 1, January 20, 2010. Christie, Chris, Executive Order No. 2, January 20, 2010. Christie, Chris, Executive Order No. 3, January 20, 2010.

Department of Environmental Protection, Rules & Regulations web page, http://www.nj.gov/dep/rules

Guadagno, Kim, Executive Order No. 41, September 23, 2010.

Guadagno, Kim, et.al., *Red Tape Review Group Findings and Recommendations*, April 19, 2010.

Guadagno, Kim, et.al., *Red Tape Review Commission: Findings and Recommendations*, February 2012.

New Jersey Administrative Code, Title 1, Chapter 30 (Rules for Agency Rulemaking), http://www.lexisnexis.com/njoal.

New Jersey Administrative Code, Title 13 (Law and Public Safety) §13:20-30.5, http://www.lexisnexis.com/njoal

New Mexico

New Mexico Statutes Annotated

Chapter 12 (Miscellaneous Public Affairs Matters), Article 8 (Administrative Procedures Act): §12-8-3, §12-8-4, §12-8-8, and §12-8-16.

Chapter 14 (Records, Legal Notices and Oaths)

Article 4 (State Rules): §14-4-7.1.

Article 4A (Small Business Regulatory Relief Act): §14-4A-3, §14-4A-4, §14-4A-5, and §14-4A-6.

Administrative Law Division, Rules Training website, http://www.nmcpr.state

Office of Business Advocacy web page, http://www.gonm.biz/Office_Business_Advocacy.aspx.

Commission of Public Records, Public Law Division, New Mexico Register, http://www.nmcpr.state

Dannemann, Merilee, *Small Business Needs a Real Relief Act*, February 7, 2011, http://www.triplespacedagain.com/wordpress/?p=109.

Economic Development Department, *Small Business-Friendly Task Force Report, April 1, 2011.*

Martinez, Susana, Executive Order 2011-001, *Formation of a Small Business-Friendly Task Force; Establishing a 90-Day Review Period for All Proposed and Pending Rules and Regulations*, January 1, 2011.

New York

New York Statutes

Legislative, Article 5-B (Legislative Review of Administrative Regulations): §87 and §88. State Administrative Procedures Act:

Article 1 (General Provisions): §102 and §102-A.

Article 2 (Rule Making): §202, §202-A, §202-B, §202-D, §202-E, §205, and §207.

Cuomo, Andrew, Executive Order No. 2, *Review, Continuation and Expiration of Prior Executive Orders*, January 1, 2011.

New York State Senate, Administrative Regulations Review Commission web page, http://www.nysenate.gov/committee/administrative-regulations

Pataki, George E., Executive Order 20, *Establishing the Position of State Director of Regulatory Reform*, November 30, 1995.

Department of State, Division of Administrative Rules, *New York State Register*, http://www.dos.ny.gov/info/register.htm.

Department of State, Division of Administrative Rules, Regulatory Flexibility Analysis for Small Businesses and Local Governments web page, http://www.dos.ny.gov/info/pdfs/FMT-RFA.pdf.

Department of State, Division of Administrative Rules, Regulatory Impact Statement web page, http://www.dos.ny.gov/info/pdfs/FMT-RIS.pdf.

Department of State, Division of Administrative Rules, *Rule Making in New York Manual*, http://www.dos.ny.gov/info/rulemakingmanual.html.

Department of State, Division of Administrative Rules website, http://www.dos.ny.gov/info/index.html.

North Carolina

North Carolina General Statutes

Chapter 150B (Administrative Procedure Act): §150B-21.2, §150B-21.26, §150B-21.4, §150B-21.8, §150B-21.9, §150B-21.11, §150B-21.10, §150B-21.12, §150B-21.13, §150B-21.16, and §150B-21.43.

North Carolina Administrative Code, Title 26 (Administrative Hearings), Chapter 02 (Rules Division), SubChapter C, *Submission Procedure for Rules and other Documents.*

Office of Administrative Hearings, Rules Review Commission, *North Carolina Register*, http://www.ncoah.com/rules

Office of Administrative Hearings, Rules Review Commission website, http://www.ncoah.com/rules

Perdue, Beverly Eaves, Executive Order No. 70, *Rules Modification and Improvement Program*, October 21, 2010.

North Dakota

North Dakota Century Code

Title 28 (Judicial Procedure, Civil), Chapter 32 (Administrative Agencies Practice Act): §28-32-08, §28-32-08.1, §28-32-10, §28-32-11, §28-32-12, §28-32-17, §28-32-18, §28-32-18.1, §28-32-42, and §28-32-46.

Legislative Council, *Administrative Rules Drafting Manual*, 2008. Legislative Council web page, http://www.legis.nd.gov/legislative-council.

Administrative Rules Committee web page, http://www.legis.nd.gov/assembly/63-2013/committees/interim/administrative-rules

Ohio

Ohio Revised Code

Title I (State Government):

Chapter 119 (Administrative Procedure): §119.03, §119.031, §119.0311, §119.032, and §119.035.

Chapter 121 (State Departments): §121.24.

Chapter 122 (Department of Development): §122.08.

Chapter 127 (Controlling Board): §127.18

Senate Bill 2 of the 129th General Assembly.
Common Sense Initiative, CSI Business Impact Analysis Form web page, http://www.governor 28.doc%29.docx.
Common Sense Initiative webpage, http://www.governor
Joint Committee on Agency Rule Review, *Procedures Manual*, Revised: September 7, 2011.
Joint Committee on Agency Rule Review website, https://www.jcarr.state.
Kaisch, John R., Executive Order 2011-01K, *Establishing the Common Sense Initiative*, January 10, 2011.
Legislative Services Commission, *Register of Ohio*, http://www.registerofohio.state. Ohio Business Gateway, Regulatory Reform web page, http://business.ohio.gov/reform
Strickland, Ted, Executive Order 2008-04S, *Implementing Common Sense Business Regulation*, February 12, 2008.

Oklahoma

Oklahoma Statutes
Title 75 (Statutes and Reports): §75-250.2, §75-250.5, §75-303, §75-303.1, §75-303.2, §75-306, §75-307.1, §75-308, §75-502, §75-503, §75-504, and §75-505.
Office of Administrative Rules, *Administrative Rules on Rulemaking*, Effective as of July 1, 2004.
Office of Administrative Rules, *Oklahoma Administrative Code and Register,* http://www.oar.state75tnm2shfcdnm8pb4dthj0chedppmcbq8dtmmak31ctijujrgcln50ob7c kj42tbkdt374 obdcli00_.
Department of Commerce, Businesses and Employers Downloads, *Small Business Advocacy*, http://www.okcommerce.gov/Businesses-And-Employers/Downloads/Small-Business-Advocacy.
Department of Commerce, Businesses and Employers Downloads, *Small Business Regulatory Fairness Act Reports*, http://www.okcommerce.gov/Businesses-AndEmployers /Down loads/SBRFA-Rule-Reports.
Office of Small Business Advocacy web page, http://dev3.okcommerce.gov/v2/Businesses-And-Employers/Small-Business-Advocacy.

Oregon

Oregon Revised Statutes
Chapter 183 (Administrative Procedures Act; Legislative Review of Rules; Civil): §183.310, §183.335, §183.336, §183.400, §183.405, §183.540, §183.715, §183.720, and §183.722.
Governor's Office Economic Revitalization Team, *Biennial Report to the 76th Legislative Assembly*, January 2011.
Kulongoski, Theodore R., Executive Order 03-01, *Regulatory Streamlining*, February 20, 2003.
Kulongoski, Theodore R., *Executive Order 09-10: Amending Executive Order 03-01 Regarding Regulatory Streamlining*, June 25, 2009.
Legislative Council, Administrative Rule Review web page, http://www.lc.state.
Secretary of State, About Oregon Administrative Rules and the Oregon Bulletin, http://arcweb.sos.state

Secretary of State, Oregon Administrative Rules website, http://arcweb.sos.state
Secretary of State, *Oregon Bulletin*, http://arcweb.sos.state

Pennsylvania

Pennsylvania Law
Regulatory Review Act: §5, §5.1, §5.2, §6, and §7. Commonwealth Documents Law: §201 and §204.
Department of Environmental Protection, Small Business Assistance Program web page, http://www.dep.state
Independent Regulatory Review Commission, Agency Toolbox web page, http://www.irrc.state
Independent Regulatory Review Commission, *2010 Annual Report.*
Independent Regulatory Review Commission, *The Regulatory Review Process in Pennsylvania*, 2011.
Independent Regulatory Review Commission website, http://www.irrc.state.
Legislative Reference Bureau, *Pennsylvania Bulletin*, http://www.pabulletin.com/index.asp.
Legislative Reference Bureau, *Pennsylvania Code & Bulletin Style Manual*, 4th ed., 2003.
Ridge, Thomas J., Executive Order 1996-1, *Regulatory Review and Promulgation*, February 6, 1996.

Rhode Island

Rhode Island General Laws
Title 42 (State Affairs and Government):
Chapter 42-35 (Administrative Procedures): §42-35-1, §42-35.1-5, §42-35-2.1, §42-35-2.2, §42-35-2.5, §42-35-3, §42-35-3.3, §42-35-3.4, and §42-35-4.2. Chapter 42-64 (Rhode Island Economic Development Corporation): §42-64.13, §42-64.13-8, and §42-64-34.
Office of Regulatory Reform web page, http://www.riedc.com/business-services
Rhode Island Economic Develop Commission, *Making It Easier to do Business in Rhode Island: Office of Regulatory Reform's Annual Report to Governor Lincoln D. Chafee and The Rhode Island General Assembly*, August 2011.
Rhode Island Economic Development Commission website, http://www.riedc.com. Secretary of State, Rules and Regulations web page, http://www.sos.ri.gov/rules

South Carolina

South Carolina Code of Laws
Title 1 (Administration of the Government), Chapter 23 (State Agency Rulemaking and Adjudication of Contested Cases): §1-23-40, §1-23-110, §1-23-111, §1-23-115, §1-23-120,
§1-23-125, §1-23-270, §1-23-280, and §1-23-290.
Department of Health and Environmental Control, Regulation Development Update web page, http://www.scdhec.gov/administration/regs/reg-update.htm#air.

Legislative Council, *Standards Manual for Drafting and Filing Regulations*, 2011.
Legislative Council, *State Register*, http://www.scstatehouse.gov/state
South Carolina Legislature, State Register and Regulations web page, http://www.scstatehouse.gov/registerandregs.php.
Small Business Regulatory Review Committee, *2005-2011Committee Report.*
Small Business Regulatory Review Committee web page, http://sccommerce.com/your-small-business-advocate.

South Dakota

South Dakota Codified Laws
Title 1 (State Affairs and Government), Chapter 26 (Administrative Procedure and Rules):
§1-26-1, §1-26-1.1, §1-26-1.2, §1-26-2.1, §1-26-4, §1-26-4.1, §1-26-6, and §1-26-14.
Legislative Research Council, *Register*, http://legis.state
Legislative Research Council, *Guide to Form and Style for Administrative Rules of South Dakota*, Revised: April 10, 2012.
Legislative Research Council website, http://legis.state.
Rules Review Committee agendas and minutes,
http://legis.state

Tennessee

Tennessee Code Annotated
Title 4 (State Government), Chapter 5 (Uniform Administrative Procedures Act), Part 2 (Rulemaking and Publications): §4-5-203, §4-5-205, §4-5-211, §4-5-220, §4-5-222, §4-5-225, §4-5-226, §4-5-227, §4-5-402, and §4-5-403.
Phil Bredesen, Executive Order No. 38, *An Executive Order Requiring State Agencies to Assess the Impact of New Regulations on Small Business*, May 22, 2006.
Department of Economic and Community Development, Jobs4TN Rollout website, http://www.tn.gov/ecd/Jobs4TN.html.
Department of Economic and Community Development, *Regulatory Reform Report*, January 2012.
Joint Committee on Government Operations website,
http://www.capitol.tn.gov/joint/committees/gov-opps.
Department of State, *Administrative Register*, http://www.tn.gov/sos/pub/tar
Department of State, Division of Publications, *Rulemaking Guidelines*, July 2010.
Department of State, Rules and Regulations web page,
http://www.tn.gov/sos/rules

Texas

Texas Statutes
Government Code, Title 10 (General Government):
Chapter 2001 (Administrative Procedure): §2001.007, §2001.023, §2001.024, and §2001.026.
Chapter 2006 (Agency Actions Affecting Small Businesses): §2006.002, §2006.011, §2006.029, §2006.031, §2006.032, §2006.038, and §2006.039.

Office of the Attorney General, *HB 3430 Small Business Impact Final Guidelines*, June 2008. https://www.oag.state
Secretary of State, Liaison Center webpage, http://www.sos.state
Secretary of State, State Rules and Open Meetings website, http://www.sos.state
Secretary of State, *Texas Register,* http://www.sos.state. http://www.sos.state.tx.us/texreg/pdf/backview/index.shtml. http://texashistory.unt.edu/explore/collections/TR.

Utah

Utah Code
Title 63G (General Government), Chapter 3 (Utah Administrative Rulemaking Act): §63G-3-102, §63G-3-201, §63G-3-301, §63G-3-302, §63G-3-304, §63G-3-501, §63G-3-501, and §63G-3-602.
Department of Administration, Division of Administrative Rules, *Utah State Bulletin*, http://www.rules
Department of Administration, Division of Administrative Rules, Administrative Rules website, http://www.rules
Department of Administration, Division of Administrative Rules, Administrative Rules Review Committee website, http://www.rules
Bangerter, Norman H., Governor's Executive Order, 2/3/1986. Bangerter, Norman H., Governor's Executive Order, 3/22/1988.
Herbert, Gary R., Governor's Executive Order 013-2011, *Establishing Effective Oversight Over State Agency Rulemaking*, December 6, 2011.

Vermont

Vermont Statutes Annotated
Title 03 (Executive), Chapter 25 (Administrative Procedure): §801, §807, §817, §820, §834, §832a, §838, §839, §840, and §842.
Secretary of State, APA/Rules website, http://vermont-archives.org/aparules.
Secretary of State, *Rule on Rulemaking*, http://www.vermont-archives.org/aparules/RuleOnRulemaking.pdf.
Secretary of State, Proposed Rules Posting web page, https://secure.vermont.gov/SOS/rules

Virginia

Code of Virginia
Title 2.2 (Administration of Government), Chapter 40 (Administrative Process Act): §2.2-4007.01, §2.2-4007.02, §2.2-4007.03, §2.2-4007.04, §2.2-4007.06, §2.2-4007.1, §2.2-4012.1, §2.2-4013, §2.2-4014, and §2.2-4027.
Division of Legislative Services website, http://dls.virginia.gov/index.html.
Office of the Lieutenant Governor, *Lieutenant Governor Bolling Named Co-Chair of Attorney General's Government and Regulatory Reform Task Force*, June 20, 2008, http://www.ltgov.virginia.gov/news/viewArticle.aspx?articleID=482&articleType=P.
McDonnell, Robert F., Executive Order Number Fourteen, *Development and Review of Regulations Proposed By State Agencies*, June 29, 2010.

Virginia Department of Planning and Budget, Economic and Regulatory Analysis Section, *Economic Impact Analysis of Virginia Regulations*, September 1, 1995.

Office of Registrar, *Form, Style and Procedure Manual for Publication of Virginia Regulations.*

Office of Registrar, Regulation Information System, http://register.dls.virginia.gov/documents/agency_resources. http://register.dls.virginia.gov/documents/agency_resources/DocumentUploadInstructions.pdf.

Office of Registrar, Virginia Register of Regulations, http://register.dls.virginia.gov. Virginia Regulatory Town Hall, http://townhall.virginia.gov.

Virginia Regulatory Town Hall, Browse Regulations web page, http://townhall.virginia.gov/L/ListBoards.cfm

Virginia Regulatory Town Hall, Guidance Documents web page, http://townhall.virginia.gov/L/GDocs.cfm.

Virginia Regulatory Town Hall, Meetings and Public Hearings web page, http://townhall.virginia.gov/L/meetings.cfm?time=future.

Virginia Regulatory Town Hall, Public Comment Forums web page, http://townhall.virginia.gov/L/Forums.cfm.

Virginia Regulatory Town Hall, Regulatory Activity web page, http://townhall.virginia.gov/L/NowInProgress.cfm.

Virginia Regulatory Town Hall, Search Tool, http://townhall.virginia.gov/l/search.cfm.

Virginia Regulatory Town Hall User Manual, http://townhall.virginia.gov/um/toc.cfm.

Washington

Revised Code of Washington

Title 19 (Business Regulations – Miscellaneous), Chapter 19.85 (Regulatory Fairness Act):

§19.85.020, §19.85.030, §19.85.050, and §19.85.070.

Title 34 (Administrative Law), Chapter 34.05 (Administrative Procedure Act): §34.05.110,

§34.05.260, §34.05.270, §34.05.310, §34.05.312, §34.05.314, §34.05.320,§34.05.325, §34.05.328, §34.05.570, §34.05.610, §34.05.620,§34.05.640, §34.05.650, §34.05.655, and §34.05.671.

Office of Financial Management and Office of Regulatory Assistance, 2001 Implementation of Executive Order 10-06: Suspending Non-Critical Rule Development and Adoption, June 2012.

Governor's Office of Regulatory Assistance, *First Annual Report, 2006: Improving and simplifying Washington's regulatory systems; Assisting those who do business in our state,* December 15, 2006.

Governor's Office of Regulatory Assistance, *Fiscal Year 2008 Performance and Accountability Report: Assist and Improve*, June 1, 2008

Governor's Office of Regulatory Assistance, *Impacts of Significant Legislative Rule-Making Requirements (2010-11)*, January 2012.

Governor's Office of Regulatory Assistance Rulemaking web page, http://www.ora.wa.gov/regulatory/rulemaking.asp.

Gregoire, Christine O., Executive Order 06-02, *Regulatory Improvement: Improve, Simplify and Assist*, February 2006.

Gregoire, Christine O., Executive Order 10-06, *Suspending Non-Critical Rule Development and Adoption*, November 17, 2010.

Joint Administrative Rules Review Committee website, http://www.leg.wa.gov/jointcommittees/jarrc/Pages/default.aspx.

Office of the Code Reviser, *Instructions on Style for the Washington Administrative Code*, 2009.

Office of the Code Reviser, *Washington State Register*, http://www.leg.wa.gov/codereviser/pages/washington state register.aspx.

West Virginia

West Virginia Code

Chapter 29A (State Administrative procedures Act:

Article 3 (Rulemaking): §29A-3-4, §29A-3-5, §29A-3-10, §29A-3-11, and §29A-3-12.

Article 4 (Declaratory Rulings and Declaratory Judgments): §29A-4-2.

Secretary of State, Administrative Law Division website, http://www.sos.wv.gov/administrative-law/Pages/default.aspx.

Secretary of State, *State Register*, http://apps.sos.wv.gov/adlaw/registers. Wise, Bob, Executive Order No. 20-03, August 27, 2003.

Wisconsin

Wisconsin Statutes

Chapter 15. (Structure of the Executive Branch): §15.155.

Chapter 227 (Administrative Procedure and Review): §227.13, §227.14, §227.15, §227.16, §227.17, §227.19, §227.26, §227.30, §227.40, §227.114, §227.135, §227.137, and §227.185.

2011 Wisconsin Act 21.

2011 Wisconsin Act 46.

Legislative Council, *Administrative Rules Procedures Manual*, November 2011

Legislative Council, *2010 Annual Report, Legislative Council Rules Clearinghouse*, February 2011.

Legislative Council Administrative Rules web page, http://legis.wisconsin.gov/lc/adminrules/index.html.

Legislative Reference Bureau *Administrative Register*, http://docs.legis.wisconsin.gov/code/register.

Legislative Reference Bureau, Wisconsin Administrative Code and Register website http://legis.wisconsin.gov/rsb/code.htm.

Walker, Scott, Executive Order # 50, *Relating to Guidelines for the Promulgation of Administrative Rules*, November 2, 2011.

Wyoming

Wyoming Statutes

Title 16 (City, County, State and Local Powers), Chapter 3 (Administrative Procedure): §16-3-103 and §16-3-114.

Title 28 (Legislature), Chapter 9 (Administrative Regulation Review): §28-9-102, §28-9-103, §28-9-104, and §28-9-106.
Legislative Service Office, *Administrative Rule Review Handbook*, April 2004.
Legislative Service Office, Legal Services Division web page, http://legisweb.state
Secretary of State, Rules and Regulations web page, http://soswy.state

APPENDIX A: SBA MODEL REGULATORY FLEXIBILITY ACT LEGISLATION[496]

A Bill

To improve state rulemaking by creating procedures to analyze the availability of more flexible regulatory approaches for small businesses.

Findings

1. A vibrant and growing small business sector is critical to creating jobs in a dynamic economy;
2. Small businesses bear a disproportionate share of regulatory costs and burdens;
3. Fundamental changes that are needed in the regulatory and enforcement culture of state agencies to make them more responsive to small business can be made without compromising the statutory missions of the agencies;
4. When adopting regulations to protect the health, safety, and economic welfare of [State], state agencies should seek to achieve statutory goals as effectively and efficiently as possible without imposing unnecessary burdens on small employers;
5. Uniform regulatory and reporting requirements can impose unnecessary and disproportionately burdensome demands including legal, accounting and consulting costs upon small businesses with limited resources;
6. The failure to recognize differences in the scale and resources of regulated businesses can adversely affect competition in the marketplace, discourage innovation, and restrict improvements in productivity;
7. Unnecessary regulations create entry barriers in many industries and discourage potential entrepreneurs from introducing beneficial products and processes;
8. The practice of treating all regulated businesses as equivalent may lead to inefficient use of regulatory agency resources, enforcement problems, and, in some cases, to actions inconsistent with the legislative intent of health, safety, environmental, and economic welfare legislation;
9. Alternative regulatory approaches which do not conflict with the stated objective of applicable statutes may be available to minimize the significant economic impact of rules on small businesses;

10. The process by which state regulations are developed and adopted should be reformed to require agencies to solicit the ideas and comments of small businesses, to examine the impact of proposed and existing rules on such businesses, and to review the continued need for existing rules.

Section 1. Short Title

This act may be cited as the Regulatory Flexibility Act of [2006].

Section 2. Definitions

(a) As used in this section:

(1) "Agency" means each state board, commission, department, or officer authorized by law to make regulations or to determine contested cases;

(2) "Proposed regulation" means a proposal by an agency for a new regulation or for a change in, addition to, or repeal of an existing regulation;

(3) "Regulation" means each agency statement of general applicability, without regard to its designation, that implements, interprets, or prescribes law or policy, or describes the organization, procedure, or practice requirements of any agency. The term includes the amendment or repeal of a prior regulation, but does not include (A) statements concerning only the internal management of any agency and not affecting private rights or procedures available to the public, (B) declaratory rulings, or (C) intra-agency or interagency memoranda;

(4) "Small business" means a business entity, including its affiliates, that (A) is independently owned and operated and (B) employs fewer than [five hundred] full-time employees or has gross annual sales of less than [six] million dollars.

Section 3. Economic Impact Statements

(a) Prior to the adoption of any proposed regulation that may have an adverse impact on small businesses, each agency shall prepare an economic impact statement that includes the following:

(1) An identification and estimate of the number of the small businesses subject to the proposed regulation;

(2) The projected reporting, recordkeeping, and other administrative costs required for compliance with the proposed regulation, including the type of professional skills necessary for preparation of the report or record;

(3) A statement of the probable effect on impacted small businesses;

(4) A description of any less intrusive or less costly alternative methods of achieving the purpose of the proposed regulation.

Section 4. Regulatory Flexibility Analysis

(a) Prior to the adoption of any proposed regulation on and after [January 1, 2007], each agency shall prepare a regulatory flexibility analysis in which the agency shall, where consistent with health, safety, environmental, and economic welfare, consider utilizing regulatory methods that will accomplish the objectives of applicable statutes while minimizing adverse impact on small businesses. The agency shall consider, without limitation, each of the following methods of reducing the impact of the proposed regulation on small businesses:

(1) The establishment of less stringent compliance or reporting requirements for small businesses;

(2) The establishment of less stringent schedules or deadlines for compliance or reporting requirements for small businesses;

(3) The consolidation or simplification of compliance or reporting requirements for small businesses;

(4) The establishment of performance standards for small businesses to replace design or operational standards required in the proposed regulation; and

(5) The exemption of small businesses from all or any part of the requirements contained in the proposed regulation.

(b) Prior to the adoption of any proposed regulation that may have an adverse impact on small businesses, each agency shall notify the [Department of Economic and Community Development or similar state department or council that exists to review regulations] of its intent to adopt the proposed regulation. The [Department of Economic and Community Development or similar state department or council that exists to review regulations] shall advise and assist agencies in complying with the provisions of this section.

Section 5. Judicial Review

(a) For any regulation subject to this section, a small business that is adversely affected or aggrieved by final agency action is entitled to judicial review of agency compliance with the requirements of this section.

(b) A small business may seek such review during the period beginning on the date of final agency action and ending one year later.

Section 6. Periodic Review of Rules

(a) Within four years of the enactment of this law, each agency shall review all agency rules existing at the time of enactment to determine whether such rules should be continued without change, or should be amended or rescinded, consistent with the stated objectives of those statutes, to minimize economic impact of the rules on small businesses in a manner consistent with the stated objective of applicable statutes. If the head of the agency determines that completion of the review of existing rules is not feasible by the established date, the agency shall publish a statement certifying that determination. The agency may extend the completion date by one year at a time for a total of not more than five years.

(b) Rules adopted after the enactment of this law should be reviewed every five years of the publication of such rules as the final rule to ensure that they minimize economic impact on small businesses in a manner consistent with the stated objectives of applicable statutes.

(c) In reviewing rules to minimize economic impact of the rule on small businesses, the agency shall consider the following factors:

(1) The continued need for the rule;

(2) The nature of complaints or comments received concerning the rule from the public;

(3) The complexity of the rule;

(4) The extent to which the rule overlaps, duplicates, or conflicts with other Federal, State, and local governmental rules; and

(5) The length of time since the rule has been evaluated or the degree to which technology, economic conditions, or other factors have changed in the area affected by the rule.

APPENDIX B: STATE GUIDANCE, TEMPLATES, AND FORMS

Arkansas

Economic Impact Statement Form[497]

Benefits of the Proposed Rule or Regulation

1. Explain the need for the proposed change(s). Did any complaints motivate you to pursue regulatory action? If so, please explain the nature of such complaints.
2. What are the top three benefits of the proposed rule or regulation?
3. What, in your estimation, would be the consequence of taking no action, thereby maintaining the status quo?
4. Describe market-based alternatives or voluntary standards that were considered in place of the proposed regulation and state the reason(s) for not selecting these alternatives.
5. Impact of Proposed Rule or Regulation
6. Estimate the cost to state government of collecting information, completing paperwork, filing, recordkeeping, auditing and inspecting associated with this new rule or regulation.
7. What types of small businesses will be required to comply with the new rule or regulation? Please estimate the number of small businesses affected.
8. Does the proposed regulation create barriers to entry? If so, please describe those barriers and why those barriers are necessary.
9. Explain the additional requirements with which small business owners will have to comply and estimate the costs associated with compliance.
10. State whether the regulation contains different requirements for different-sized entities, and explain why this is, or is not, necessary.
11. Describe your understanding of the ability of small business owners to implement changes required by the proposed regulation.

12. How does this rule or regulation compare to similar rules or regulations in other states or the federal government?
13. Provide a summary of the input your agency has received from small business advocates about the proposed rule or regulation.

Excerpts from Regulatory Flexibility FAQ Sheet

Q. Question 12 of the Economic Impact Statement asks that we provide a summary of input our agency has received from small business or small business advocates. Does this imply that we will already have completed the rule-making procedures outlined in the Administrative Procedures Act?

A. *No. You should complete the process outlined in the regulatory flexibility process before taking the steps outlined in the Administrative Procedures Act. This question deals with informal feedback your agency has received.*

Q. Are there guidelines on how to estimate the cost to state government and cost of compliance, as referenced in questions 5 and 8 of the Economic Impact Statement?

A. *We suggest each agency consider the cost of staff time, postage, etc. the state will incur as a result of implementing and monitoring new rules and regulations. The cost to small businesses can be determined by consulting with trade organizations or small business owners themselves.*

California

Office of Administrative Law Checklist[498]

INFORMATIVE DIGEST/POLICY STATEMENT OVERVIEW (11346.5(a)(3)): Is the format similar to the Legislative Counsel's digest?

Is it in plain English?

Does it include a clear and concise summary of existing laws, and regulations (if any) related directly to the proposed rulemaking?

Does it include a clear and concise summary of the effect of the proposed rulemaking?

If there is a substantial difference from an existing, comparable federal regulation or statute, are significant differences briefly described?

If so, is a full citation to federal regulation or statute included? (11346.5(a)(3)(B))

Does it include a policy statement overview explaining the broad objectives of the regulation AND explaining the specific benefits anticipated from the proposed action, including, to the extent applicable, non-monetary benefits such as the protection of public health and safety, worker safety, or the environment, the prevention of discrimination, the promotion of fairness or social equity, and the increase in transparency in business and government? Does it include an evaluation of whether the proposed regulation is inconsistent or incompatible with existing state regulations?

SIGNIFICANT STATEWIDE ADVERSE ECONOMIC IMPACT DIRECTLY AFFECTING BUSINESS, INCLUDING ABILITY TO COMPETE (11346.3(a); 11346.5(a)(7); 11346.5(a)(8)): *If agency makes initial determination that proposal may have such an impact, does the determination:* --Identify types of businesses affected? --Describe projected compliance requirements? --Solicit proposed alternatives using boilerplate at 11346.5(a)(7)(C)? *If agency makes initial determination that proposal will not have such an impact,* does Notice make a declaration to that effect? (11346.5(a)(8))

STATEMENT OF THE RESULTS OF THE ECONOMIC IMPACT ASSESSMENT (11346.5(a)(10))
Is a statement of the results of the economic impact assessment included?
Does it specify whether and to what extent the proposed regulation will affect:
Creation of jobs within California
Elimination of jobs within California
Creation of new businesses within California
Elimination of existing businesses within California
Expansion of businesses currently doing business within the state
Benefits of the regulation to the health and welfare of California residents, worker safety, and the state's environment
COST IMPACTS ON REPRESENTATIVE PERSON OR BUSINESS (11346.5(a)(9)):
Is a description included of all cost impacts known to the agency that a representative person or business would necessarily incur in reasonable compliance with the proposed action? *If no cost impacts are known to the agency* does the notice say: "The agency is not aware of any cost impacts that a representative private person or business would necessarily incur in reasonable compliance with the proposed action?"
BUSINESS REPORT (11346.5(a)(11); 11346.3(d)):
Does the regulation require a report to be made?
Does the report requirement apply to business?
--*If "yes,"* is there a finding that: "It is necessary for the health, safety, or welfare of the people of the state that the regulation apply to businesses"?
SMALL BUSINESS (1 CCR 4(a) and (b)):
Is a statement included that the proposed action does/does not affect small businesses? (1 CCR 4(a)) If "does not affect" determination is made, is a brief explanation included? (1 CCR 4(b))
ALTERNATIVES STATEMENT (11346.5(a)(13)): Does the notice include the following statement: A rulemaking agency must determine that no reasonable alternative considered by the agency or that has otherwise been identified and brought to the attention of the agency would be more effective in carrying out the purpose for which the action is proposed, would be as effective and less burdensome to affected private persons than the proposed action, or would be more cost-effective to affected private persons and equally effective in implementing the statutory policy or other provision of law.

Economic Impact Statement[499]

A. ESTIMATED PRIVATE SECTOR COST IMPACTS (Include calculations and assumptions in the rulemaking record.)

1. Check the appropriate box(es) below to indicate whether this regulation:

a.Impacts businesses and/or employees
b. Impacts small businesses
c. Impacts jobs or occupations g. Impacts individuals

d. Impacts California competitiveness

e. Imposes reporting requirements

f. Imposes prescriptive instead of performance

g. Impacts individuals

h. None of the above (Explain below. Complete the Fiscal Impact Statement as appropriate.) (If any box in Items 1 a through g is checked, complete this Economic Impact Statement.)

2. Enter the total number of businesses impacted:

Describe the types of businesses (Include nonprofits.):

Enter the number or percentage of total businesses impacted that are small businesses:

3. Enter the number of businesses that will be created: ___ eliminated: ___ Explain:

4. Indicate the geographic extent of impacts: Statewide ___ Local or regional (List areas.): ___

5. Enter the number of jobs created: ___ or eliminated: ___ Describe the types of jobs or occupations impacted:

6. Will the regulation affect the ability of California businesses to compete with other states by making it more costly to produce goods or services here? Yes ___ No ___ If yes, explain briefly:

B. ESTIMATED COSTS (Include calculations and assumptions in the rulemaking record.)

1. What are the total statewide dollar costs that businesses and individuals may incur to comply with this regulation over its lifetime? $___

a. Initial costs for a small business: $___ Annual ongoing costs: $___ Years: ___

b. Initial costs for a typical business: $___ Annual ongoing costs: $___ Years: ___

c. Initial costs for an individual: $___ Annual ongoing costs: $___ Years: ___

d. Describe other economic costs that may occur:

2. If multiple industries are impacted, enter the share of total costs for each industry:

3. If the regulation imposes reporting requirements, enter the annual costs a typical business may incur to comply with these requirements. (Include the dollar costs to do programming, record keeping, reporting, and other paperwork, whether or not the paperwork must be submitted.): $ ___

4. Will this regulation directly impact housing costs? Yes___ No ___

If yes, enter the annual dollar cost per housing unit: ___ and the number of units: ___

5. Are there comparable Federal regulations? Yes ___ No ___

Explain the need for State regulation given the existence or absence of Federal regulations: Enter any additional costs to businesses and/or individuals that may be due to State - Federal differences: $

C. ESTIMATED BENEFITS (Estimation of the dollar value of benefits is not specifically required by rulemaking law, but encouraged.)

1. Briefly summarize the benefits that may result from this regulation and who will benefit:

2. Are the benefits the result of : __ specific statutory requirements, or __goals developed by the agency based on broad statutory authority? Explain:

3. What are the total statewide benefits from this regulation over its lifetime? $ ___

D. ALTERNATIVES TO THE REGULATION (Include calculations and assumptions in the rulemaking record. Estimation of the dollar value of benefits is not specifically required by

1. List alternatives considered and describe them below. If no alternatives were considered, explain why not:

2. Summarize the total statewide costs and benefits from this regulation and each alternative considered:

Regulation: Benefit: $ ___ Cost: $ ___

Alternative 1: Benefit: $ ___ Cost: $ ___

Alternative 2: Benefit: $ ___ Cost: $ ___

3. Briefly discuss any quantification issues that are relevant to a comparison of estimated costs and benefits for this regulation or alternatives:

4. Rulemaking law requires agencies to consider performance standards as an alternative, if a regulation mandates the use of specific technologies or equipment, or prescribes specific actions or procedures. Were performance standards considered to lower compliance costs?

Yes ___ No ___ Explain:

E. MAJOR REGULATIONS (Include calculations and assumptions in the rulemaking record.) Cal/EPA boards, offices, and departments are subject to the following additional requirements per Health and Safety Code section 57005.

1. Will the estimated costs of this regulation to California business enterprises exceed $10 million ? Yes ___ No ___ (If No, skip the rest of this section.)

2. Briefly describe each equally as an effective alternative, or combination of alternatives, for which a cost-effectiveness analysis was performed:

Alternative 1: Alternative 2:

3. For the regulation, and each alternative just described, enter the estimated total cost and overall cost-effectiveness ratio: Regulation: $ ___ Cost-effectiveness ratio: $ ___

Alternative 1: $ Cost-effectiveness ratio: $ ______

Alternative 2: $ ___ Cost-effectiveness ratio: $ ___

Indiana

Excerpts from DEM Fiscal Impact Statement Guidance[500]

Fiscal Impact Statement

Cost-Benefit Analysis

- Statement of Need
- Federal or state statutory requirement; alleged market failure; and/or serve a public need
- Number of individuals and businesses affected by the rule:
- Policy rationale or goal behind the proposed rule, including an analysis of the following:
  - o Conduct and its frequency of occurrence that the rule is designed to change or address:

    - Harm resulting from the conduct that the rule is designed to change
    - Involved regulated entities in rule development
  - Description of the methodology used in making the above determinations.
- Evaluation of Costs and Benefits
  - Primary and direct benefits of the rule, by type
  - Secondary or indirect benefits of the rule and an explanation of linkage of rule to benefits
  - Compliance costs for regulated entities, by type of cost
  - Administrative expenses, by type
  - Any cost savings to regulated entities as a result of the proposed rule
- Examination of Alternatives
  - Alternatives considered in the rulemaking workgroup process
    - Applicability:
    - De minimis:
    - Unused/available loading capacity required under rule
    - Pollutants of concern or regulated pollutants
    - Exemptions and how much information is to be required to justify eligibility for exemption
  - Alternatives defined by statute: Specific statutory requirement and statutory discretion
  - Feasibility of market-oriented approaches,
  - Measures to improve the availability of information, as an alternative to regulation;
  - Various alternative enforcement methods
  - Performance standards rather than design standards.
  - Different requirements for different sized regulated entities
  - Baseline - how the world would look without the proposed rule.
  - Different compliance dates
  - Redundancy.
- $500,000 Fiscal Impact
- Sources used in determining costs and benefits

Small Business Economic Impact Statement

- Estimate the number of small businesses, classified by industry sector, subject to the proposed rule:
- Estimate the average annual small business reporting, record keeping, and other administrative costs
- Estimate the total annual economic impact of compliance on all small businesses subject to the rule:
- Justify any requirement or cost imposed on small business by the rule not expressly required by law:

- Regulatory Flexibility Analysis
  - Less stringent compliance or reporting requirements for small businesses
  - Less stringent compliance deadlines or reporting requirements for small businesses:
  - Consolidation or simplification of compliance or reporting requirements for small businesses:
  - Performance standards for small businesses instead of design or operational standards
  - Any exemptions for small businesses from any requirements or costs
  - If no listed alternative is implemented, explain the reasons for not choosing the alternatives

Kentucky

Tiering: Statutory Provision

13A.210 Tiering of administrative regulations.

(1) When promulgating administrative regulations and reviewing existing ones, administrative bodies shall, whenever possible, tier their administrative regulations to reduce disproportionate impacts on certain classes of regulated entities, including government or small business, or both, and to avoid regulating entities that do not contribute significantly to the problem the administrative regulation was designed to address. The tiers, however, shall be based upon reasonable criteria and uniformly applied to an entire class. Administrative bodies shall use any number of tiers that will solve most efficiently and effectively the problem the administrative regulation addresses. A written statement shall be submitted to the Legislative Research Commission explaining why tiering was or was not used.

(2) Administrative bodies may use, but shall not be limited to, the following methods of tiering administrative regulations:

(a) Reduce or modify substantive regulatory requirements;

(b) Eliminate some requirements entirely;

(c) Simplify and reduce reporting and recordkeeping requirements;

(d) Provide exemptions from reporting and recordkeeping requirements;

(e) Reduce the frequency of inspections;

(f) Provide exemptions from inspections and other compliance activities;

(g) Delay compliance timetables;

h() Reduce, modify, or waive fines or other penalties for noncompliance; and

(i) Address and alleviate special problems of individuals and small businesses in complying with an administrative regulation.

(3) When tiering regulatory requirements, administrative bodies may use, but shall not be limited to, size and nonsize variables. Size variables include number of citizens, number of employees, level of operating revenues, level of assets, and market shares. Nonsize variables include degree of risk posed to humans, technological and economic ability to comply, geographic locations, and level of federal funding.

(4) When modifying tiers, administrative bodies shall monitor, but shall not be limited to, the following variables:

(a) Changing demographic characteristics;

(b) Changes in the composition of the work force;

(c) Changes in the inflation rate requiring revisions of dollar-denominated tiers;

(d) Changes in market concentration and segmentation;

(e) Advances in technology; and

(f) Changes in legislation.

Tiering: Guidance in Kentucky Administrative Regulations[501]

The following form shall be used for the regulatory impact analysis and tiering statement:

REGULATORY IMPACT ANALYSIS AND TIERING STATEMENT

Administrative Regulation #: Contact person

(1) Provide a brief summary of:

(a) What this administrative regulation does:

(b) The necessity of this administrative regulation:

(c) How this administrative regulation conforms to the content of the authorizing statutes:

(d) How this administrative regulation currently assists or will assist in the effective administration of the statutes:

(2) If this is an amendment to an existing administrative regulation, provide a brief summary of:

(a) How the amendment will change this existing administrative regulation:

(b) The necessity of the amendment to this administrative regulation:

(c) How the amendment conforms to the content of the authorizing statutes:

(d) How the amendment will assist in the effective administration of the statutes:

(3) List the type and number of individuals, businesses, organizations, or state and local governments affected by this administrative regulation:

(4) Provide an analysis of how the entities identified in question (3) will be impacted by either the implementation of this administrative regulation, if new, or by the change, if it is an amendment, including:

(a) List the actions that each of the regulated entities identified in question (3) will have to take to comply with this administrative regulation or amendment:

(b) In complying with this administrative regulation or amendment, how much will it cost each of the entities identified in question (3):

(c) As a result of compliance, what benefits will accrue to the entities identified in question (3):

(5) Provide an estimate of how much it will cost the administrative body to implement this administrative regulation:

(a) Initially:

(b) On a continuing basis:

(6) What is the source of the funding to be used for the implementation and enforcement of this administrative regulation:

(7) Provide an assessment of whether an increase in fees or funding will be necessary to implement this administrative regulation, if new, or by the change if it is an amendment:

(8) State whether or not this administrative regulation established any fees or directly or indirectly increased any fees:

(9) TIERING: Is tiering applied?

Louisiana

Excerpt from the Louisiana Administrative Code Handbook[502]

▸ Regulatory Flexibility Analysis/Small Business Economic Impact Statement

Every Rule must have an accompanying Small Business Analysis (R.S. 49:956.6). If you choose, you may print your analysis with Notice of Intent for public viewing.

Small Business Statement

In accordance with R.S. 49:965.6, the Department of Revenue has conducted a Regulatory Flexibility Analysis and found that the proposed amending of this Rule will have a negligible effect on small businesses.

If the results of the regulatory flexibility analysis required by R.S. 49:965.6 indicates an adverse impact on small businesses, the agency needs to complete a Small Business Economic Statement, pursuant to R.S. 49:965.5, and file it with the Department of Economic Development.

Massachusetts

Small Business Impact Statement Template[503]

In order to accurately predict the impact the adoption, amendment, or repeal of a regulation will have on small businesses, the promulgating authority must conduct a thorough analysis that not only considers the potential effects of the action but also quantifies the costs, if any, associated with each. The questions below are designed to aid promulgating authorities in conducting their analysis. A careful review of the questions is recommended before beginning to draft the regulation and then again at each stage of the process.

Agency Submitting Regulation:

Date:

Subject Matter of Regulation:

Regulation No:

Statutory Authority:

Other Agencies Affected:

Other Regulations That May Duplicate or Conflict with the Regulation:

Describe the Scope and Objectives of the Regulation:

Business Industry(ies) Affected by the Regulation:

Types of Businesses Included in the Industry(ies):

Total Number of Small Businesses Included in the Regulated Industry(ies): Unknown

Number of Small Businesses Potentially Subject to the Proposed Regulation:

Effective Date Used In Cost Estimate:

Estimate Prepared By:
Telephone No.:

Yes No N/A

*Note: For each question, explain why you answered "yes," "no," or "not applicable." Where the answer to any of the following questions is "yes," in addition to explaining your answer, provide a fair estimate of the expected cost of the requirement, or a reasonable basis for assuming the cost will be de minimis or insignificant. This estimate may be based on any facts, data, views, arguments, input from small businesses and/or small business advocacy groups, or any other sources that quantify the cost associated with the regulation.

Will small businesses have to create, file, or issue additional reports?

Will small businesses have to implement additional recordkeeping procedures? Will small businesses have to provide additional administrative oversight?

Will small businesses have to hire additional employees in order to comply with the proposed regulation?

Does compliance with the regulation require small businesses to hire other professionals (e.g. a lawyer, accountant, engineer, etc.)?

Does the regulation require small businesses to purchase a product or make any other capital investments in order to comply with the regulation?

Are performance standards more appropriate than design standards?

Does the regulation require small businesses to cooperate with audits, inspections, or other regulatory enforcement activities?

Will the regulation have the effect of creating additional taxes and/or fees for small businesses?

Does the regulation require small businesses to provide educational services to keep up to date with regulatory requirements?

Is the regulation likely to encourage the formation of small businesses in Massachusetts?

Can the regulation provide for less stringent compliance or reporting requirements for small businesses?

Can the regulation establish less stringent schedules or deadlines for compliance or reporting requirements for small businesses?

Can the compliance or reporting requirements be consolidated or simplified for small businesses?

Can performance standards for small businesses replace design or operational standards? Performance, design, and operational standards are not addressed by this regulation.

Are there alternative regulatory methods that would minimize the adverse impact on small businesses?

Michigan

"Administrative Rules Process in a Nutshell"[504]

Request for Rulemaking (RFR) (2 days)

Requests to commence rulemaking can come from professional boards/commissions, the department, or the public. The RAO sends an RFR electronically to ORR.

Draft Rules (Dept. draft = 4-12 months; ORR approval = 1-2 weeks; LSB editing = 30-40 days)

- Board/commission (and department) approves; Regulatory Affairs Officer (RAO) of department/agency approves.
- ORR approves (legal/policy); sends to LSB.
- LSB edits and returns to ORR; ORR returns to department/agency for correction.

Public Hearing (1-2 months)
- Regulatory Impact Statement and Cost Benefit Analysis (the "why" and "$" document) is approved by the RAO and sent to ORR for approval.
- Rulemaking Policy Analysis Form is sent to ORR.
- Public hearing notice and LSB-corrected rules are sent by RAO to ORR.
- Newspaper ads (hearing notice secured by RAO).
- *Michigan Register* (ORR publishes notice and rules).
- Court reporter (secured by RAO).
- Public comment period beyond hearing noted.

Draft Rules (2-4 months)
- Board/commission (and department) approves rules.
- Department submits to ORR for approval.
- ORR submits the final rules to LSB, and LSB has 21 days to certify the rules for form, classification, and arrangement.
- ORR legally certifies (and can also certify for form if LSB did not complete the task in 21 days).

Joint Committee on Administrative Rules (JCAR) - The 1-stop in the legislature (15 session days)
- The rules must be submitted to JCAR within one year from the hearing.
- JCAR report summarizes changes made after hearing.
- JCAR has 15 session days to meet and object.

Department/Agency Adopts the Rules (1 week)
- Department director adopts rules; or, the agency or commission adopts if it is a Type I agency/commission.
- Rules can be filed by ORR with Great Seal after 15 JCAR session days expires, unless JCAR files a notice of objection, which gives them 15 more session days to pass rules-stopping legislation and present it to the Governor.
- ORR enters the filing date at the top of the first page of the rules and sends an electronic copy of the final rules to the Great Seal and to the RAO.

The rules may become effective immediately upon filing or at a later date specified in the rules.

***Excerpts from Regulatory Impact and Cost-Benefit Analysis Form*[505]**

Small Business Impact Statement:

(15) Describe whether and how the agency considered exempting small businesses from the proposed rules.

(16) If small businesses are not exempt, describe (a) the manner in which the agency reduced the economic impact of the proposed rule(s) on small businesses, including a detailed recitation of the efforts of the agency to comply with the mandate to reduce the disproportionate impact of the rule(s) upon small businesses as described below (in accordance with MCL 24.240(1)(A-D)), or (b) the reasons such a reduction was not lawful or feasible.

(A) Identify and estimate the number of small businesses affected by the proposed rule(s) and the probable effect on small business.

(B) Describe how the agency established differing compliance or reporting requirements or timetables for small businesses under the rule after projecting the required reporting, record-keeping, and other administrative costs.

(C) Describe how the agency consolidated or simplified the compliance and reporting requirements and identify the skills necessary to comply with the reporting requirements.

(D) Describe how the agency established performance standards to replace design or operation standards required by the proposed rules.

(17) Identify any disproportionate impact the proposed rule(s) may have on small businesses because of their size or geographic location.

(18) Identify the nature of any report and the estimated cost of its preparation by small business required to comply with the proposed rule(s).

(19) Analyze the costs of compliance for all small businesses affected by the proposed rule(s), including costs of equipment, supplies, labor, and increased administrative costs.

(20) Identify the nature and estimated cost of any legal, consulting, or accounting services that small businesses would incur in complying with the proposed rule(s).

(21) Estimate the ability of small businesses to absorb the costs without suffering economic harm and without adversely affecting competition in the marketplace.

(22) Estimate the cost, if any, to the agency of administering or enforcing a rule that exempts or sets lesser standards for compliance by small businesses.

(23) Identify the impact on the public interest of exempting or setting lesser standards of compliance for small businesses.

(24) Describe whether and how the agency has involved small businesses in the development of the proposed rule(s). If small business was involved in the development of the rule(s), please identify the business(es).

Cost-Benefit Analysis of Rules (independent of statutory impact):

(25) Estimate the actual statewide compliance costs of the rule amendments on businesses or groups. Identify the businesses or groups who will be directly affected by, bear the cost of, or directly benefit from the proposed rule(s). What additional costs will be imposed on businesses and other groups as a result of these proposed rules (i.e. new equipment, supplies, labor, accounting, or recordkeeping)? Please identify the types and number of businesses and groups. Be sure to quantify how each entity will be affected.

(26) Estimate the actual statewide compliance costs of the proposed rule(s) on individuals (regulated individuals or the public). Please include the costs of education, training, application fees, examination fees, license fees, new equipment, supplies, labor, accounting, or recordkeeping). How many and what category of individuals will be affected by the rules? What qualitative and quantitative impact does the proposed change in rule(s) have on these individuals?

(27) Quantify any cost reductions to businesses, individuals, groups of individuals, or governmental units as a result of the proposed rule(s).

(28) Estimate the primary and direct benefits and any secondary or indirect benefits of the proposed rule(s). Please provide both quantitative and qualitative information, as well as your assumptions.

(29) Explain how the proposed rule(s) will impact business growth and job creation (or elimination) in Michigan.

(30) Identify any individuals or businesses who will be disproportionately affected by the rules as a result of their industrial sector, segment of the public, business size, or geographic location.

(31) Identify the sources the agency relied upon in compiling the regulatory impact statement, including the methodology utilized in determining the existence and extent of the impact of a proposed rule(s) and a cost-benefit analysis of the proposed rule(s). How were estimates made, and what were your assumptions? Include internal and external sources, published reports, information provided by associations or organizations, etc., which demonstrate a need for the proposed rule(s).

Alternatives to Regulation:

(32) Identify any reasonable alternatives to the proposed rule(s) that would achieve the same or similar goals. In enumerating your alternatives, please include any statutory amendments that may be necessary to achieve such alternatives.

(33) Discuss the feasibility of establishing a regulatory program similar to that proposed in the rule(s) that would operate through private market-based mechanisms. Please include a discussion of private market-based systems utilized by other states.

(34) Discuss all significant alternatives the agency considered during rule development and why they were not incorporated into the rule(s). This section should include ideas considered both during internal discussions and discussions with stakeholders, affected parties, or advisory groups.

Missouri

Small Business Regulatory Fairness Board Small Business Impact Statement[506]

Date:

Rule Number:

Name of Agency Preparing Statement: Name of Person Preparing Statement:

Phone Number: Email:

Name of Person Approving Statement:

Please describe the methods your agency considered or used to reduce the impact on small businesses *(examples: consolidation, simplification, differing compliance, differing reporting requirements, less stringent deadlines, performance rather than design standards, exemption, or any other mitigating technique).*

Please explain how your agency has involved small businesses in the development of the proposed rule.

Please list the probable monetary costs and benefits to your agency and any other agencies affected. Please include the estimated total amount your agency expects to collect from additionally imposed fees and how the moneys will be used.

Please describe small businesses that will be required to comply with the proposed rule and how they may be adversely affected.

Please list direct and indirect costs (in dollars amounts) associated with compliance.

Please list types of business that will be directly affected by, bear the cost of, or directly benefit from the proposed rule.

Does the proposed rule include provisions that are more stringent than those mandated by comparable or related federal, state, or county standards?

Yes___ No___

If yes, please explain the reason for imposing a more stringent standard.

New York

Format Guidance

Regulatory Impact Statement[507]

1. Statutory authority: (Explain the rationale used by your agency to determine that the statutory authority authorizes the rule.)

2. Legislative objectives: (Explain how the proposal accords with the public policy objectives the Legislature sought to advance by enacting the statutory authority.)

3. Needs and benefits: (Explain the purpose of, the necessity for, and benefits derived from the rule. A citation and summary, not to exceed 500 words, for each scientific or statistical study, report or analysis that served as the basis for the rule, an explanation of how it was used to determine the necessity for and benefits derived from the rule, and the name of the person that produced each study, report or analysis.)

4. Costs: (A statement detailing the projected costs of the rule, including responses to a, b and c; or d:

a. costs to regulated parties for the implementation of and continuing compliance with the rule;

b. costs to the agency, the state and local governments for the implementation and continuation of the rule; and

c. the information, including the source(s) of such information and the methodology upon which the cost analysis is based;

OR d. where an agency finds that it cannot fully provide a statement of costs, a statement setting forth the agency's best estimate, which shall indicate the information and methodology upon which the estimate is based and the reason(s) why a complete cost statement cannot be provided.)

5. Local government mandates: (Describe any program, service, duty or responsibility imposed by the rule upon any county, city, tow n, village, school district, fire district or other special district.)

6. Paperwork: (Describe the need for any reporting requirements, including forms and other paperwork that would be required as a result of the rule.)

7. Duplication: (Identify relevant rules and other legal requirements of the state and federal governments, including those that may duplicate, overlap or conflict with the rule. Identify efforts agency has or will undertake to resolve or minimize the impact of any duplication, overlap or conflict on regulated persons, including but not limited to seeking waivers or amendments of or exemptions from such other rules or legal requirements, or entering into a memorandum of understanding or other agreement regarding same.)

8. Alternatives: (Describe any significant alternative proposals that were given consideration before deciding on the final proposal and for each alternative, explain why the alternatives were rejected in favor of this proposal. If there were no significant alternatives to be considered, state that fact.)

9. Federal standards: (Identify whether the rule exceeds any minimum standards of the federal government for the same or similar subject areas and, if so, provide an explanation of why the rule exceeds such standards.)

10. Compliance schedule: (Indicate the estimated period of time needed to enable regulated persons to achieve compliance with the rule.)

Regulatory Flexibility Analysis for Small Businesses and Local Governments[508]

1. Effect of rule: (Describe the types of small businesses and local governments and provide an estimate of the number of each such small business or local government that will be affected by the rule.)

2. Compliance requirements: (Describe the reporting, recordkeeping or other affirmative acts that a small business or local government will have to undertake to comply with the rule.)

3. Professional services: (Describe the types of professional services that a small business or local government is likely to need to comply with the rule.)

4. Compliance costs: (Estimate the initial capital costs that will be incurred by a regulated business or industry or local government to comply with the rule; estimate the annual cost for continuing compliance with the rule; and indicate whether or not the initial or continuing compliance costs will vary for small businesses or local governments depending on the type and/or size of such business or local government.)

5. Economic and technological feasibility: (Provide an assessment of the economic and technological feasibility of compliance with such rule by small businesses and local governments.)

6. Minimizing adverse impact: (Explain how the rule is designed to minimize any adverse economic impact the rule may have on small businesses or local governments. In this respect, an agency should consider the approaches suggested by the Legislature in SAPA §202-b(1). If the rule could not be designed to minimize the adverse economic impact on small businesses or local governments, explain why. If the rule will have no adverse economic impact on small businesses or local governments, explain the reasons for that finding. In addition, this section must contain a statement indicating whether the approaches for minimizing adverse economic impact suggested in SAPA §202-b(1) or other similar approaches were considered.)

7. Small business and local government participation: (Explain how your agency complied with SAPA §202-b(6), which requires that agencies ensure that small businesses and local governments have an opportunity to participate in the rule making process.)

8. (IF APPLICABLE) For rules that either establish or modify a violation or penalties associated with a violation: (If the rule text does not include a cure period or other opportunity for ameliorative action, the successful completion of which will prevent the imposition of penalties on the party or parties subject to enforcement, explain why no such cure period was included in the rule.)

Ohio

CSI Business Impact Analysis Template[509]

Regulatory Intent

1. Please briefly describe the draft regulation in plain language.

Please include the key provisions of the regulation as well as any proposed amendments.

2. Please list the Ohio statute authorizing the Agency to adopt this regulation.

3. Does the regulation implement a federal requirement? Is the proposed regulation being adopted or amended to enable the state to obtain or maintain approval to administer and enforce a federal law or to participate in a federal program?

If yes, please briefly explain the source and substance of the federal requirement.

4. If the regulation includes provisions not specifically required by the federal government, please explain the rationale for exceeding the federal requirement.

5. What is the public purpose for this regulation (i.e., why does the Agency feel that there needs to be any regulation in this area at all)?

6. How will the Agency measure the success of this regulation in terms of outputs and/or outcomes?

Development of the Regulation

7. Please list the stakeholders included by the Agency in the development or initial review of the draft regulation.

If applicable, please include the date and medium by which the stakeholders were initially contacted.

8. What input was provided by the stakeholders, and how did that input affect the draft regulation being proposed by the Agency?

9. What scientific data was used to develop the rule or the measurable outcomes of the rule? How does this data support the regulation being proposed?

10. What alternative regulations (or specific provisions within the regulation) did the Agency consider, and why did it determine that these alternatives were not appropriate? If none, why didn't the Agency consider regulatory alternatives?

11. Did the Agency specifically consider a performance-based regulation? Please explain.

Performance-based regulations define the required outcome, but don't dictate the process the regulated stakeholders must use to achieve compliance.

12. What measures did the Agency take to ensure that this regulation does not duplicate an existing Ohio regulation?

13. Please describe the Agency's plan for implementation of the regulation, including any measures to ensure that the regulation is applied consistently and predictably for the regulated community.

Adverse Impact to Business

14. Provide a summary of the estimated cost of compliance with the rule. Specifically, please do the following:

a. Identify the scope of the impacted business community;

b. Identify the nature of the adverse impact (e.g., license fees, fines, employer time for compliance); and

c. Quantify the expected adverse impact from the regulation.

Pennsylvania

Summary of the Regulatory Analysis Form Contents[510]

1. The title of the regulation, the name of the agency, and the names and telephone numbers of agency officials responsible for responding to questions and receiving comments.
2. A concise, nontechnical explanation of the regulation.
3. A citation to the Federal or State statute or regulation, or the decision of a federal or state court, authorizing or affecting the regulation.
4. An explanation of the compelling public interest that justifies the regulation.
5. A statement of the public health, safety, environmental or general welfare risks associated with non-regulation.
6. An identification of the types of persons, businesses and organizations who will need to comply with the regulation and who will benefit or be adversely affected.
7. Estimates of the direct and indirect costs to the regulated community, the Commonwealth and its political subdivisions.
8. A description of required legal, accounting or consulting procedures, additional reporting, recordkeeping or other paperwork and measures taken to minimize these requirements.
9. A listing of provisions that are more stringent than federal standards and the compelling Pennsylvania interest that demands stronger regulation.
10. A description of how the regulation compares to regulations in other states and whether the regulation will put Pennsylvania at a competitive disadvantage.
11. A description of alternatives which have been considered and rejected, and a statement that the regulation is the least burdensome alternative.
12. A description of the input solicited during the development of the regulation, a schedule of any hearings, and the anticipated effective date.
13. A description of special provisions developed to meet the needs of affected persons, including minorities, elderly, small businesses and farmers.
14. A description of the plan developed for evaluating the continuing effectiveness of the regulation after its implementation.

South Dakota

Small Business Impact Statement Form[511]
See SDCL 1-26-2.1

(NOTE: This form must be signed by either the head of the agency or the presiding officer of the board or commission empowered to adopt the rules. Check your statutes to see who is authorized to promulgate rules. A small business is defined as any business with 25 or fewer full-time employees. When a set of rules is proposed, a general summary shall be provided; each proposed rule amendment shall also be explained thoroughly. In the case of a large set of proposed rules which all have a single purpose and impact, one explanation is sufficient. The law makes it clear that agencies or commissions shall use readily available information and existing resources to prepare the impact statement.)

1. Our agency has determined that the rule/s we are proposing have the following type of impact on small businesses:

□ Direct impact *(please complete remainder of form)*

□ Indirect impact *(please provide a brief explanation, then sign, date, and submit form. Questions 2 through 8 do not need to be answered)*

□ No impact *(please provide a brief explanation, sign, date, and submit form - Questions 2 through 8 do not need to be answered)*

2. A general narrative and overview of the effect of the rule(s) on small business - written in plain, easy to read language:

3. What is the basis for the enactment of the rules(s)?

□ Required to meet changes in federal law

□ Required to meet changes in state law

□Required solely due to changes in date (i.e. must be changed annually)

Other: ____

4. Why is the rule(s) needed?

5. What small businesses or types of small businesses would be subject to the rule?

6. Estimate the number of small businesses that would be subject to the rule.

□ 1-99　□ 100-499　□ 500-999　□ 1,000-4,999　□ More than 5,000

□ Unknown - please explain ______________________________

7. Are small businesses required to file or maintain any reports or records under this rule?

□Yes　□ No

a. If "yes," how many reports must a small business submit to the state on an annual basis?

b. If "yes," how much ongoing recordkeeping within the business is necessary?

c. If "yes," what type of professional skills would be necessary to prepare the reports or records?

□ The average owner of a small business should be able to complete the reports and/or records with no assistance

□ It is likely that a bookkeeper for a small business should be able to complete the reports and/or records

□ It is likely that a small business person would need the assistance of a CPA to complete the reports and/or records

□ It is likely that a small business person would need the assistance of an attorney to complete the reports and/or records

□ Other ____

□ Unknown - please explain ____

8. Are there any less intrusive or less costly methods to achieve the purpose of the rule (i.e. fewer reports, less recordkeeping, lower penalties)?

□ No - please explain ____

□ Yes - please explain ____

Dated ____________ Authorized Signature ___________ Name of Agency _________

Tennessee

Excerpts from

Rulemaking Guidelines[512]

Responses to Public Hearing Comments. For *Rulemaking Hearing Rules only*, agencies shall include only their responses to public hearing comments which shall be summarized. Space is provided in the rule making hearing form for these responses. No letters of inquiry from parties questioning the rule will be accepted. Minutes or transcripts of the meeting will not be accepted. When no comments are received at the public hearing, the agency need only include a statement stating such in this section.

Impact on Local Governments Statement. Pursuant to T.C.A. 4-5-220 and 4-5-228, “any rule proposed to be promulgated shall state in a simple declarative sentence, without additional comments on the merits of the policy of the rules or regulation, whether the rule or regulation may have a projected impact on local governments.” (See Public Chapter Number 1070 (http://state.tn.us/sos/acts/106/pub/pc1070.pdf) of the 2010 Session of the General Assembly).

Regulatory Flexibility Statement. As part of the rulemaking process for any proposed rule that may have an impact on small businesses, each agency shall prepare an economic impact statement as an addendum for each rule that is deemed to affect small businesses (T.C.A. 4-5- 403), The statement shall include the following:

- The type or types of small business and an identification and estimate of the number of small businesses subject to the proposed rule that would bear the cost of, or directly benefit from the proposed rule,
- The projected reporting, recordkeeping and other administrative costs required for compliance with the proposed rule, including the type of professional skills necessary for preparation of the report or record,
- A statement of the probable effect on impacted small businesses and consumers,
- A description of any less burdensome, less intrusive or less costly alternative methods of achieving the purpose and objectives of the proposed rule that may exist, and to what extent the alternative means might be less burdensome to small business,
- A comparison of the proposed rule with any federal or state counterparts, and
- Analysis of the effect of the possible exemption of small businesses from all or any part of the requirements contained in the proposed rule.

Texas

Excerpts from
HB 3430 SMALL BUSINESS IMPACT FINAL GUIDELINES[513]

II. Outline of Required Steps

Is an Economic Impact Statement required:

- Would the proposed rule have:
  1) An adverse economic effect;
  2) On small business?

If the answer to both questions is yes, then an Economic Impact Statement must be prepared that includes:

- An estimate of the number of small businesses subject to the proposed rule;
- A projection of the economic impact of the proposed rule on small businesses, and;
- A regulatory Flexibility Analysis, which reflects an agency's consideration of the alternative methods described in the Economic Impact Statement, must include:
  - Consideration of the use of regulatory methods that will achieve the purpose of the proposed rule while minimizing adverse impacts on small businesses, if consistent with the health, safety, environmental and economic welfare of the state; and
  - An analysis of several proposed methods of reducing the adverse impact of the proposed rule on small business.

Notice and Comment is required:

- Include the Economic Impact Statement and the Regulatory Flexibility Analysis in the notice of the proposed rule in the *Texas Register*
- Provide copies to the standing committees of each house of the legislature that is charged with reviewing the proposed rule

- Respond to any comments on the Economic Impact Statement and Regulatory Flexibility Analysis as required in any adoption preamble.

III. What Is a Small Business?

As provided under § 2006.001(2), as amended by HB 3430, a small business is an entity that is:

1) For profit,

2) Independently owned and operated, and

3) Has fewer than 100 employees or less than $6 million in annual gross receipts. Each of these three elements should be met in order for an entity to qualify as a small business under HB 3430. A business must be operated for profit. Consequently, rules that apply exclusively to non-profit and governmental entities need not comply with HB 3430.

Independently owned and operated businesses are self-controlling entities that are not subsidiaries of other entities or otherwise subject to control by other entities and entities that are not publicly traded. To qualify as a small business, an entity must have either fewer than 100 employees or less than $6 million in annual gross receipts. Practically, the standard of fewer than 100 employees will be the easiest to determine and implement. Data on an entity's annual gross receipts is generally not publicly available.

In some cases, individual persons licensed by an agency might be considered to be small businesses. Whether an individual licensee might be a small business will depend upon the nature of the regulated profession or trade and the governing statute. An agency should look to see if any of its licensees might practice as small businesses.

IV. Adverse Economic Effect

Section 2006.002(c) requires that "[b]efore adopting a rule that may have an adverse economic effect on small businesses, a state agency shall prepare" an Economic Impact Statement and Regulatory Flexibility Analysis. One of an agency's first inquiries should be whether a proposed rule may have an adverse economic effect on small businesses.[514]

If a proposed rule will not have an adverse economic effect on small business, an agency should include a finding to that effect in the notice of the proposed rule. An agency is not required to prepare an Economic Impact Statement and Regulatory Flexibility Analysis if there is no adverse economic effect.[515] An agency should, however, provide a reasoned explanation in the preamble for the proposed rule as to why an Economic Impact Statement and Regulatory Flexibility Analysis is not required for the proposed rule.[516]

Adverse economic effects can include the costs to a small business for compliance with a proposed rule and may include a loss of business opportunities as the result of regulatory limits. What constitutes an adverse economic impact may depend upon the characteristics of a regulated industry and upon the effect of a proposed rule. However, an agency need only consider direct adverse economic effects. An agency need not consider indirect economic effects, such as impacts on small businesses that are not regulated entities.[517] Generally, there is no need to examine the indirect effect of a proposed rule on entities outside of an agency's regulatory jurisdiction. However, an agency should carefully evaluate a proposed rule where indirect effect may be of particular concern, such as the impact of a proposed rule on other regulated entities.

Adverse economic effects need not be limited to regulatory programs. Adverse economic effects can also be associated with grant programs or other voluntary programs.

V. Economic Impact Statement and Regulatory Flexibility Analysis

Agencies should make reasonable, good-faith effort to prepare an Economic Impact Statement and Regulatory Flexibility Analysis that will provide the public and the affected small businesses with information about the potential adverse effects of the proposed rule and about potentially less-burdensome alternatives.[518] Substantial compliance requires that the Economic Impact Statement provide interested persons with an opportunity to comment intelligently on the basis for an agency's projected economic impact of a proposed rule on small business.[519]

An agency should individually analyze the impacts of each proposed rule or rule amendment. While an agency may be able to take advantage of the data and analysis compiled as part of an Economic Impact Statement for a prior rule making, the agency should confirm that the data is appropriate for each proposed rule.

A. Determining the Number of Small Businesses

To k now whether a proposed rule affects a number of small businesses, an agency must first know how many regulated entities exist and which are small businesses. For some agencies that regulate only one industry or profession, this may require determining only how many of the businesses that the agency regulates meet the standards for small businesses. For some agencies, most of their regulated individuals and entities, if not nearly all, may qualify as small businesses.

The most readily determinable factor will be whether a business has less than 100 employees. If a business does, then it is clearly a small business and an economic impact statement ad regulatory flexibility analysis should be prepared. With regard to businesses with more than 100 employees, but less than $6 million in annual gross receipts, further information may be obtained by consulting.

The Comptroller of Public Accounts has developed a web site to assist agencies in determining a proposed rule's potential adverse economic effect on small businesses (https://fmx.cpa.state. Additional information on employers with fewer than 100 employees is available from the Texas Workforce Commission's TRACER web site (www.tracer2.com).[520]

An agency that regulates only one industry or profession may only need to conduct this analysis once to determine the number and/or percentage of small businesses that it regulates. That analysis can then be used in future rulemakings, however, the analysis should be reviewed and updated periodically to reflect changes in the number of regulated businesses or changes to the agency's jurisdiction.

Agencies that adopt rules affecting multiple industries will likely need to determine for each proposed rule the number of small businesses that may be affected. The first step in this analysis would be to identify the industry sectors to be regulated. In the past, many ag3encies used the Standard Industrial Classification (SIC) codes to categorize regulated businesses on an industryby-industry basis. In 1999, the SIC system was replaced by the North American Industry Classification System (NAICS), which breaks down industry sectors in much greater detail.

For a grant program or other voluntary program, an agency can develop an estimate of the number of small businesses affected by anticipating the potential number of applicants and potential number of grant recipients. The number of applicants from past years of a program could be used as examples, or the number of applicants for similar programs can be used as the basis for an estimate. An agency should strive to provide some reasoned explanation for an estimate of the number of applicants and the methodology and quality of the data used to derive the estimate.

An agency does not need to provide an exact accounting of the number of small businesses that a proposed rule may affect.[521] The number of businesses may be reported as an approximation such as "more than," or a range such as: 1-100, 101-500, 501-1000, 1001-5000, 5001-10,000, or 10,000+.

In some instances, an agency may regulate businesses that are located outside of Texas. In such a case, an agency should look to see whether any of these businesses are small businesses that should be included in the number that the proposed rule might affect. However, an agency need only assess the general adverse effect of a proposed rule on small businesses doing business in Texas; it need not perform a detailed analysis of how a proposed rule might have a different effect, if any, on small businesses that are located outside of Texas.

B. Projecting the Economic Impact

Under § 2006.002(c)(1), an agency is required to project the economic impact of a proposed rule on small businesses. Every rule is different. The level, scope, and complexity of analysis may vary significantly depending on the characteristics and composition of the industry or small-entity sectors to be regulated. The projection need only assess the potential adverse economic effects on small businesses.

Agencies are also required , under § 2006.002(f), to reduce the adverse effect of rules on micro-businesses. Under § 2006.001(1), a micro-business is defined as an entity with not more than 20 employees. Consequently, the number of micro-businesses in a regulated industry or profession is a subset of the number of small businesses. In some instances, however, a proposed rule may have a disparate effect on micro-businesses as compared to small businesses. An agency's projection of economic impact should include an analysis as to whether a proposed rule may have an adverse effect on micro-businesses distinct from any potential adverse effect on small business.

Examples of the costs associated with a proposed rule may include:

- Recordkeeping;
- Reporting;
- Required professional expertise, such as lawyer, accounting, or engineering;
- Capital costs for any required equipment;
- Costs for modifying any existing processes and procedures;
- Lost sales and profits resulting from the proposed rule;
- Changes in market competition as a result of the proposed rule and its effect on the balance between specific submarkets;
- Extra tax costs;
- Additional employees that may need to be hired; and
- Required fees.

C. Regulatory Flexibility Analysis

In preparing the Regulatory Flexibility Analysis, as required under § 2006.002(c)(2), an agency must consider alternative methods of achieving the purpose of the proposed rule. As provided under § 2006.002(c-1), the alternative should:

- Be consistent with the health, safety, and environmental and economic welfare of the state;
- Accomplish the objectives of the rule; and
- Minimize adverse impacts on small business.

An agency must also include in the analysis several proposed methods of reducing the adverse impact of a proposed rule on a small business. The Regulatory Flexibility Analysis and Economic Impact Statement can be combined into a single report.

1. Exception for the Public Health, Safety, and Welfare

Under § 2006.002(c-1), an agency must "consider, if consistent with the health, safety, and environmental and economic welfare of the state, using regulatory methods that will accomplish the objectives of applicable rules while minimizing adverse impacts on small business."

An agency is not required to consider alternatives that, while possibly minimizing adverse impacts on small business would not be protective of the health, safety and environmental and economic welfare of the state.[522] One common example would appear to fit within this exception. Agencies may be required to adopt as rules specific fees or specific standards and procedures under a legislative or federal mandate. In such a situation, the mandated language may be considered *per se* consistent with the health, safety, or environmental and economic welfare of the state and the agency need not consider other regulatory methods.

Other situation may not be as clear, and each agency should exercise professional discretion and expertise in making this determination. It is reasonable to conclude that this *per se* exception should be narrowly applied, and it should only be applied in situations where the governing standard has left the agency with no discretion as to the standard to be applied and the method for implementing the rule.

2. Alternatives Analysis

The kinds of alternatives that are possible will vary based on the particular regulatory objective and the characteristics of the regulated industry. Examples of alternatives that an agency may identify and evaluate include:

- Establishment of different compliance or reporting requirements for small entities or timetables that take into account the resources available to small entities.
- Clarification, consolidation, or simplification of compliance and reporting requirements for small entities.
- Use of performance rather than design standards.
- Implementation of different requirements or standards for micro-businesses.
- Exemption for certain or all small entities from coverage of the rule, in whole or in part.
- Adopting different standards for the size of business.
- Modifying the types of equipment that are required for large and small entities.
- The effect of not adopting the proposed regulation, a "no action" alternative.

An agency must include the analysis several methods of reducing the adverse impact of a proposed rule on a small business. A common meaning of "several" is "more than two but fewer than many," with "many" meaning "a large number of persons or things."

Virginia

Excerpts from Template for Proposed Regulation Agency Background Document[523]

Economic Impact

Please identify the anticipated economic impact of the proposed new regulations or amendments to the existing regulation. When describing a particular economic impact, please specify which new requirement or change in requirements creates the anticipated economic impact.

- Projected cost to the state to implement and enforce the proposed regulation, including (a) fund source, and (b) a delineation of one-time versus on-going expenditures.
- Projected cost of the *new regulations or changes to existing regulations* on localities.
- Description of the individuals, businesses or other entities likely to be affected by the *new regulations or changes to existing regulations.*
- Agency's best estimate of the number of such entities that will be affected. Please include an estimate of the number of small businesses affected. Small business means a business entity, including its affiliates, that (i) is independently owned and operated and (ii) employs fewer than 500 full-time employees or has gross annual sales of less than $6 million.
- All projected costs of the *new regulations or changes to existing regulations* for affected individuals, businesses, or other entities. Please be specific and include all costs. Be sure to include the projected reporting, recordkeeping, and other administrative costs required for compliance by small businesses. Specify any costs related to the development of real estate for commercial or residential purposes that are a consequence of the proposed regulatory changes or new regulations.
- Beneficial impact the regulation is designed to produce.

Alternatives

Please describe any viable alternatives to the proposal considered and the rationale used by the agency to select the least burdensome or intrusive alternative that meets the essential purpose of the action. Also, include discussion of less intrusive or less costly alternatives for small businesses, as defined in §2.2-4007.1 of the Code of Virginia, of achieving the purpose of the regulation.

Regulatory Flexibility Analysis

Please describe the agency's analysis of alternative regulatory methods, consistent with health, safety, environmental, and economic welfare, that will accomplish the objectives of applicable law while minimizing the adverse impact on small business. Alternative regulatory methods include, at a minimum:

1. the establishment of less stringent compliance or reporting requirements;
2. the establishment of less stringent schedules or deadlines for compliance or reporting requirements;
3. the consolidation or simplification of compliance or reporting requirements;
4. the establishment of performance standards for small businesses to replace design or operational standards required in the proposed regulation; and
5. the exemption of small businesses from all or any part of the requirements contained in the proposed regulation.

End Notes

[1] Public Law 96-354 – Sept. 19, 1980.

[2] Public Law 104-121 – March 29, 1996.

[3] These included:

- Definition of small business,
- Analysis of economic impacts,
- Regulatory flexibility analysis of alternatives,
- Designation of a state review agency to "advise and assist" in regulatory flexibility analysis,
- Judicial review, and
- Periodic review of rules.

[4] In practice, "available" meant posted on line. The types of information available varied widely and included (among other things) background information, notices, guidance, reports, analyses, review criteria, agendas, and minutes.

[5] Some procedures, such as notification and comment, are already in the state Administrative Procedures Act.

[6] Processes for involving stakeholders before the Notice of Proposed Rule often fall in this category.

[7] An initial regulatory flexibility analysis is required for all regulations, but a final regulatory flexibility analysis is not required if a regulation does not have a significant impact on a substantial number of small entities.

[8] In such cases, dashes or blanks (without explanation) are common on the regulatory flexibility analysis forms.

[9] Missouri has an executive order that stipulates an aggregate impact of $500, which many rules do not exceed. This illustrates the issue, as it was merely an attempt to provide an operational definition for "affects small business."

[10] These generally involve expedited proceeding without a hearing on regulations thought to be non-controversial (for which a hearing would be a waste of resources), unless comments indicate some level of demand for a hearing.

[11] This should include

- A brief summary of the purpose and need for the rule;
- A brief explanation of what the rule will change and how it will be changed; and
- A brief description of effects known at the time.

[12] This includes the full text of the proposed rule, any analyses, other docket materials, and agency contacts.

[13] Most often, this is the Secretary of State's office or the staff of a legislative bureau.

[14] Virginia sets the standard with a Regulatory Town Hall website that provides background information on the regulatory process, notices, hearing schedules, documentation, status information on individual rules, pages for subscribing for notices and making comment, posting of comments – and more – all in one place.

[15] Examples include advisory committees, formal notices earlier in the rulemaking than the NPRM, and negotiated rulemaking.

[16] SBA published separate guidance, which does not appear to have percolated to the state level. The first two paragraphs in the *Forward* of SBA's *State Guide to Regulatory Flexibility for Small Business* provide a better orientation to regulatory flexibility analysis than anything found in state guidance.

[17] Regulatory flexibility guidance for state agencies should be expanded in at least three basic directions.

- Background on what regulatory flexibility is about is needed.
- The mechanics of estimating cost impacts need to be explained.

- Illustrative examples, particularly for regulatory flexibility alternatives and criteria for revising rules on periodic review, are most helpful for understanding.

[18] This function is inadequately addressed in SBA's model legislation, which says only that "each agency shall notify the... state department... that exists to review regulations of its intent to adopt the proposed regulation. The department... shall advise and assist agencies in complying with the provisions of this section."

[19] Public Law 96-354 – Sept. 19, 1980.

[20] Public Law 104-121 – March 29, 1996.

[21] The model legislation is discussed further in Chapter II. The text is in Appendix A.

[22] SBA Office of Advocacy, Small Business Regulatory Flexibility Model Legislation Initiative, September 2005.

[23] SBA Office of Advocacy, State Guide to Regulatory Flexibility for Small Businesses, March 2007.

[24] Most of the Findings, for example, are taken verbatim from the Regulatory Flexibility Act, except for word changes such as "state" for "Federal."

[25] This discussion is based on:

- Lists in the text and a map as of mid-2005 in Small Business Regulatory Flexibility Model Legislation Initiative;
- A map as of early 2007 in State Guide to Regulatory Flexibility for Small Businesses; and
- The latest available data from the SBA website. These data are probably mostly no later than 2008, as they are given a date of August 2010 but are annotated "this information may not reflect updates from the past two legislative sessions."

[26] These states are shown on the 2005 map as having legislation but not described in the text as having considered or adopted legislation since 2002.

[27] These states are mentioned in the 2005 text as considering legislation since 2002, and are shown on the2005 map as having it, but are not mentioned in the text as having adopted it since 2002.

[28] Five governors issued executive orders, but two of the states subsequently passed legislation which was included in the previous figures.

[29] For simplicity, the District of Columbia is counted as a territory, along with Guam, Puerto Rico, and the Virgin Islands.

[30] One fact sheet is a map; the other an older version of the list - all conveying the same information.

[31] Some analysis documents, for example, were sent directly to a legislative review committee and were not openly published. Documents that were available upon request during a rulemaking, usually were not conveniently archived.

[32] In a few cases, an executive order was germane, but most of the earlier executive orders incorporated SBA's model legislation, some are no longer in force, and some made little change to regulatory flexibility legislation.

[33] These included:

- Definition of small business,
- Analysis of economic impacts,
- Regulatory flexibility analysis of alternatives,
- Designation of a state review agency to "advise and assist" in regulatory flexibility analysis,
- Judicial review, and
- Periodic review of rules.

[34] Most states, for example, were more concerned with fiscal impacts on local government than business impacts.

[35] The model legislation requires only notification of the regulatory review agency, while the Regulatory Flexibility Act requires publication of a regulatory flexibility agenda that is available to the public.

[36] For simplification, we focused on and standard rulemaking process and not emergency rules or other processes. Similarly, we also did not consider most aspects of scheduling, other than length of the comment period.

[37] Specific sources included websites of:

- The entity that publishes the *Register* and/or with whom documents were officially "filed,"
- The executive agency involved in regulatory flexibility (usually the department of commerce and/or economic development, and sometimes the small business office within that department),
- The agency that published the state rulemaking manual,
- The agency that provides guidance and information on rulemaking to agency staff and/or the public,
- Committees or commissions (both legislative and independent) that review regulations, and/or
- Agencies that promulgated regulations.

In most states one agency performed more than one of these functions.

[38] Arkansas provides an example. When an internet search for the Regulatory Review Committee turned up nothing, we contacted the person "designated as the point of contact for regulatory flexibility" for information. She had none.

[39] Alaska, Delaware, Illinois, Massachusetts, Oklahoma, Rhode Island, Virginia

[40] The model legislation suggests [in brackets] common SBA size standards of 500 employees and $6 million.

[41] The model legislation suggests [Department of Economic and Community Development] as a possibility.

[42] State APAs are influenced to a greater or lesser degree by a model Administrative Procedures Act – adopted in 1981 by the National Conference of Commissioners on Uniform State Laws (NCCUSL) - which provides states with guidance for adopting procedures for promulgating administrative regulations and for adjudicating disputes before administrative bodies. The NCCUSL has since developed a revised model APA, which it adopted in July 2010.

[43] For states that use a revenue standard, the standard is generally a much larger percentage of the SBA standard than is the employment standard.

[44] Connecticut, Delaware, Illinois, Iowa, Minnesota, New Hampshire, New Mexico, North Dakota, Oklahoma, Oregon, Utah, South Dakota, Vermont, Washington, and Wisconsin.

[45] Alaska, Arizona, Arkansas, Georgia, Missouri, New Jersey, New York, South Carolina, and Texas.

[46] Colorado, Florida, Indiana, Michigan, Nevada, Ohio, and Virginia.

[47] Massachusetts and Rhode Island.

[48] Specific industries and standards include:

- Agriculture ($1,000,000),
- Utility, water company, or power transmission company (4.5 million kilowatt hours),
- General construction ($9,500,000),
- Special trade construction ($5,000,000),
- Manufacturing (250 employees),
- Retail trade ($2,000,000),
- Wholesale trade ($9,500,000),
- Transportation and warehousing ($1,500,000), and
- Services ($2,000,000),
- Health care facility (150 beds or $1,500,000). (California Code, §11342.610(c))

[49] Arizona and Illinois.

[50] Massachusetts, Michigan, New Jersey, and New York.

[51] Indiana.

[52] These include the following:

- Kentucky allows "any number of tiers that will solve most efficiently and effectively the problem the administrative regulation addresses."
- Maryland allows agencies to "adopt 1 or more regulations that apply differently to classes of businesses."
- Connecticut (with a size standard of 500 employees) allows any smaller size standard "as necessary."
- Michigan (size standard of 250 employees) allows alternative classifications of 0-9, 10-49, or 50-249 employees.

[53] Alaska, California, Illinois, Indiana, Iowa, Maine, Michigan, Oregon, Rhode Island, South Carolina, Tennessee, Washington, and Wisconsin

[54] Arizona, Connecticut, Florida, Georgia, Louisiana, Utah, and Virginia.

[55] Georgia focused on alternatives analysis in a way that only implicitly referred to regulatory flexibility: In the formulation and adoption of any rule, an agency shall choose an alternative that does not impose excessive regulatory costs on any regulated person or entity which costs could be reduced by a less expensive alternative that fully accomplishes the stated objectives of the statutes which are the basis of the proposed rule. (Official Code of Georgia Annotated, §50-13-4(a)(3))

[56] Nevada, New Jersey, and New York.

[57] New York and New Jersey (using identical language) omit "consolidation or simplification of requirements." Nevada includes only different compliance standards and simplification, but adds modification of fees or fines. Vermont directs "an agency [to] consider creative, innovative, or flexible methods of compliance with the rule." West Virginia has SBA Section 3 as a requirement by executive order.

[58] North Dakota and South Dakota.

[59] In Colorado: "Such cost-benefit analysis *shall* include... at least two alternatives to the proposed rule or amendment that can be identified by the submitting agency or a member of the public, including the costs and

benefits of pursuing each of the alternatives identified." [emphasis added] (Colorado Revised Statutes, §24-4-103(2.5))

In Delaware: "Whenever... it is lawful, desirable and feasible to exempt... small businesses or to set lesser standards of compliance by... or small businesses, the agency *shall* issue a rule or regulation containing an appropriate exemption for such... small businesses or setting lesser standards for compliance by... small businesses." [emphasis added] (Delaware Code, Title 29, §10406)

60 Arkansas, Hawaii, and Missouri.

61 Hawaii's Small Business Regulatory Review Board and Missouri's Small Business Regulatory Fairness Board both have clear statutory functions and appear to be functioning reasonably well. The website of the Arkansas Economic Development Commission's Small and Minority Development Division has a web page devoted to regulatory flexibility, but no sign of the Regulatory Review Committee (established by statute in 2009) could be found.

62 Kentucky, Maryland, and Oklahoma.

63 New Mexico and Ohio.

64 New Hampshire's fiscal impact statement requires:

An analysis of the general impact of the proposed rule upon any independently owned businesses, including a description of the specific reporting and recordkeeping requirements upon small businesses which employ fewer than 10 employees. (New Hampshire Revised Statutes, §541-A:5)

Pennsylvania's regulatory analysis requirements include:

A description of any special provisions which have been developed to meet the particular needs of affected groups and persons, including minorities, the elderly, small businesses and farmers. (Pennsylvania P.L. 633, No. 181, §5(b))

65 If the annual cost of the rule exceeds $25,000 (as determined by the agency or an administrative law judge), a small business (or small city) "may [with some exceptions] file a written statement with the agency claiming a temporary exemption from the rules. Upon filing of such a statement with the agency, the rules do not apply to that business or that city until the rules are approved by a law [subsequently] enacted." (Minnesota Statutes §14.127)

66 Hawaii's version: "Any agency authorized to assess civil penalties or fines upon a small business shall waive or reduce any penalty or fine... for a violation of any statute, ordinance, or rules by a small business under the following conditions:

(a) The small business corrects the violation within a minimum of thirty days after receipt of a notice of violation or citation; and

(b) The violation was unintentional or the result of excusable neglect; or

(c) The violation was the result of an excusable misunderstanding of an agency's interpretation of a rule." (Hawaii Revised Statutes §201M-7)

67 Alabama, Idaho, Kansas, Mississippi, Montana, Nebraska, and North Carolina.

68 In Alabama, "At a minimum, the fiscal note... shall include the following:

(1) A determination of the need for the regulation and the expected benefit of the regulation.

(2) A determination of the costs and benefits associated with the regulation and an explanation of why the regulation is considered to be the most cost effective, efficient, and feasible means for allocating public and private resources and for achieving the stated purpose.

(3) The effect of the regulation on competition.

(4) The effect of the regulation on the cost of living and doing business in the geographical area in which the regulation would be implemented.

(5) The effect of the regulation on employment in the geographical area in which the regulation would be implemented.

(6) The source of revenue to be used for implementing and enforcing the regulation.

(7) A conclusion on the short-term and long-term economic impact upon all persons substantially affected by the regulation, including an analysis containing a description of which persons will bear the costs of the regulation and which persons will benefit directly and indirectly from the regulation.

(8) The uncertainties associated with the estimation of particular benefits and burdens and the difficulties involved in the comparison of qualitatively and quantitatively dissimilar benefits and burdens. A determination of the need for the regulation shall consider qualitative and quantitative benefits and burdens.

(9) The effect of the regulation on the environment and public health.

(10) The detrimental effect on the environment and public health if the regulation is not implemented." (Code of Alabama, §41-22-23(f))

[69] Examples include: Arizona, Connecticut, Florida, Kentucky, Maryland, Nebraska, New Jersey, New York, North Carolina, Ohio, Pennsylvania, South Dakota, Virginia, and Wisconsin.

[70] Examples include: Delaware, Florida, Kentucky, Louisiana, Michigan, Minnesota, North Dakota, and Virginia.

[71] Examples include: Arizona, Connecticut, Florida, Indiana, Kentucky, Maryland, Minnesota, Nebraska, North Carolina, North Dakota, Ohio, Pennsylvania, and West Virginia.

[72] Examples include: Hawaii, Kansas, Minnesota, Missouri, New York, North Carolina, Washington, and Texas.

[73] Examples include: Alabama, California, Colorado, Louisiana, and New Jersey.

[74] Examples include: Alabama, Colorado, and Louisiana.

[75] Examples include: Arizona, Maine, Mississippi, New Hampshire, Pennsylvania, and Washington.

[76] Examples include: Alabama, Idaho, South Carolina, and Vermont.

[77] Examples include: Hawaii, Michigan, Missouri, Oregon, and Pennsylvania.

[78] The following examples generally do not include the function of preparing written guidance for rulemaking.

[79] Alaska and Connecticut fit this pattern.

[80] Arkansas, Georgia, Illinois, Indiana, and Michigan are cases in point. For example, the Indiana Economic Development Commission makes comments that may

- Recommend that the agency implement regulatory alternatives found in the statute;
- Suggest regulatory alternatives not considered by the agency;
- Recommend any other changes to the proposed rule to minimize the economic impact of the proposed rule on small businesses; or
- Recommend that the agency abandon or delay the rulemaking action until more data on small-business can be gathered and evaluated or less intrusive or less costly alternative methods of achieving the proposed rule's purpose can be implemented. (Indiana Code, §22-2.1-6)

[81] Texas Statutes, §2006.002(g)

[82] Arizona, Hawaii, Missouri, Pennsylvania, South Carolina, and Wisconsin. New York had such an office, created by executive order.

[83] Florida, Maine, and Rhode Island have this position, which was established by statute, and Indiana's Ombudsman has a similar function. Massachusetts has such a position, created and appointed by the Governor.

[84] Florida, Kentucky New Mexico, and Oklahoma.

[85] Hawaii provides general statutory authority, but other states encourage this on a more piecemeal basis.

[86] Is there a continued need for the rule?

What has been the nature of complaints or comments received concerning the rule from the public?

How complex is the rule?

To what extent does the rule overlap, duplicate, or conflict with other Federal, State, and local governmental rules?

How long has it been since the rule has been evaluated?

To what degree have technology, economic conditions, or other factors changed in the area affected by the rule?

[87] Setting a time frame for reviewing rules existing at the time the legislation was enacted is fairly common.

[88] Massachusetts (review required every 12 years), Mississippi, New Mexico, Oregon, South Carolina, and Virginia.

[89] New York and Rhode Island.

[90] Arizona, Florida, Montana (review required every 2 years), and Nevada.

[91] Georgia and Pennsylvania.

[92] Minnesota, Missouri, and Ohio.

[93] Arizona and Hawaii.

[94] Alaska, California, Maryland, North Dakota, Oklahoma, and Vermont.

[95] Indiana, New Hampshire, New Jersey, and Texas.

[96] Colorado, Kentucky, and Utah.

[97] Arkansas and North Carolina.

[98] Illinois, Iowa, Kentucky, Michigan, and Washington.

[99] These criteria for review are discussed further below under legislative review.

[100] Washington is a notable exception. Not only does its statute quote the SBA model Findings, it makes its own: The legislature finds that administrative rules adopted by state agencies can have a disproportionate impact on the state's small businesses because of the size of those businesses. This disproportionate impact reduces competition, innovation, employment, and new employment opportunities, and threatens the very existence of some small businesses. The legislature therefore enacts the Regulatory Fairness Act with the intent of reducing

the disproportionate impact of state administrative rules on small business. (Revised Code of Washington, §19.85.011)

Michigan and Kentucky also have the concept of disproportionality in their statutory language.

[101] Examples include Rhode Island (Office of Regulatory Reform) and Washington (Office of Regulatory Assistance).

[102] Oregon's pamphlet, for example, covers the following topics:

- General Information
- Background on Oregon Administrative Rules
- How to Cite
- Understanding an Administrative Rule's "History"
- Locating the Most Recent Version of an Administrative Rule
- Locating Administrative Rules Unit Publications
- 2011–2012 *Oregon Bulletin* Submission and Publication Schedule. (Oregon Secretary of State, *About Oregon Administrative Rules and the Oregon Bulletin*, http://arcweb.sos.state.or.us/pages/rules/bulletin/about.html.

[103] Mississippi's Frequently Asked Questions, for example, are:

1. What is the normal process for submitting a rule for publication in the Administrative Bulletin and Code?
2. What if I have an emergency need to adopt rules prior to the mandatory notice periods?
3. How long must an agency wait before holding a Public Comment Hearing?
4. How long do rules have to be proposed before I can file final rules?
5. How long do rules have to be filed as final rules before they are effective?
6. Where can I find the Administrative Bulletin and Code?

(http://www.sos.ms.gov/regulation_and_enforcement_adminjrocedures_faqs.aspx)

[104] An example from Michigan is provided in Appendix B.

[105] Nebraska Secretary of State's website (http://www.sos.ne.gov/dyindex.html#boxingName)

[106] The organization of New York's Manual, for example is:

- Using this Manual
- Introduction
- Pre-Proposal Rule Review
- Chapter 1. How to Propose a Rule
- Chapter 2. How to Revise or Withdraw a Proposal
- Chapter 3. How to Adopt a Rule
- Chapter 4. How to Adopt an Emergency Rule
- Chapter 5. How to Incorporate by Reference
- Chapter 6. How to Publish a Regulatory Agenda
- Chapter 7. Five Year Review of Existing Rules
- Chapter 8. Guidance Documents (Department of State, Division of Administrative Rules, *Rule Making in New York Manual*, http://www.dos.ny.gov/info/rulemakingmanual.html)

[107] Even this reference is obscure. A small business impact is not required when small businesses are affected. The statute requires one when there is a "significant statewide adverse economic impact directly affecting business."

[108] The requirement for the Initial Statement of Reasons is described as:

A description of reasonable alternatives to the regulation that would lessen any adverse impact on small business and the agency's reasons for rejecting those alternatives. Similarly, the Final Statement of Reasons requirement is described as:

An explanation setting forth the reasons for rejecting any proposed alternatives that would lessen the adverse economic impact on small businesses. (Office of Administrative Law, *OAL Checklist Notice Review*, http://www.oal.ca.gov/res/docs/pdf/checklist/NoticeReviewChecklist.PDF)

[109] The sections (each basically a paragraph long) address:

- Relevant definitions,
- Procedures for dealing with comments on proposed rules,
- Appearance Before House and Senate Committees,
- Periodic five-year review of rules, and
- Provision of public information. (Joint Committee on Agency Rule Review, *Procedures Manual*, Revised: September 7, 2011, pp. 25-26)

[110] Kansas' guidance is helpful in thinking through cost analysis - but Kansas does not have regulatory flexibility. Think broadly when trying to identify potential economic impacts of proposed regulations. Consider whether or not there are less obvious, indirect economic impacts or hidden costs. For example, the economic impact of an increase in the number of continuing education units required for renewal of a license would clearly involve registration costs for the additional training. However, the increase in required continuing education is likely to have a number of other less obvious costs, including travel costs and lost productivity due to time away from work.

While it is preferable to develop dollar estimates of the economic impact, agencies may not always have adequate data to do so. In those instances, be sure to describe the nature and anticipated extent of the economic impact. (Department of Administration, *Policy and Procedure Manual for the Filing of Kansas Administrative Regulations*, Revised: January 2010, p. 9)

[111] The Guidelines also reference SBA's State Guide to Regulatory Flexibility for Small Businesses.

[112] Texas also is unique in that this guidance was prepared by the Attorney General. The Guidelines are unusual in that they went through their own notice and comment process.

[113] Three seminar topics are taught in rotation:

- Rulewriting 101
- Five-year Review Report Basics
- Preparing an Economic, Small Business, and Consumer Impact Statement

[114] The Course Agenda includes:

- Introduction
- Statutes and Regulations
- APA Background
- An Overview of the Rulemaking Process
- Underground Regulations(rules meeting the APA definition of a "regulation" but not adopted under the APA)
- Preliminary Activities for Rulemaking
- Special Considerations
- Internet demo: OAL and the CCR on-line
- Preparing the Initial Statement of Reasons
- Drafting the Notice of Proposed Rulemaking
- Publishing/Issuing the Notice
- Conducting the Public Hearing
- Preparing the Rulemaking Record
- Emergency Regulations and Non-Regulatory Changes
- Fiscal Impact Statement (Form 399) : Department of Finance and State Mandates Commission
- OAL Review
- The Six APA Standards: Authority, Reference, Consistency, Clarity, Nonduplication, and Necessity (California Office of Administrative Law, *Rulemaking Course Under California's APA: Course Agenda*, http://www.oal.ca.gov/res/docs/pdf/3-DayCourseAgenda.pdf)

[115] The Small Business Regulatory Fairness Board (SBRFB) course is developed around an simple model of the regulatory flexibility analysis process that asks three key questions:

- Preliminary Analysis: Will there be an effect on small business?
- Small Business Impact Statement: What is the potential economic impact of the rule on small business?
- Regulatory Fairness Analysis: What can be done to minimize the economic impact of the rule on small business?

  The presentation goes through the analytical process, raising specific issues that need to be addressed and providing guidelines and techniques for answering them. Communicating with the public – early, often, and attentively – is emphasized, and the forms and templates that have been developed are proffered as tools.

Training is designed to be done in and by each agency. The SBRFB recommends that each agency

- Provide formal training, on an annual basis, for all rule development, enforcement and compliance staff
- Assign division-level liaisons to ensure proper attention to and distribution of small business regulatory requirements.

The SBRFB has developed a State Agency Compliance Training Form to track agency performance. (Small Business Regulatory Fairness Board website, http://www.sbrfb.ded.mo.gov)

[116] "This workshop will explore the ins and outs of writing rules. The content covers the entire rulemaking process, from legislative delegation to replacement pages for ARM [Administrative Rules of Montana]. It includes practical exercises on style, reasonable necessity, and responding to comments." Montana has no regulatory flexibility program. (Montana Professional Development Center, Writing Administrative Rules, http://pdc.mt.gov/default.mcpx)

[117] These courses are:

- New Mexico State Rules and Rulemaking: An Introduction, which "provides a basic overview of what rules are, who can issue them, how they are created, and where they can be found."
- NMAC Advanced Training for Rule Filers, which "covers the specific details of writing and formatting rules." (Administrative Law Division, Rules Training website, http://www.nmcpr.state.nm.us /rules/training.htm)

[118] According to Division summary data, 31 people took this course in FY2011.

[119] Texas defines both small businesses and micro-businesses. Kentucky and Maryland have flexible definitions of small that allow for several classes, but these are rarely, if ever used.

[120] Texas (Appendix B) is a striking exception.

[121] California (Appendix B) is an example.

[122] In some states the titles "advocate" and "ombudsman" are reversed, but the usage here seems the most common.

[123] Rhode Island General Laws, Chapter 42-64.13

[124] Indiana Code, §5-28-17-5

[125] Illinois Office of Regulatory Flexibility website, http://www.ildceo.net/dceo/Bureaus/Entrepreneurship+and+Small+Business/Regulatory+Compliance+Assistance/RegFlex.htm

[126] Arizona Governor's Regulatory Review Council website, http://www.grrc.state.az.us/default.asp

[127] Florida Office of Small Business Advocate & Small Business Regulatory Advisory Council, *FY 2009-10 Annual Report*

[128] Hawaii Small Business Regulatory Review Board website, http://hawaii.gov/dbedt/programs/sbrrb

[129] Kentucky Revised Statutes, §11.200(2)

[130] Missouri Small Business Regulatory Fairness Board website, http://www.sbrfb.ded.mo.gov

[131] The IRRC "acts as an independent and critical eye to review regulations and offer constructive input and alternatives to promulgating agencies. This is accomplished through the review of the regulation and the consideration of input by the regulated public, the legislature, and other interested parties who often bear distinctive perspectives on the appropriateness and effectiveness of the proposed regulation." (Independent Regulatory Review Commission, *2010 Annual Report*, p. 2.

[132] Minutes of meetings from 2004 and 2005, for example, show representatives from half a dozen agencies present and discussing the affairs of the agencies. (http://www.okcommerce.gov/Businesses-And-Employers/Downloads/Small-Business-Advocacy)

[133] The Chairman, who was named 2009 Small Business Champion of Oklahoma by the NFIB and reportedly served on a federal small business committee at some previous time.

[134] Members of the General Assembly also have the authority to require these analyses.

[135] South Carolina Small Business Regulatory Review Committee, *2005-2011Committee Report*

[136] This is the only use of this phrase found at the state level. (2011 Wisconsin Act 21)

[137] Wisconsin Statutes, 227.14(2g)

[138] Recent legislation sponsored by Governor Walker, has added a seventh small business representative and removed all of the departmental representatives. (2011 Wisconsin Act 46)

[139] Chris Christie, Executive Order No. 1, January 20, 2010.

[140] Theodore R. Kulongoski, Executive Order 03-01, *Regulatory Streamlining*, February 1, 2003.

[141] Christine O.Gregoire, Executive Order 06-02, *Regulatory Improvement: Improve, Simplify and Assist*, February 2006.

[142] Connecticut General Statutes, §4-168a.

[143] Sonny Perdue, Executive Order, *Small Business Regulatory Reform Initiative*, March 6, 2006.

[144] Relatively recent legislation established a Regulatory Review Committee, appointed by the Director, to review rules, but in this study no trace of a Regulatory Review Committee was found.

[145] Michigan Compiled Laws, §24-234. A recent executive order reorganized ORR and renamed it "Office of Regulatory Reinvention." Review is now done by Advisory Rules Committees, established "with the expectation that a broad spectrum of stakeholders, including members of the regulated community and the general public, will be included in their membership." The Advisory Rules Committees review rules and submit reports of findings and recommendations to ORR. The committees are appointed for 120 (or 240) days

and then dissolve, and this lack of permanence is not conducive to advocacy. (Richard D. Snyder, Executive Order 2011-5, *Executive Reorganization*, February 23, 2011)

[146] Arizona Ombudsman – Citizens' Aide website, About Us web page, http://www.azleg.gov/ombudsman/about.asp

[147] As the ombudsman function is not directly a part of the rulemaking function, this study made no particular attempt to identify an ombudsman in any given state.

[148] Florida Statutes, §288.70015.

[149] Indiana Code, §5-28-17-5.

[150] New Mexico Office of Business Advocacy web page, http://www.gonm.biz/Office_Business_Advocacy.aspx.

[151] Kentucky Revised Statutes, §11.175.

[152] Ted Strickland, Executive Order 2008-04S, *Implementing Common Sense Business Regulation*, February 12, 2008.

[153] "What Does the Small Business Ombudsman Do?

- Serves as the primary advocate for small businesses within the Department of Environmental Protection (DEP);
- Serves as the DEP spokesperson to the small business community;
- Assists small businesses in realizing the potential cost savings of pollution prevention versus pollution control;
- Reviews pending regulations and ensures that the impact on small businesses is considered;
- Investigates complaints from small businesses about DEP;
- Provides confidential assistance to small businesses within the commonwealth needing help with environmental issues;
- Reports annually to the Governor and the U.S. EPA regarding the performance of the Small Business Assistance Program;
- Provides compliance assistance and pollution prevention pamphlets and fact sheets for small businesses;
- Provides information to small businesses needing financial assistance to implement pollution prevention practices and comply with environmental regulations."

(Department of Environmental Protection, Small Business Assistance Program web page, http://www.dep.state.pa.us/dep/deputate/airwaste/aq/small_business/small_business.htm)

[154] Ohio Executive Order 2008-04S also ordered agencies to "treat those affected by their rules and regulatory processes as customers."

[155] The legislation establishing this program adopted SBA's model Section 3 and Section 4 verbatim. Alaska was featured as an exemplary program in SBA's *State Guide to Regulatory Flexibility for Small Businesses* (2007).

[156] "In an informal survey... 75 percent of the regulators that responded want the Program to sunset." (Alaska Department of Commerce, Community, and Economic Development - Office of Economic Development, *AS 44.62.218. Regulations Affecting Small Businesses, 2005: A Program Report*, April 2, 2008, p. 3.)

[157] Excerpts from the report include:

- "The Program is increasing the Department's ability to deliver consistently good customer service with follow-up and tangible results to the public... The program is addressing one need identified in the 2006 Transition Report that stated 'the Department had no established procedure for handling consumer complaints'."
- "The Program is helping to establish the Department as a player and a leader in small business services in Alaska."
- "Through increased interagency collaboration, the Program is increasing the quality of the Department's customer service to small businesses and entrepreneurs. In order to better serve callers and walk-ins to the Department, and in collaboration with the staff from the Office of Economic Development, the Program helped launch the Small Business Assistance Center (Center)—a website with over 150 direct links to small business resources throughout Alaska and Outside." (*Ibid.*, pp. 8-10.)

[158] This includes:

- A summary of regulatory flexibility requirements,
- A link to Act 143 of 2007 (the Arkansas Regulatory Flexibility Act),
- A link to a schematic of the regulatory flexibility process, which shows the Economic Impact Statement and review by the Department of Economic Development before publication of the notice of intent,
- A Regulation Economic Impact Statement Form, and
- A Regulatory Flexibility FAQ sheet that provides practical advice.

(Arkansas Economic Development Commission, Small and Minority Business Development Division regulatory flexibility website, http://arkansasedc.com/entrepreneurs/regulatory-flexibility)

[159] Delaware Code, Chapter 104.

[160] Delaware Department of Natural Resources & Environmental Control, Delaware Small Business, Secretary's Order No. 2007-F-0004, *Re: Application of Regulatory Flexibility Act to Regulation 3215, Horseshoe Crab Harvest Moratorium*, February 5, 2007.

[161] Official Code of Georgia Annotated, §50-13-4(a)(3).

[162] "If the rule would have a substantial impact on small business and if, within thirty-two days after the published notice of proposed rule adoption, a written request for analysis is submitted to the agency by the administrative rules review committee, the administrative rules coordinator, at least twenty-five persons signing that request who each qualify as a small business or by an organization representing at least twenty-five such persons." (Iowa Code, §17A.4(1)-(3))

[163] By contrast, a fiscal impact statement must be filed with the NPRM, and fiscal statements regularly appear on the Iowa Administrative Rules webpage. (https://www.legis.iowa.gov/IowaLaw/AdminCode/adminLaw.aspx)

[164] Louisiana Revised Statutes, §49:965.5.

[165] Office of the State Register, *LAC Handbook*, October 2011.

[166] "The commission may:

(1) provide state agencies with input regarding proposed rules that may adversely affect small business;

(2) consider requests from small business owners to review rules adopted by an agency;

(3) review rules promulgated by an agency to determine whether a rule places an unnecessary burden on small business and make recommendations to the agency to mitigate the adverse effects; and

(4) provide an annual evaluation report to the governor and the legislature, including recommendations and evaluations of agencies regarding regulatory fairness for small businesses." Office of the State Register, *LAC Handbook*, October 2011.

[167] Five members were appointed by the governor, for example, and two each appointed by the speaker of the house of representatives and the president pro tempore of the senate.

[168] "After [the Small Business Regulatory Relief Act] was enacted [in 2005], I tried several times to find information about the commission and what, if anything, it was doing. It was attached to the Economic Development Department, but I found no mention of it on the department's Web site. More than a year later, I telephoned the department and talked with a staff member assigned to this commission. I learned that commission members had been appointed, and a couple of meetings had taken place. But nothing of substance had been done.

Some time later, I met a commission member. The members, initially committed and enthusiastic, had been forced to spend several meetings trying to figure out how to get the information they needed from state agencies, she said, and never got much past that point.

Frustrated members started missing meetings. Without a quorum the commission couldn't take official actions. Then members started resigning." (Merilee Dannemann, *Small Business Needs a Real Relief Act*, February 7, 2011, http://www.triplespacedagain.com/wordpress/?p=109)

[169] North Dakota Century Code §28-32-08 and §28-32-08.1.

[170] Legislative Council, Administrative Rules Drafting Manual, 2008.

[171] North Dakota Legislature, Administrative Rules Committee web page, http://www.legis.nd.gov/assembly/63-2013/committees/interim/administrative-rules-committee

[172] Among other things, analyses do not even consistently use the same terminology to differentiate between the regulatory analysis and the small business economic impact statement. Other examples:

- Three analyses of Human Services regulations reported impacts of over $50,000 (the threshold for analysis) but did not clarify on whom the impacts fell.
- A number of small business impact statements indicated "N/A" rather than providing a response.
- One report summed up the process: "The purpose of this small entity requirement is to fulfill the requirements of N. D. C. C. §28-32-08.1(2)."

[173] Sixty days in Kansas and Minnesota; 90 days in Louisiana.

[174] Florida, Idaho, and South Carolina.

[175] For simplicity, this publication will be referred to as *Register* whatever its actual title.

[176] In Connecticut, notices are published in the *Connecticut Law Journal*. In Arkansas, only final rules are published in the hard-copy Register, presumably as a step toward inclusion in the CAR.

[177] Massachusetts and South Carolina.

[178] A quaint provision in a Massachusetts statute illustrates the significance of on-line publication:

Each agency shall purchase a copy or copies of the issues of the register which contain regulations or notices of that agency and make at least one copy readily available in a prominent place at each of the agency's offices for the purpose of public inspection and copying. (General Laws of Massachusetts Chapter, 30A §6B)

179 In almost all states where a *Register* has both a hard-copy edition and an on-line edition, the hard-copy edition is the official one. Washington, which declares its on-line edition "official," is the only exception.

180 Another advantage having the proposed rule on a separate web page is that the marked up proposed rule can use different colors for additions (underlined) and deletions (strike-outs) – but that takes additional programming.

181 For example: "The Georgia Technology Authority... shall develop a Georgia Rules and Regulations website that... indexes all State Agency rules and regulations including proposed regulatory changes and is kept current by the relevant agency." (Sonny Perdue, Executive Order, *Small Business Regulatory Reform Initiative*, March 6, 2006)

182 In Minnesota, for example, the search for a proposed rule, beginning at an agency home page, can go:

- Home → Division → Driver and Vehicle Services → News → Public Notices
- Home → Statutes and rules → Rulemaking → Construction Codes → Visit the Plumbing Board Web page → Rulemaking Dockets
- Home → Elections & Voting → Election Administration → Rulemaking

In Hawaii, the search from the home page may begin with Overview, About Us, Department Info, Administrative Division, or Publications → Library → Find a Law.

183 Over a quarter of the links leading to proposed rules pages that had no entries (always a legitimate possibility). Four agencies had no such page and listed only existing rules. (Office of the Lieutenant Governor, *Administrative Rules Proposed Changes,* http://ltgov.hawaii.gov/the-office/administrative-rules/proposed-changes)

184 Department of Regulatory Agencies, Office of Policy, Research & Regulatory Reform website, http://www.colorado.gov/cs/Satellite/DORA-OPRRR/CBON/DORA/1251614750683.

185 "A direct link to the agency's rule-making page must be displayed on the agency's homepage. The rule-making web site shall include the complete text of all proposed rules, emergency rules, and permanent rules proposed or adopted within the past twelve months, or include a direct link to the index page on the Washington State Register web site that contains links to the complete text of all proposed rules, emergency rules, and permanent rules proposed or adopted within the past twelve months by that state agency. For proposed rules, the time, date, and place for the rule-making hearing and the procedures and timelines for submitting written comments and supporting data must be posted on the web site." (Revised Code of Washington, §34.05.270)

186 If a hearing will be held, a contact person for anyone needing assistance must be included.

187 This particular language is fairly commonly used. Other ways of stating this requirement include:

- An informative summary of the proposed subject of agency action,
- A statement of the topic of the proposed rule or a general description of the subjects involved,
- A description of the nature of the proceedings including a brief synopsis of the subject, substance, issues, possible terms of the agency action,
- An easily readable and understandable summary of the overall nature and effect of the proposed rule,
- A synopsis of the proposed rule, which must contain a statement of the purpose and the main features of the proposed rule,
- A short, plain explanation of the purpose and effect of the proposed rule,
- A statement of the need for the rule and a statement of how the rule is intended to meet the need,
- An explanation of the people, enterprises and governmental entities affected by the rule, and
- An informative digest drafted in plain English in a format [which] shall include the following:
  (A) A concise and clear summary of existing laws and regulations, and of the effect of the proposed action.
  (B) A brief description of [any] significant differences [from comparable] federal regulations or statutes.
  (C) A policy statement overview explaining the broad objectives of the regulation and... the specific objectives.

188 Even without boilerplate, a notice that uses only paragraphs of narrative loses clarity if the layout minimizes white space (as government publications tend to) or lacks adequate headings.

189 Some interpretation of statutes is required. Hyperlinks must be construed as fulfilling the requirement to include the full text of a proposed rule or explain "how interested persons may review the text of the rule."

190 In Michigan, for example, depending on how far the rulemaking has progressed the history includes dates for:

- Request for Rule-making Filed with ORR,
- Request for Rule-making Approved by ORR,

- Draft Rule to ORR,
- Draft Rule Approved by ORR,
- Regulatory Impact Statement to ORR,
- Public Hearings,
- Rules Certified by LSB,
- Rules Submitted to ORR,
- Rules Certified by ORR, and
- Rules Filed with JCAR.

(Office of Regulatory Reinvention, Pending Rule Changes, http://www.michigan.gov/lara/0,4601,7-154-35738_5695---,00.html)

[191] RSS is known colloquially as Really Simple Syndication.

[192] "How does RegAlert Work?

1. The SBRRB electronically mails a RegAlert to small business membership associations.
2. The business association, in turn, may send the rules to its members who can review the rules.
3. The small businesses may then email their testimonies on the rules to DBEDT via the SBRRB at sbrrb@dbedt.hawaii.gov.
4. The SBRRB will review the small businesses' testimonies at an upcoming scheduled Board meeting.
5. Upon review of the testimonies, the SBRRB will provide commentary to the rule-making agency."

(Department of Business, Economic Development and Tourism, RegAlert Description, http://hawaii.gov/dbedt/programs/sbrrb/regalert/FOLDER_NOTE.2008-07-11.2333/view?searchterm=RegAlert)

[193] Colorado's Department of Regulatory Agencies, on the other hand has so many different opportunities to register on its website that navigation has its comical moments.

[194] New Hampshire specifies all persons regulated by the proposed rules who hold occupational licenses.

New Jersey requires distributed to the news media maintaining a press office to cover the State House Complex.

[195] Joint Committee on Administrative Rules, *Illinois Regulation (The Flinn Report)*, weekly.

[196] Ohio Business Gateway, Regulatory Reform web page, http://business.ohio.gov/reform

[197] Specifications include "newspapers of record," "newspapers of general circulation," and "at least the accepting newspaper of largest paid circulation that is published [or circulated] in each county."

[198] The statute reads:

"The agency shall at the time of giving the notice of intent to act upon a regulation...

(a) Deposit one copy of the notice and text of the proposed regulation with the State Library and Archives Administrator;

(b) Keep at least one copy of the notice and text available in each of its offices from the date of the notice to the date of the hearing, for inspection and copying by the public; and

(c) If the agency does not maintain an office in a county, deposit one copy of the notice and text with the librarian of the main public library in the county." (Nevada Revised Statutes §233B.0607) An appendix to the Attorney General's guide, *Administrative Rulemaking* lists all Nevada public libraries.

[199] Department of Regulatory Agencies, Office of Policy, Research & Regulatory Reform, *loc. cit.*

[200] Office of the Secretary of State website, http://www.azsos.gov/Info/Office.htm.

[201] Arizona Governor's Regulatory Review Council website, http://www.grrc.state.az.us/default.asp.

[202] Office of Administrative Law, P:ublic Participation web page, http://www.oal.ca.gov/Public Participation.htm.

[203] Governor's Office of Regulatory Assistance Rulemaking web page, http://www.ora.wa.gov/regulatory/rulemaking.asp.

[204] These include:

- Notice of administrative rules open for public comment (comment due dates and contacts)
- Notice of administrative rules open for public comment (summary of each rule filing open for public comment)
- Notice of administrative rules open for public comment that affect state government or state employees
- Notice of emergency administrative rules in effect
- Notice of administrative rule hearings published in the Utah State Bulletin

[205] Department of Administration, Division of Administrative Rules, Administrative Rules website, http://www.rules.utah.gov/index.htm.

[206] Virginia Regulatory Town Hall, http://townhall.virginia.gov.

[207] "This search includes titles of regulations, regulatory actions, meetings, guidance documents, mandates, petitions for rulemaking, and general notices." (Virginia Regulatory Town Hall, Search Tool, http://townhall.virginia.gov/l/search.cfm)

[208] Virginia Regulatory Town Hall, Public Comment Forums web page, http://townhall.virginia.gov/L/Forums.cfm.

[209] Virginia Regulatory Town Hall User Manual, http://townhall.virginia.gov/um/toc.cfm

[210] This is organized by secretariat, board and agency within each secretariat, and VAC Citation. Each record provides the chapter title, date of the last action, and date or stage of periodic review and a link to a page that summarizes current actions, past (most recent) action, and (most recent) withdrawn action. (Virginia Regulatory Town Hall, Browse Regulations web page, http://townhall.virginia.gov/L/ListBoards.cfm.

[211] Actions are sorted into legislative mandates, petitions for regulation, actions underway, and periodic reviews and organized by agency. (Virginia Regulatory Town Hall, Regulatory Activity web page, http://townhall.virginia.gov/L/NowInProgress.cfm)

[212] Information includes the agency, the title of the meeting, and a link to a summary notice of the meeting that includes (among other things) the date, time, and place, a statement of the purpose of the meeting; a link to agency website; and an agenda (if any). (Virginia Regulatory Town Hall, Meetings and Public Hearings web page, http://townhall.virginia.gov/L/meetings.cfm?time=future)

[213] Virginia Regulatory Town Hall, Guidance Documents web page, http://townhall.virginia.gov/L/GDocs.cfm.

[214] Links lead to pages that provide discussions on:

- Frequently asked questions about rulemaking,
- Executive branch review of regulatory actions,
- Types of regulatory actions,
- Public participation in rulemaking,
- Flow charts of regulatory processes, and
- Legal basis for rulemaking.

[215] Links lead to pages that provide discussions on:

- Overview of the Town Hall Website,
- Public Users,
- State Agency Users,
- How to find what you're looking for, and
- Regulatory Forms and Templates.

[216] Links lead to pages that provide discussions on:

- Meetings,
- Guidance Documents,
- Petitions for Rulemaking,
- Legislative Mandates,
- Periodic Reviews,
- General Notices,
- Public Comment Forums, and
- Public Comment Policy.

[217] Links lead to pages that provide guidance on:

- How to write a regulation,
- Before you submit a regulatory action,
- How to start and submit a regulatory action,
- After you have started a regulatory action, and
- Uploading and Replacing Documents.

[218] Links lead to pages that provide guidance on:

- For regulatory coordinators: How to manage the Town Hall users for your agency,
- Agency mailing list,
- Withdrawing an action or a stage. What are the implications, and
- How to indicate that a regulatory action has been suspended.

[219] The standard entries under stage include:

- A statement as to whether the action is exempt from APA,
- DPB Review,
- Secretary Review,
- Governor's Review,

- Virginia Registrar, and
- Comment Period, particularly the closing date.

[220] Standard documents include the:

- Proposed Text,
- Agency Statement,
- Attorney General Certification,
- Economic Impact Analysis (performed by the Virginia Department of Budget and Planning),
- Agency Response to EIA, and
- Governor's Approval Memo.

[221] Code of Alabama, §41-22-5(a)(2).

[222] Florida, New York, and Virginia are examples.

[223] "A substantially affected person... may [timely] submit to an agency a good faith written proposal for a lower cost regulatory alternative to a proposed rule which substantially accomplishes the objectives of the law being implemented.... The agency shall prepare... or... revise its... statement of estimated regulatory costs, and either adopt the alternative or give a statement of the reasons for rejecting the alternative in favor of the proposed rule." (Florida Statutes, §120.541 (1))

[224] Examples include Arizona (Governor's Regulatory Review Council), Michigan (Office of Regulatory Reinvention), New York (Governor's Office of Regulatory Reform), and Pennsylvania (Independent Regulatory Review Committee).

[225] "No rule or regulation shall be adopted, amended, or repealed by any agency except after public hearing." (Nebraska)

[226] In Colorado, for example, a hearing must be held "unless the agency deems it unnecessary."

[227] In some states a smaller number – 10 or 15 persons – is specified. Some states specify "directly affected persons."

[228] Virginia has a distinctive tiered system that includes a double notice: a Notice of Intended Action and (30 days later) a NPRM. The NPRM has a 60-day comment period, giving a total of 90 days for comment. There is a Fast-Track procedure for "rules that are expected to be noncontroversial." With approval of the Governor and notification to the legislature, a Fast-Track rule requires only a NPRM with a 30-day comment period, and the rule may become effective 15 days after the comment period ends. If ten persons or any member of the legislature objects, however, the rule reverts to the normal procedure, with the Fast-Track NPRM in effect serving as the standard Notice of Intended Action. (Code of Virginia, §2.2-4007.03(A) and §2.2-4012.1)

[229] A hearing may be required, for example, if requested by 5 interested persons or by "any affected person" or simply if "a timely request" is made.

[230] Formulations include a "substantive regulation" or a rule that is of "significant" or "sufficient" interest to the public.

[231] Ohio's statutory requirements are a bit more explicit than most. Any person affected by the proposed rule "may appear [at a hearing], may present the person's position, arguments, or contentions, orally or in writing, offer and examine witnesses, and present evidence tending to show that the proposed rule... if adopted or effectuated, will be unreasonable or unlawful." (Ohio Revised Code, §119.03(C))

[232] This includes actions taken in response to comments as well as for other reasons.

[233] This occurs in Minnesota and South Carolina.

[234] In California the extension is 15 days; in Virginia it is 30 days.

[235] In New York, this notice must "contain:

(i) a summary and an analysis of the issues raised and significant alternatives suggested by any such comments;

(ii) a statement of the reasons why any significant alternatives were not incorporated into the rule; and

(iii) a description of any changes made in the rule as a result of such comments." (New York State Administrative Procedures Act, §202(4-a(b)))

[236] The wording is California's; the concept much more widespread.

[237] New York. Other states that require regulatory agendas are Arizona, Florida (by executive order), Illinois, Maine, Washington, Rhode Island, and Pennsylvania (by executive order).

[238] This is New Jersey's version. Texas and Wisconsin use virtually the same language.

[239] These guidelines included:

Before drafting a regulation, agencies, where practical, shall undertake extensive public outreach to those who are likely to be affected by the regulation. Creating advisory committees, using regulatory negotiation, and developing other creative procedures are encouraged as means to solicit the public's input during the regulatory development process.

Those to be affected by the regulation should continue to be consulted during the drafting process. When appropriate, members of the regulated community should be involved with the formulation of language, the development of standards, and any other areas in which the regulated community has an interest and/or can provide insight.

Each agency shall develop its own policies regarding public involvement tailored best to meet the needs of the agency and the regulated community. (Thomas J. Ridge, Executive Order 1996-1, *Regulatory Review and Promulgation*, February 6, 1996)

[240] New York, for example, requires "a statement indicating how the agency complied with subdivision six of this section," which states, "When any rule is proposed for which a regulatory flexibility analysis is required, the agency shall assure that small businesses and local governments have been given an opportunity to participate in the rule making through such activities as:

(a) the publication of a general notice for the proposed rule making in publications likely to be obtained by small businesses and local governments of the types affected by the proposed rule;

(b) the direct notification of interested small businesses and local governments affected by the proposed rule;

(c) the conduct of special open conferences concerning the proposed rule for small businesses and local governments affected by the rule; and

(d) the adoption or modification of agency procedural rules to reduce the cost or complexity of participation in the rule making by small businesses and local governments.

(New York State Administrative Procedures Act, §202-B)

[241] Florida, Nebraska, New York, and Washington.

[242] Florida encourages agencies to consider the process

- "when complex rules are being drafted or strong opposition to the rules is anticipated,
- [if] a balanced committee of interested persons who will negotiate in good faith can be assembled;
- [if] the agency is willing to support the work of the negotiating committee, and
- [if] the agency can use the group consensus as the basis for its proposed rule." (Florida Statutes, §120.54 (2)(d))

[243] Statutory criteria for appropriateness include the following:

(a) There is a need for a rule;

(b) There are a limited number of identifiable interests that will be significantly affected by the rule;

(c) There is a reasonable likelihood that a committee can be convened with a balanced representation of persons who:

(i) Can adequately represent the interests identified; and

(ii) Are willing to negotiate in good faith to reach a consensus on the proposed rule;

(d) There is a reasonable likelihood that a committee will reach a consensus on the proposed rule within a fixed period of time;

(e) The negotiated rulemaking procedure will not unreasonably delay the notice of proposed formal rulemaking and the issuance of the final rule pursuant to the Administrative Procedure Act;

(f) The agency has adequate resources and is willing to commit those resources, including technical assistance, to the committee; and

(g) The agency, to the maximum extent possible consistent with the legal obligations of the agency, will use the consensus of the committee as the basis for the rule proposed by the agency in the formal rulemaking process of the Administrative Procedure Act. (Nebraska Revised Statutes, §84-922)

[244] Among other information, this notice includes:

- A description of the subject and scope of the rule to be developed and the issues to be considered,
- A list of interests likely to be significantly affected by the proposed rule,
- A list of the persons proposed to represent the affected interests and the agency, and
- An explanation of how a person may apply for or nominate another person for membership on the committee. (Nebraska Revised Statutes, §84-926)

[245] Alaska, Arizona, Arkansas, Connecticut, Hawaii, Illinois, Indiana, Missouri, Rhode Island, Tennessee, Vermont, Virginia, West Virginia (executive order), and Wisconsin.

[246] Louisiana, Maine, New Mexico, Oklahoma, and Texas.

[247] "This section shall not apply to any proposed rule which the agency finds would not impose reporting, record-keeping, or other compliance requirements on small businesses." (New Jersey) New York's wording is quite similar – one of a number of instances where one state's statute appears to have copied from the other's.

[248] Examples include:

- "Direct impact on small business" (South Dakota)
- "If the agency reasonably expects [after consideration and comment] that a proposed rule will have a measurable negative fiscal impact on small businesses" (Utah)
- "may have a negative impact on economic competitiveness or on small business" (Colorado)
- Massachusetts requires an analysis for regulations that require a hearing (i.e., violations could result in a fine).

[249] Examples include:

- "In the case of a rule that would have a substantial impact on small business," (Iowa)
- "If the agency reasonably expects [after consideration and comment] that a proposed rule will have a measurable negative fiscal impact on small businesses" (Utah)
- "Whenever the results of such consideration by an agency indicate that it is lawful, desirable and feasible to exempt... or to set lesser standards of compliance by... small businesses, the agency shall issue a rule or regulation containing an appropriate exemption... or setting lesser standards." (Delaware)
- "Before a[n agency] adopts a proposed regulation, the [agency] shall evaluate whether the proposed regulation has any impact on businesses... On the basis of the evaluation, the unit may adopt 1 or more regulations that apply differently to classes of businesses." (Maryland)
- "An agency shall determine whether the proposed regulation is likely to:
  (a) Impose a direct and significant economic burden upon a small business; or
  (b) Directly restrict the formation, operation or expansion of a small business." (Nevada)

[250] Examples include:

- "Any state agency filing a notice of proposed rulemaking [which] would require an expenditure of money by or a reduction in income for any... business entity of any kind or character which is estimated to cost more than five hundred dollars in the aggregate" (Missouri)
- $50,000 in cost to the regulated community triggers an economic impact statement - but not a regulatory flexibility analysis. (North Dakota)
- $100,000 defines a "significant impact." (Mississippi – which has no regulatory flexibility requirements)
- $500,000 is the threshold for legislative review. (Indiana)

[251] These include:

- $25,000 per entity, with the determination subject to review by an administrative law judge, is a threshold over which a small entity can get an exemption. (Minnesota)
- If the proposed rule will impose more than minor costs on businesses in an industry, where "'minor cost' means a cost per business that is less than three-tenths of one percent of annual revenue or income, or one hundred dollars, whichever is greater, or one percent of annual payroll." (Washington)
- If during the public comment period an agency receives comment that the proposed rule will cost small business more than one day's annual average gross receipts, and the agency had not previously performed the [regulatory flexibility] analysis [of alternatives], the agency shall perform the analysis. (Utah)

[252] In Arizona, for example:

- For one agency, "annual cost/revenue changes are designated as minimal when less than $5,000, moderate when between $5,000 and $10,000, and substantial when greater than $10,000."
- One agency described a $25 increase to a $975 license fee to raise more funds for the agency as "minimal."

[253] These include the following:

- "When an agency proposes to adopt a rule that will apply to a small business and the rule will have a disproportionate impact on small businesses because of the size of those businesses..." (Michigan)
- "Each agency, before the adoption, amendment, or repeal of a rule, shall consider the impact of the rule on small businesses... Whenever practicable, an agency shall tier its rules to reduce disproportionate impacts on small businesses... to avoid regulating small businesses... that do not contribute significantly to the problem the rule is designed to address." (Florida)
- An agency is required, "whenever possible, [to] tier their administrative regulations to reduce disproportionate impacts on... small business... and to avoid regulating entities that do not contribute significantly to the problem the administrative regulation was designed to address. (Kentucky)

[254] "A 'significant legislative rule' is a rule other than a procedural or interpretive rule that

(A) adopts substantive provisions of law pursuant to delegated legislative authority, the violation of which subjects a violator of such rule to a penalty or sanction;

(B) establishes, alters, or revokes any qualification or standard for the issuance, suspension, or revocation of a license or permit; or

(C) adopts a new, or makes significant amendments to, a policy or regulatory program." (Revised Code of Washington, §34.05.328(5)(c)(iii))

[255] Some assessment of alternatives is part of the economic impact statement, but the only real requirements related to small business are determinations of whether they are affected and whether this threshold is exceeded.

[256] California Code, §11346.5(a)(7).

[257] Among other examples:

- In Colorado, no analyses are required with the NPRM, but
  - An agency must issue a regulatory analysis or a proposed rule "upon request of any person, at least fifteen days prior to the hearing," (Colorado Revised Statutes, §24-4-103(4.5)(a))
  - DORA, after reviewing the proposed rule, "may order the agency to perform a cost-benefit analysis." A cost-benefit analysis must be requested at least 20 days before a hearing and completed at least five days before the hearing. (Colorado Revised Statutes, §24-4-103(2.5))
- In Iowa, an agency must publish a regulatory analysis of a proposed rule "if the rule would have a substantial impact on small business and if, within thirty-two days after the published notice of proposed rule adoption, a written request for analysis is submitted to the agency by the administrative rules review committee, the administrative rules coordinator, at least twenty-five persons signing that request who each qualify as a small business or by an organization representing at least twenty-five such persons." (Iowa Code, §17A.4(1)-(3))
- In North Dakota, the governor or a member of the legislature may file a "timely" written request for a regulatory analysis after the NPRM has been published. (North Dakota Century Code, §28-32-08)
- In Utah, an agency must consider methods of reducing small business impact in the NPRM if it "reasonably expects that a proposed rule will have a measurable negative fiscal impact on small businesses." Subsequently, a more specific criterion comes into play: "If during the public comment period an agency receives comment that the proposed rule will cost small business more than one day's annual average gross receipts, and the agency had not previously performed the analysis." (Utah Code, §63G-3-301)

[258] Department of Regulatory Agencies, *Cutting Red Tape in Colorado State Government*, Omnibus Report to the Governor on the "Pits and Peeves" Roundtable Initiative, December 2011, pp. 18-19.

[259] Nothing was available in 21 states and small business impact statements were not available in 11.

[260] The following are among the explanations often found:

- The rule affects only the promulgating agency or other public entity.
- The only impacts of the rule are fiscal impacts at the state level.
- The rule affects only large businesses.
- The rule affects only individuals.
- The rule repeals an existing rule.
- The rule replaces or extends an expired rule without making substantive changes.
- The rule only makes a clarification, correction, or formatting change.
- The rule makes only minor change with no cost and possibly a benefit.
- The action required is no more costly that what businesses are currently doing.
- The rule benefits small businesses by reducing burden or enhancing revenue.

[261] Examples include the following:

- In Iowa, 58 out of 59 impact statements that addressed the impact on jobs made exactly the same statement: "After analysis and review of the rulemaking, no adverse impact on jobs has been found."
- In Florida, 90 of 92 NPRMs stated that a Statement of Estimated Regulatory Cost was not needed and had not been done. The explanation usually was boilerplate. One of the two most common formats: During discussion of the economic impact of this rule the Department, based upon the expertise and experience of its members, determined that a Statement of Estimated Regulatory Cost (SERC) was not necessary and that these rule amendments will not require ratification by the Legislature. No person or interested party submitted additional information regarding the economic impact at that time. The rule will not have an adverse impact on small business, or likely increase regulatory costs in excess of $200,000 in the aggregate within 1 year after implementation of the rule.
- Of 101 Maryland NPRMs reviewed:
  - 86 analyses stated both that the proposed action had "no economic impact," and

- 12 analyses included an estimate of economic impacts, but

All of these analyses stated that there was "minimal or no economic impact on small businesses."

[262] Examples include the following:

- California agencies have to address two simple questions concerning small business and several questions about other impacts. Forty impact statements were reviewed. Responses were sketchy:
- As to whether there would be a significant statewide impact,
  - 29 analyses stated that there would not be, and
  - 11 analyses did not address the issue.
- As to whether there would be impacts on small business,
  - 23 analyses stated that small businesses would not be affected, although six of these did not provide a statutorily required explanation,
  - Three analyses stated that small businesses "will be" affected,
  - Eight analyses stated that small businesses "may be" affected, and
  - Six analyses did not address the issue.
- As to whether there would be any of the specific types of impacts,
  - 29 analyses stated that none of these impacts would occur,
  - Two analyses projected employment impacts, and
  - 11 analyses did not address the issue.
- In 31 of 50 Tennessee rules reviewed, there was no Regulatory Flexibility Statement. These included:
  - Nine rules for which the Regulatory Flexibility Addendum part of the form was omitted;
  - Three rules for which the Regulatory Flexibility Addendum was entirely blank;
  - Seven rules for which the Regulatory Flexibility Addendum was filled out N/A;
  - Three rules where an explanation was given instead of an analysis; and
  - Nine rules where it was stated that there would be no impact on small businesses.

[263] Arizona is an interesting special case. The Governor requires her office's approval of any regulation (with a few types exempted), and it is unlikely that any regulation with more than minimal costs would be approved.

[264] Examples include the following:

- One proffered explanation for there being no costs to a regulation was that it was merely implementing a federal or state statute. Thus the *regulation* did not impose costs. There is some logic to this view with respect to a federal statute or regulation. The state cannot do anything about those costs of compliance, and an impact analysis is largely pointless (and some states provided an exemption). Indeed, a very common issue in reviewing such a regulation is whether it exceeds the minimum federal requirements. If state law is imposing costs, however, they ought to be estimated and reported to the legislature, not zeroed out.
- In a number of rulemakings, a permanent rule replaced an emergency rule. In one sense there was no impact, because the rule was its own baseline, but (because it was "temporary") the emergency rule's impacts had not been analyzed.
- One rule dismissed impacts on commercial fishermen by saying that these costs would be offset by benefits to businesses that supplied the fishermen with required gear.

[265] A regulation on municipal recycling, for example, stated:

Where there is an increased participation in recycling programs or services, this regulation may lead to financial impacts on certain small businesses, such as recycling haulers or property management businesses that choose to provide recycling services.

[266] A fish and wildlife regulation for commercial fishermen, for example, listed "compliance with the handling, labeling, and tracking requirements" and then stated only that the required permit would have no cost.

[267] States differ in their opinions as to whether licensed professions are businesses or individuals. On one hand, licensees are individuals; on the other, they may be self-employed or their employers may be the ones actually paying the fees.

[268] Examples include the following:

- In one state, three Human Services regulations reported impacts over $50,000, but the regulatory analyses failed to clarify on whom the impacts fell, and the impacts on small businesses either were unclear.
- One analysis estimated that a utility filing fee was $25,000 to $50,000 but provided no further discussion.

[269] A Louisiana regulation imposed a $1,000 fee, plus $100 annually on out-of-state pharmacists performing cognitive services for Louisiana residents, for example, was considered not to have any impacts on small businesses.

[270] Examples include the following:

- Two TennCare rules (one for standard care, one for Medicaid) reportedly saved the government $1,721,500, but the regulatory impact analysis stated that the rule would have no effect on small business.
- A Louisiana regulation reduced the reimbursement for nursing facilities by an annual amount estimated to be $200,951,212. The impact on nursing homes was not considered, as there was no Small Business Impact Statement. The Family Impact Statement, on the other hand, stated:
  It is anticipated that this proposed Rule may have an adverse impact on family functioning, stability and autonomy as described in R.S. 49:972 in the event that provider participation in the Medicaid Program is diminished as a result of reduced reimbursement rates.

[271] For example:

- A Tennessee rule, which imposed substantial costs by increasing formal educational requirements for a licensed counselor, had no Regulatory Flexibility Statement.
- A Louisiana rule amendment that will "have some indeterminate impact on continuing education providers, as the demand for course credit will diminish by roughly half" had no Small Business Impact Statement.

[272] Michigan, Missouri, New Jersey, New York, and Oregon were among the best performing states in this respect.

[273] One New Jersey rule, for example, allowed commercial advertising on school busses. The analysis explained that this did not entail regulatory burdens:
The proposed rules impose some reporting, recordkeeping and compliance requirements. However, their impact is minimal. The recordkeeping required by these rules fall within the scope of what is necessary to conduct advertising, and are not materially changed by these proposed rules.

[274] One of the better examples was a Nevada environmental regulation that required training for operators of underground waste storage tanks. Estimated training costs were $75 to $150 per operator. The rule incorporated several measures to minimize impacts by providing maximum flexibility, including:

- Allowing multiple options for training,
- Allowing operators with training to oversee multiple systems,
- Allowing "appropriate persons" to serve as two classes of operator, and
- Not requiring renewals except for compliance retraining.

[275] These measures included:

- Modification of net marking requirements for commercial fishermen;
- An exemption for very small operations;
- Conditional licenses that give operators time to come into compliance,
- Provision of cost-sharing technical support,
- Issuance of "broad incidental take permit/authorization" to avoid high costs of avoiding very minor, unintentional violations; and
- Provision of technical assistance by University of Wisconsin personnel.

[276] Examples from Indiana included:

- The Board of Animal health "considered adopting very detailed and specific standards of [animal] care [but instead required] core principles of care [that] focused on the outcome of the care provided."
- The Department of Health used design standards (i.e., specification of screening practices), but also used performance standards, allowed flexibility for coming into compliance, and used grant funds to purchase equipment as free "loaner equipment" for facilities having difficulty obtaining their own new equipment.
- The Natural Resources Commission "uses performance standards to meet biological needs to manage pests and pathogens," "recognizes and adopts the USDA/APHIS compliance agreement to meet state needs for the small business," and "develops its own agreements "with the intent to fit the requirements to each business operation to have minimal... impacts [and be] as flexible as biologically possible."

Examples from Texas included:

- In a rule required that operators of "certain programs for minors" train employees on sexual abuse and child molestation, the agency approved three options:
  - Choose a free already-approved training program for staff (at a cost of one hour of each employee's time),
  - Choose an already-approved training program for staff that charges a fee, or
  - Develop and get approval of a new training program for staff, at an approval fee of $125.

- A rule amending regulations "concerning Importation of Waste from a Non-Compact Generator for Disposal" had "undetermined" costs, because the costs would depend on fees for disposal that had not yet been set. "In an attempt to address cost issues for small generators, the proposed rule allows for waste brokers to assemble wastes from generators. While there will be fees paid for the services of brokers, the fees will be less than if each individual generator were required to make an application for disposal. The Compact Commission is also proposing to suspend its current requirement that there be an application fee."

[277] This list included:

- Alternatives are prohibited by specific requirements in the statute.
- Rule requirements are necessary to achieve the objectives of the rule.
- No available alternatives are less burdensome than the proposed rule.

In Kentucky, which has a distinctive tiering alternative (and apparently fairly diligent oversight), tiering was addressed (but not adopted) in all but one notice reviewed. Explanations included:

- Tiering is not appropriate because the regulation inherently applies equally to all individuals or entities,
- "Tiering was not used because this regulation should not disproportionately affect any particular group of people, and
- Tiering is basically a violation of equal protection under the law (a concern about discrimination).

[278] In one rulemaking, for example, an agency attempted to estimate the number of business vehicles that would be affected by a ten-cent increase in a bridge toll.

[279] California seems an apt example. Although its guidance focused on how to say that there are not small business impacts, significant statewide adverse economic impacts, or useful alternatives, when it came to the determination that might trigger a regulatory flexibility analysis, 11 of 40 analyses simply left it blank.

[280] Although it has been cited above, one agency response bears repeating:

The purpose of this small entity requirement is to fulfill the requirements of N. D. C. C. §28-32-08.1(2)

[281] *Approval* needs some clarification. It will be used to refer to completion of changes made by the agency in response to input during the comment period, which may be prior to or coincident with filing for publication.

[282] Depending on the state, this review may occur before the final rule is filed for publication or possibly after publication and before the effective date. In some states the review procedures merge with review of existing, effective rules.

[283] These include Alaska, Connecticut, Georgia, Illinois, and Indiana.

[284] Among other activities, the Director:

- "May elicit views and information from, and shall serve as the point of contact for, small business organizations and associations, state and federal agencies, and other parties who have comments, objections, or opinions concerning the proposed rule;"
- "If appropriate... shall convey these communications to the agency;" and
- "Shall provide detailed information in writing to the agency regarding
  - whether... the agency has satisfactorily completed the economic impact statement and
  - whether the agency has taken sufficient measures to balance the objectives of the proposed rule with the interests of the affected small businesses." (Arkansas Code, §25-15-303(d))

[285] This legislation apparently has not been implemented.

[286] As noted above, the time frame for this analysis is extremely short.

[287] Headings for the report include:

- Project compliance required,
- Types and Number of Small Businesses Affected,
- Estimate of economic impact, and
- Possible Alternatives to the Rule.

[288] Michigan Compiled Laws, §24-234.

[289] These reflect much of the language in SBA's model legislation but do not explicitly mention small business.

[290] To this end, ORR has developed a set of FIRST Principles:

- Fair - The regulatory system balances the cost and benefits to all affected parties with quantitative and qualitative measures.
- Innovative - The regulatory process considers the latest technology, economic incentives and market practices in deciding how to regulate.
- Responsive - Regulators engage stakeholders as they would customers.
- Simple - Regulations are written in plain language and easy to understand.

- Transparent - The regulatory process is time bound, rational and consistent ensuring that stakeholders can engage the process at any time.

(Rhode Island Economic Develop Commission, Making It Easier to do Business in Rhode Island: Office of Regulatory Reform's Annual Report to Governor Lincoln D. Chafee and The Rhode Island General Assembly, August 2011, p. 8.)

291 "ORA's core mission [is] to help agencies improve service delivery and "make life a little easier" for those who do business in Washington.." (Governor's Office of Regulatory Assistance, First Annual Report, 2006: *Improving and simplifying Washington's regulatory systems; Assisting those who do business in our state,* December 15, 2006.

292 Texas, where the Attorney General plays a much broader role, is an exception.

293 For example: "The Secretary of State shall... reject those notices which are not in substantial compliance with the provisions of this section, give prompt notice of such rejection to the agency, and advise such agency on the corrective action required." (New York State Administrative Procedures Act, §202(9(a))

294 For example:

- In Wisconsin the governor must approve the scope of a regulation before it is developed.
- In Nebraska, the Governor may – after review – waive the requirement for a public hearing.

295 In Iowa the Governor may rescind a new rule by executive order within 70 days of its effective date.

296 Kentucky and Maryland.

297 The Council has six members appointed by the Governor, who include a small business representative, a public interest representative, at least one attorney, and two non-legislators from lists nominated by the legislature. The director (or assistant director) of the department of administration serves as chair. The Council has a staff of four. (Arizona Revised Statutes, Article 5)

298 Arkansas Code, §25-15-303 and §25-15-304.

299 The Council is made up of nine current or small business owners appointed (three each) by the Governor, the President of the Senate, and the Speaker of the House. The Council is housed within the Florida Small Business Development Center Network. (Florida Statutes, §120.7001)

300 The Board has 11 members, appointed by the Governor, who represent different types of business (no more than two from any one type). It is sited within the Department of Business, Economic Development, and Tourism. (Hawaii Revised Statutes, §201M-5)

301 The Commission has 30 members, most of whom are appointed by the Governor from lists of nominees, including 17 business association representatives, the four classes of city, non-profit development organizations (2), and four cabinet departments. The Commission is attached to the Department for Existing Business Development. (Kentucky Revised Statutes, §11.200(2))

302 The Board has nine members, including the chair of the minority business advocacy commission (which had been established for years before the SBRFB was created), four members appointed by the Governor, and four members appointed by legislative leaders. The Department of Economic Development provides staff support for the Board. (Missouri Revised Statutes, §536.305 and §536.310)

303 Of the nine members, five were appointed by the governor, and four by legislative leaders. The Board was administratively attached to the Economic Development Department. (New Mexico Statutes Annotated, §14-4A-5)

304 George E. Pataki, Executive Order 20, Establishing the Position of State Director of Regulatory Reform, November 30, 1995.

305 Andrew Cuomo, Executive Order No. 2, Review, Continuation and Expiration of Prior Executive Orders, January 1, 2011

306 The Committee has 11 members. Five are appointed by the Governor, two by the Lieutenant Governor, and three by each house of the legislature. All are current or former small business owners or officers. The Committee is supported by the Department of Commerce. (Oklahoma Statutes, §75-503)

307 The Commission five members. Four are appointed (one each) by the President pro tem of the Senate, the Speaker of the House of Representative, and the Minority Leaders of each house, and one by the Governor. (Pennsylvania P.L. 633, No. 181, §5.1)

308 The agency's options are similar to those following legislative review. It may modify the rule and report to the Commission, withdraw the rule, or wait for the legislative committees' review and response to the Commission's disapproval (adopting the rule if there is no further adverse action). (Pennsylvania P.L. 633, No. 181, §6)

309 The Committee has 11 voting members. Five members (and the chairman) are appointed by the Governor, and three (each) by the President Pro Tempore of the Senate and the Speaker of the House of Representatives. The

Chairmen of the Senate and House Commerce and Industry and Labor Committees are nonvoting, ex officio members of the committee. The Committee is housed within the Department of Commerce. South Carolina Code of Laws, §1-23-280(A))

[310] A press release at the time the Act was signed described the vision for the Committee as follows:

- The Small Business Regulatory Review Committee can:
  - Determine if a state agency regulation has a significant adverse impact on small businesses
  - Request the promulgating agency to prepare an economic impact statement and a regulatory flexibility analysis to assess its potential impact.
  - Request the Budget and Control Board's Office of Research and Statistics to issue a final assessment report.
- The Committee is focused on two main objectives:
  - The ability of small businesses to communicate their concerns about the adverse impact of agency regulations to the Committee, and
  - The ability of state agencies to address the concerns of small businesses as they relate to existing and future regulations.
- To accomplish these two objectives means the Committee must:
  - Get inputs from small businesses on what existing agency regulations need to be reviewed.
  - Create and perpetuate a good working relationship with state agencies in an effort to change regulations that create an adverse impact on small businesses by supporting their efforts with a set of guidelines.

[311] The Board originally had 17 members: representatives of nine cabinet departments, six Governor-appointed small business representatives, and the chairs of one senate and one assembly committee concerned with small businesses. (Wisconsin Statutes, §227.14(2g)) Recent legislation changed the composition of the Board, adding a seventh small business representative and eliminating all of the departmental representatives. (2011 Wisconsin Act 46) The Board is housed min the Department of Commerce.

[312] In South Carolina, minutes from September 2011 meeting reflected a discussion "that South Carolina small businesses do not know the charge for the SBRRC and there needs to be a better way to let businesses know the Committee's purpose."

[313] Rule reports have a standard structure:

- Summary of new/amended rules,
- Potential impact on small businesses, and
- Recommended action to be taken on the proposed rule.

[314] Minutes show two or three DBEBT staff members present; one has been with the SBRRB since at least 2003.

[315] The SBRFB has statutory authority to:

- Provide state agencies with input regarding rules that adversely affect small businesses,
- Solicit input and conduct hearings from small business owners and state agencies regarding any rules proposed by a state agency, and submit an evaluation report to the governor and the general assembly regarding small business comments, agency response, and public testimony on rules,
- Provide an evaluation report to the governor and the general assembly, including any recommendations and evaluations of state agencies regarding regulatory fairness for Missouri's small businesses,
- Conduct inquiries based on the request of a small business owner and make recommendations, based on periodic-review and small-business-impact criteria.
- Provide agencies with lists of any rules adopted by the agency that affect small business and have generated complaints or concerns – to which the agencies must at least respond in writing.

(Missouri Revised Statutes, §536.310)

[316] Depending on its specific activities, it may have any of several other names.

[317] This is really distinct from disapproval only if the parts approved are practicably separable and if there are no possible ways of amending the disapproved parts.

[318] "The reference shall be removed from a rule published in the Washington Administrative Code if a subsequent adjudicatory proceeding determines that the rule is within the intent of the legislature or was adopted in accordance with all applicable laws, whichever was the objection of the rules review committee." (Revised Code of Washington, §34.05.640)

[319] In Tennessee, if an agency does not comply with a committee's "request," the committee "may vote to request the general assembly to suspend any or all of such agency's rulemaking authority for any reasonable period of time or with respect to any particular subject matter." (Tennessee Code Annotated, §4-5-226)

[320] "If the Commission or Subcommittee objects to the regulation after determining that...
(a) The regulation is not required pursuant to a federal statute or regulation [as was claimed];
(b) The regulation does not conform to statutory authority; or
(c) The regulation does not carry out legislative intent,
the Legislative Counsel shall attach to the regulation a written notice of the objection, including, if practicable, a statement of the reasons for the objection, and shall promptly return the regulation to the agency." (Nevada Revised Statutes, §233B.067)

[321] The most notable case is Pennsylvania's IRRC, which functions almost as an agent of the legislature.

[322] Suspension can be until the end of the next legislative session. In Virginia rules can be suspended by joint actin of the Governor and the legislature to give the legislature time to act and/or the agency more time to make changes.

[323] "Interim" refers to the period between sessions of the legislature. This mechanism is used mostly in sparsely populated states with extremely short legislative sessions, particularly the northern plains states. In such states, as one legislator put it, during the session legislators may be too busy with other matters to review rules.

[324] "When appropriate, the committee shall prepare and arrange for the introduction of a bill to clarify the intent of the general assembly when the general assembly enacted a law or to correct the misapplication of a law by an agency." (Indiana Code, §2-5-18-8)

[325] Different formulations of this question may specify state law, federal law, and/or federal regulations. While compliance with federal law and regulations is a universal concern, a subsidiary issue often is whether the rule contains more than the minimal requirements for compliance. If so, a justification often is required.

[326] This issue can include technical aspects, such as form, style, and drafting requirements, as well as adhering to the actions and time-frames required by the APA.

[327] New York Statutes. Legislative, §87(1) and Utah Code §63G-3-501(2).

[328] Illinois Compiled Statutes, §100/5-110.

[329] Senate Bill 2 of the 129th General Assembly.

[330] Illinois Compiled Statutes, *loc. cit.*

[331] Vermont Statutes Annotated, §842.

[332] The review produced the following examples of JCAR objections and disapprovals – filed or otherwise:

- In Alabama, notices of two Joint Committee disapprovals were published over a 14-month period.
    - One concerned repeal of an environmental rule upon certification that the federal rule had expired.
    - One concerned sections of a Medicaid Agency rule related to eye care, eyeglasses, and billing.
- In 2011, the Florida Joint Administrative Procedures Committee filed objections to six rules, based on:
    - Modification or violation of statutory provisions (three rules, two of which involved agency procedures),
    - Invalid exercise of delegated legislative authority (two rules), and
    - Issues of arbitrariness and clarity (a rule related to administration of medications by nurses).
- The Illinois JCAR, at its December 2011 meeting, made eight objections, on the following grounds:
    - The rule exceeded statutory authority in ways that threatened the public interest (5 rules).
    - A gross delay in adopting a rule had caused policy set out in the rule to be adopted prior to authorization.
    - The rule adversely affected individuals (Medicaid recipients).
    - The rule raise clear regulatory flexibility issues (see below).
- The Iowa Administrative Rules Committee, in the latter half of 2011:
    - Ordered stays on rules involving municipal annexation, transfer of patient records, and hunting season, and
    - Objected (9 to 0) to a rule designed by the agency to reduce booking burdens for businesses, on the grounds that the rule understated benefits of job creation by state programs.
- A Kentucky Regulation Review Subcommittee meeting agenda included 20 rulemakings (35 individual sections of Administrative Code. The Committee deferred six rulemakings (10 sections) and acted on 14 (25). The ARRs voted on amendments to 22 sections whose purposes included:
    - "Conform with the drafting and formatting requirements of KRS Chapter 13A" (17 sections),
    - "Conforming amendments to correct inconsistencies between the currently effective administrative regulation and the filed proposed administrative regulation" (8 sections),
    - Change statutory citations (2 corrections, 1 insertion, and 1 deletion),
    - "Clearly state the necessity for and function served by this administrative regulation" (3sections),

- Correct form titles (2 sections),
- Correct minor drafting errors (2 sections) and
- Other technical corrections, including terminology, definitions, and typographical errors (5 sections).

- Over a 15 month period, one Louisiana oversight subcommittee filed one disapproval concerning a provision on ethics training that was considered neither in conformity with legislative intent nor advisable.
- Over one session of the Maine legislature, 15 "resolves" summaries of committee reviews of substantive legislation) were reduced. Ten recommended adoption; five recommended adoption with technical amendments. The amendments concerned definitions, inclusion of an exception related to contract payments, and meetings.
- The New Hampshire Joint Legislative Committee on Administrative Rules filed five final objections to rules over four years. The Committee objected that these rules:
  - Violated the legislative intent (all 5 rules),
  - Exceeded the agency's authority (3 rules),
  - Were contrary to the public interest by using language that was overly broad or not "clear and understandable" (3 rules), and/or
  - Was contrary to the public interest because the agency had not made changes in response to public comments.
- In four meetings over the 2011-2012 interim, the North Dakota Administrative Rules Committee voided three parts of one rule – a rescission – because the rescinded provisions were not entirely obsolete.
- In nine Ohio Joint Committee on Agency Rule Review meetings over six months, the JACC considered seven rules serious enough to invite testimony. Of these:
  - Two involved relatively minor clarifications,
  - Two involved agency actions that primarily affected individuals,
  - Two involved other actions of agency officials, and
  - One (discussed further below) had arguably serious impacts on small businesses.
- Oklahoma statute allows 30 days for legislative review, after which a rule is approved by default. Over a one-year period, in all final notices of rules the entry for "legislative approval" was: "Failure of the Legislature to disapprove the rules resulted in approval on [date]."
- In a recent meeting of the South Dakota Rules Review Committee, eight rulemakings by five agencies were considered. None involved impacts on business. (Two involved DOT signage.) All were approved 5-0 or 4-1.
- The Utah Administrative Rules Review Committee meetings in 2011 included consideration of a number of regulatory details, such as whether paper filings were still allowed or the lengthy of data storage for license plate scanning. Several discussions had an ombudsman flavor, as they were triggered by one individual. Only one health rule could be considered as having an economic impact (see below) and it was exceptional.
- The Wisconsin Legislative Council review focuses on technical issues. Of the first 46 rules reviewed in 2011:
  - 39 had comments about clarity, grammar, punctuation and use of plain language;
  - 39 had comments about form, style, and placement in the Administrative Code;
  - 23 had comments about the adequacy of references to related statutes, rules, and forms;
  - Eight had comments about statutory authority; and
  - One had a comment about conflicts with and comparability to a related federal regulation.

  Notices of Final Rules include a Summary of Comments by legislative review committees. In 57 of 59 summaries, "No comments were reported." In the other, the committee held a hearing but took no further adverse action.

[333] A North Dakota regulation concerned hydraulic fracture stimulation. An industry representative was generally supportive of the regulation but wanted the substantial compliance cost ($300,000 per well) on the public record.

[334] Of these three rules:

- One concerned fees set by the State Board of Medical Examiners,
- One concerned per diem Medicaid reimbursement rates for a residential facility under quite specific circumstances, which the agency estimated would affect about 10 patients at any given time, and

- One Indoor Clean Air Act prohibited hookahs (which heat, but do not ignite tobacco), to which a bar and grill owner was objecting (and also seeking injunctive relief).

[335] A requirement by the Ohio Livestock Care Standards Board to keep calves in larger pens with other calves – rather than 24-inch-wide stalls – after the age of 10 weeks was hotly contested by the veal industry, which predicted devastating economic impacts, particularly on Amish (i.e., small) farmers. Violation of three prongs (statutory authority, legislative intent, and incorrect data in the rule summary) were asserted. Industry and Board testimony disagreed about mortality and medication costs. Board testimony cited significant productivity gains from higher feed conversion in large pens. Significant capital costs of reconfiguration were acknowledged. Research and guidelines of the American Veterinary Medical Association and the Ohio Veterinary Medical Association were cited in support of the rule. The Ohio Farm Bureau testified to its belief that "the proposed rule is consistent with the scope of OLCSB's rulemaking authority and the legislative intent" and that "the OLCSB made appropriate decisions." In the end, a JCARR member suggested identifying a funding source to help small farms comply, and the Farm Bureau responded that discussions were already underway with USDA to identify an appropriate program.

[336] Illinois also is very unusual in that the Office of Regulatory Flexibility reports to the JCARR.

[337] These are:

(1) The continued need for the rule;

(2) The nature of complaints or comments received concerning the rule from the public;

(3) The complexity of the rule;

(4) The extent to which the rule overlaps, duplicates, or conflicts with other Federal, State, and local governmental rules; and

(5) The length of time since the rule has been evaluated or the degree to which technology, economic conditions, or other factors have changed in the area affected by the rule.

[338] Indiana, Massachusetts, New Mexico, Rhode Island, South Carolina, and Virginia.

[339] Arizona, Maryland, Mississippi, New York, Nevada, Ohio, Oregon, Texas.

[340] Mississippi.

[341] Examples include:

- Ohio requires determination of:
    - "Whether the rule should be continued without amendment, be amended, or be rescinded, taking into consideration the purpose, scope, and intent of the statute under which the rule was adopted,
    - Whether the rule needs amendment or rescission to give more flexibility at the local level,
    - Whether the rule needs amendment or rescission to eliminate unnecessary paperwork... [and
    - Whether the rule duplicates, overlaps with, or conflicts with other rules," as well as "Consider of the continued need for the rule, the nature of any complaints or comments received." (Ohio Revised Code, §119.032)
- Oregon law requires determining:
    - Whether the rule has had the intended effect,
    - Whether the anticipated fiscal impact of the rule was underestimated or overestimated,
    - Whether subsequent changes in the law require that the rule be repealed or amended; and
    - Whether there is continued need for the rule. (Oregon Revised Statutes, §183.405(1))
- In Florida, rules are reviewed "in order to:

(a) Identify and correct deficiencies in its rules;

(b) Clarify and simplify its rules;

(c) Delete obsolete or unnecessary rules;

(d) Delete rules that are redundant of statutes;

(e) Seek to improve efficiency, reduce paperwork, or decrease costs to government and the private sector;

(f) Contact agencies that have concurrent or overlapping jurisdiction to determine whether their rules can be coordinated to promote efficiency, reduce paperwork, or decrease costs to government and the private sector; and

(g) Determine whether the rules should be continued without change or should be amended or repealed to reduce the impact on small business while meeting the stated objectives of the proposed rule." (Florida Statutes, §120.74(1))

- Texas requires "an assessment of whether the reasons for initially adopting the rule continue to exist." (Texas Statutes, §2006.039)

[342] Georgia, Minnesota, Missouri, and Pennsylvania.

[343] California, Ohio, Oklahoma, and North Dakota. In California the Office of Administrative Law conducts the review.

[344] Illinois, Iowa, Vermont, and Wisconsin

[345] Review of Impact Statement. Within two years after a rule is finalized, an [affected] person... may... petition... an agency objecting to all or part of a rule on any of the following grounds:

1. The actual economic, small business or consumer impact significantly exceeded the impact estimated in the economic, small business and consumer impact statement submitted during the making of the rule.

2. The actual economic, small business or consumer impact was not estimated in the economic, small business and consumer impact statement submitted during the making of the rule and that actual impact imposes a significant burden on persons subject to the rule.

3. The agency did not select the alternative that imposes the least burden and costs to persons regulated by the rule, including paperwork and other compliance costs, necessary to achieve the underlying regulatory objective."

A person affected by the agency's decision may appeal to the Governor's Regulatory Review Council. (Arizona Revised Statutes, §41-1056.01)

[346] In Missouri, "any affected small business" also may file a petition concerning "any rule affecting small business on any of the following grounds:

- The rule creates an undue barrier to the formation, operation, and expansion of small businesses in a manner that significantly outweighs the rule's benefit to the public;
- The rule duplicates, overlaps, or conflicts with rules adopted by the agency or any other agency or violates the substantive authority under which the rule was adopted; or
- The technology, economic conditions, or other relevant factors justifying the purpose for the rule has changed or no longer exist." (Missouri Revised Statutes, §536.323(1))

[347] (Missouri Revised Statutes, §536.025(2)).

[348] A classic illustration of a regulation that defied common sense was a New Jersey rule that stated:

Any school bus that has been declared and marked "out-of-service" shall not be operated until all "out-of-service" repairs have been satisfactorily completed. The term "operate" as used in this section shall include towing the vehicle; provided, however, that vehicles marked "out-of-service" may be towed by means of a vehicle using a crane or hoist. (New Jersey Administrative Code, §13:20-30.5)

This regulation presumably was adopted to protect children from being transported in an unsafe school bus. Yet it defied common sense, as the Red Tape Review Commission's report pointed out, to require that a school bus, which was out of service because it had failed inspection, be towed – even back to the inspection station (see "satisfactorily") – when driving the bus without passengers was sufficient to ensure the safety of school children. As of publication of the report, a proposal to change this rule was pending.

[349] Among other things, repeals tend to get minimal scrutiny – if any – from reviewers.

[350] Indiana, New Hampshire, New Jersey, and Texas.

[351] The Texas statute does not use the word "expire," and it reads very much like a periodic review requirement except that "The state agency shall readopt, readopt with amendments, or repeal a rule as the result of reviewing the rule under this section." (Texas Statutes, §2006.039)

[352] There are classes of exception.

[353] In Utah:

Every agency rule that is in effect on February 28 of any calendar year expires on May 1 of that year unless it has been reauthorized by the Legislature... The Administrative Rules Review Committee shall have omnibus legislation prepared for consideration by the Legislature during its annual general session [that is] substantially in the following form: 'All rules of Utah state agencies are reauthorized except for the following:..." (Utah Code, §63G-3-502)

[354] Norman H. Bangerter, Governor's Executive Order, 2/3/1986 and Norman H. Bangerter, Governor's Executive Order, 3/22/1988.

[355] Agency heads were required to examine the following questions:

a. What statute does the rule implement or interpret?

b. Is the rule or amendment required to implement the law and legislative intent?

c. What need will be met or problem will be solved by the rule?

d. What fiscal and non-fiscal impact does the rule have on the citizens, businesses, state government, and local political subdivisions?

e. Could the length of the rule be reduced through incorporation by reference?

f. Is the rule organized in logical, understandable fashion using concise, everyday language?

g. Does the rule meet all the criteria of 63-46a-2(13) and 63-46a-3?

h. Is the rule in the format prescribed in the Rulewriting Manual for Utah?

[356] Gary R. Herbert, Governor's Executive Order 013-2011, *Establishing Effective Oversight Over State Agency Rulemaking*, December 6, 2011.

[357] These include:

- Ensure a full opportunity for public participation in the rulemaking process as prescribed by state law,
- Clearly establish and articulate the need for and purpose of each administrative rule is as part of the rule analysis,
- Ensure that the head of the agency and policy officials exercise effective oversight, and
- Minimize compliance costs, paperwork, and other burdens on the public.

[358] "WHEREAS, agencies' continual review of existing rules coupled with a process of careful consideration and assessment for new rules will improve state agencies' responsiveness to the public;"

[359] George E. Pataki, Executive Order 20, Establishing the Position of State Director of Regulatory Reform, November 30, 1995.

360 "GORR reviews agency material for compliance with the following criteria:

1. The rule:

(a) is clearly within the authority delegated by law;

(b) is consistent with and necessary to achieve a specific legislative purpose;

(c) is clearly written so that its meaning will be easily understood by those persons affected by it;

(d) does not unnecessarily duplicate or exceed existing federal or state statutes or rules;

(e) is consistent with existing state statutes and rules;

(f) consistent with state statutory requirements, will produce public benefits which will outweigh the costs, if any, imposed on affected parties;

(g) does not impose a mandate on local governments or school districts which is not fully funded, except as specifically required by state statute;

(h) prescribes methodologies or requirements that allow regulated parties flexibility and encourage innovation in meeting the legislative or administrative requirements and objectives underlying the rule;

(i) is based on credible assessments, using recognized standards, of the degree and nature of the risks which may be regulated, including a comparison with every-day risks familiar to the public;

(j) gives preference to the least costly, least burdensome regulatory and paperwork requirements needed to accomplish legislative and administrative objectives;

(k) is based upon the best scientific, technical and economic information that can reasonably and affordably be obtained; and

(l) if possible and practical, favors market-oriented solutions and performance standards over commandand-control regulation.

2. The agency has complied with SAPA §§ 202-a, 202-b and 202-bb, relating to regulatory impact statement, regulatory flexibility analysis for small businesses and rural area flexibility analysis.

If GORR concludes that any of the criteria is not met, it may require the agency to undertake additional analyses, including a cost-benefit analysis or risk assessment.

Once the information provided to GORR is complete, GORR recommends to the Secretary to the Governor, Counsel to the Governor, Deputy Secretary to the Governor and Director of the Division of the Budget whether the agency may submit the rule making for publication in the State Register.

After publication, GORR again reviews the rule for any new information or factors. If GORR concludes that any such new factors exist, the agency is notified of any deficiencies within 45 days of publication of the proposed rule (30 days of publication of a revised rule).

GORR reviews the agency response to determine whether it adequately addresses the deficiencies. If the response is adequate, the agency may proceed with the rule making. If the agency response is inadequate, GORR may notify the agency that it may not adopt the rule. This notification may then be confirmed or modified by the Governor's Senior Advisors." *New York State Register*, Vol. XXXIII, Issue No. 8, February 23, 2011.

[361] Andrew Cuomo, Executive Order No. 2, Review,C ontinuation and Expiration of Prior Executive Orders, January 1, 2011.

[362] Thomas J. Ridge, Executive Order 1996-1, *Regulatory Review and Promulgation*, February 6, 1996.

[363] The Act was adopted on June 25, 1982 (P.L. 633, No. 181) and amended on June 30, 1989 (P.L.73, No.19).

[364] "special provisions which have been developed to meet the particular needs of affected groups and persons, including minorities, the elderly, small businesses and farmers." (Pennsylvania P.L. 633, No. 181, §5(b))

[365] William Weld, Executive Order No. 384, *To Reduce Unnecessary Regulatory Burden*, February 9, 1996.

[366] "In order to find that a regulation meets this standard, the Agency must demonstrate, in its review, that:

(a) there is a specific need for governmental intervention that is clearly identified and precisely defined;

(b) the costs of the regulation do not exceed the benefits that would be effected by the regulation;

(c) less restrictive and intrusive alternatives have been considered and found less desirable based on a sound evaluation of the alternatives;

(d) the Agency has established a process and a schedule for measuring the effectiveness of the regulation; and

(e) the regulation is time-limited or provides for regular review."

[367] Mitt Romney, Executive Order No. 453 (03-11), *Promoting the Consideration of Small Businesses in Agency Rulemaking*, September 25, 2003.

[368] Deval L. Patrick, Executive Order No. 485, *Coordinating Agency Regulations*, May 25, 2007

[369] Mel Carnahan, Executive Order 96-18, October 17, 1996.

[370] "No department or agency shall transmit a proposed rule to the Secretary of State after December 1, 1996, unless it has determined whether such proposed rule will have a direct economic impact on small businesses of five hundred dollers [sic] ($500) or more in the aggregate. A small business shall be defined as an independently owned and operated business entity that employs fifty or fewer full-time employees."

[371] Bob Holden, Executive Order 3-15, August 25, 2003.

[372] In addition to the SBA model, E.O. 05-04 required:

- Detail on the types of small business that would be affected,
- Dollar estimates of compliance costs,
- Estimates of implementation costs and benefits to the agency, and
- A comparison of the proposed rule with federal and state counterparts.

[373] Theodore R. Kulongoski, Executive Order 03-01, *Regulatory Streamlining*, February 20, 2003.

[374] Theodore R. Kulongoski, Executive Order 09-10: Amending Executive Order 03-01 Regarding Regulatory Streamlining, June 25, 2009.

[375] Oregon Governor's Office Economic Revitalization Team, *Biennial Report to the 76th Legislative Assembly*, January 2011, p. 58.

[376] Bob Wise, Executive Order No. 20-03, August 27, 2003.

[377] Christine O. Gregoire, Executive Order 06-02, *Regulatory Improvement: Improve, Simplify and Assist*, February 2006.

[378] These included:

- Develop a One-Stop Business Portal
- Provide Multi-Agency Reviews for Permits
- Engage in On-going Regulatory Improvement, specifically:
  - Consult regularly with stakeholders;
  - Develop and implement innovative regulatory best practices;
  - Work with local and federal governments to develop coordinated permitting, licensing and related regulatory systems;
  - Utilize the latest technology to ensure all the work of businesses and citizens with the state is as efficient and user-friendly as possible; and
  - Report annually to the Governor on the status of regulatory improvement work plans.
- Listen to Our Clients
- Talk Clearly to the Public
- Be Accountable

[379] Christine O. Gregoire, Executive Order 10-06, *Suspending Non-Critical Rule Development and Adoption*, November 17, 2010.

[380] Review guidelines

1. Agencies shall review all rules in progress and their proposed rule making agenda for next year and identify those rules that can be suspended until after December 31, 2011.

2. In determining whether a rule should be suspended, agencies shall recognize the benefits of a stable regulatory environment. Where possible, agencies should redirect scarce resources away from rule making to front-line service delivery, including implementing and enforcing existing rules.

3. Rule making proceedings are non-critical unless the rule is:

   a. required by federal or state law or required to maintain federally delegated or authorized programs;

   b. required by court order;

   c. necessary to manage budget shortfalls, maintain fund solvency, or for revenue generating activities;

d. necessary to protect public health, safety, and welfare or necessary to avoid an immediate threat to the state's natural resources; or

e. beneficial to or requested or supported by the regulated entities, local governments or small businesses that it affects.

4. If an agency decides to proceed with a rule that has a small business impact or an impact to local government, the agency must consult with small businesses and/or governments on how the impact can be mitigated.

5. Agencies may continue to adopt rules that have been the subject of negotiated rule making or pilot rule making that involved substantial participation by interested parties before the development of the proposed rule. Agencies can also proceed to finalize permanent rule making that has previously been covered by emergency rules.

6. Agencies may continue to adopt expedited rules under RCW 34.05.353 where the proposed rules relate only to internal governmental operations.

[381] Mike Huckabee, Executive Order 05-04, February 1, 2005.

[382] Act 143 of 2007 (Arkansas Code Title 25, Chapter 15, Subchapter 2).

[383] Phil Bredesen, Executive Order No. 38, An Executive Order Requiring State Agencies to Assess the Impact of New Regulations on Small Business, May 22, 2006.

[384] The central elements of E.O. 38 were:

Section 2. Applicability. Prior to initiating a rulemaking process Under the Uniform Administrative Procedures Act... all agencies shall conduct a review of whether the rule under consideration affects small businesses... As part of this analysis, each agency shall examine whether a means exists to make the rule less costly for small businesses without compromising the objective of the rule...

Section 3. Economic Impact Statement. In conducting its review, each agency shall prepare an economic impact statement that sets forth the following:

(1) The type or types of small businesses that will be directly affected by, bear the cost of, and/or directly benefit from the proposed rule;

(2) A description of how small businesses will be adversely impacted;

Whether, and to what extent, alternative means exist for accomplishing the objectives of the proposed rule that might be less burdensome to small businesses, and why such alternatives are not being proposed; and

(3) A comparison of the proposed rule with federal or state counterparts.

[385] Acts 2007, ch. 464 (Tennessee Code Annotated Title 4, Chapter 5, Part 4).

[386] In over 60 percent of the analyses reviewed, the Regulatory Flexibility Addendum was "N/A," blank, or missing. Several rules with substantial impacts had analyses that reported no impact.

[387] Department of Economic and Community Development, Jobs4TN Rollout website, http://www.tn.gov/ecd/Jobs4TN.html.

[388] Department of Economic and Community Development, *Regulatory Reform Report*, January 2012.

[389] Specifics included departmental inefficiencies, lack of response to constituents, poor attitude, rude treatment of constituents, threats made towards constituents, and general lack of management and accountability.

[390] Sonny Perdue, Executive Order, *Small Business Regulatory Reform Initiative*, March 6, 2006.

[391] At that time, Georgia had adopted regulatory flexibility legislation, but there was no executive branch involvement.

[392] Establishing that something is not there requires indirect research techniques. In this case, indications included:

- The telephone number was out of service,
- Two links – including one to the executive order establishing the initiative – were broken,
- The FAQ page was blank, and
- Two of the four Headline pages were blank, and a third was dated 2006.

[393] A press release stated, "this committee was created by House Speaker David Ralston in January 2012 to solely focus on sustaining and growing small businesses in Georgia and thereby creating job opportunities for Georgians." (Georgia Republican Party (GAGOP), House Speaker David Ralston Charges Small Business Committee with Red Tape Watch Initiative, January 30, 2012, http://www.gagop.org/house-speaker-david-ralston-charges-small-businesscommittee-with-red-tape-watch-initiative)

[394] Alex Atwood, Session Update, *Rep. Alex Atwood Requesting Input from Business Community*, February 6, 2012, http://www.alexatwoodstaterep.com/update_feb6_2012.html.

[395] "Red Tape Watch" website, www.house.ga.gov/redtapewatch.

[396] Review criteria included:

- Does the regulation have a bona fide purpose that makes sense in the 21st century?

- Does the regulation exceed its statutory authority?
- Does the regulation conflict with another regulation on the books?
- Is the regulation redundant of the existing statute, and is the redundancy necessary?
- Is the regulation necessary to protect the safety, health, and/or welfare of the citizens of the Commonwealth?
- Do monitoring and enforcement of the regulation impose unreasonable costs on the Commonwealth? If so, can the objective be met by more effective and alternative means?
- Can reporting requirements be fulfilled more effectively through electronic or other means?

(Office of the Lieutenant Governor, *Lieutenant Governor Bolling Named Co-Chair of Attorney General's Government and Regulatory Reform Task Force*, June 20, 2008, http://www.ltgov.virginia.gov/news /viewArticle.aspx?articleID=482&articleType=P)

[397] Ted Strickland, Executive Order 2008-04S, *Implementing Common Sense Business Regulation*, February 12, 2008.

[398] Specific directives included:

- Establish rules through rulemaking, rather than use case-by-case or retroactive approaches.
- Make rules easy to comprehend, transparent, and predictable.
- Adopt federal rules unless a specific state purpose is involved.
- Focus on outcomes, rather than process.
- Minimize burdens and costs on business, including cumulative impacts.

[399] Specific directives included:

- Treat those affected as customers, and treat them consistently.
- Co-ordinate with other agencies to minimize worksite disruptions.
- Minimize processing time for permits, licenses, and other actions requiring agency response.
- Minimize information requirements.
- Provide compliance education and the ability to make compliance inquiries without risk of enforcement.
- Waive penalties for first-time or isolated paperwork or procedural noncompliance, where appropriate.
- Engage in continuous regulatory process improvement, including customer feedback.
- Establish a centralized electronic registration system to receiving notices.

[400] Specific directives included:

- Determine, as if for the first time, whether rules are needed to implement the underlying statute.
- Amend or rescind rules that are unnecessary, ineffective, contradictory, redundant, inefficient, needlessly burdensome, that unnecessarily impede economic growth, or that have had unintended negative consequences.
- Reduce or eliminate state regulation in areas where federal regulation is adequate.
- Select for earlier review those regulations that appear least consistent with common sense regulation.

[401] John R. Kaisch, Executive Order 2011-01K, *Establishing the Common Sense Initiative*, January 10, 2011.

[402] Aside from fiscal notes, the only real statutory requirement was for "a summary of the estimated cost of compliance with the rule to all directly affected persons." (Ohio Revised Code, §127.18(B))

[403] The rule development directives in E.O. 2008-04S were phrased as preparation for JCARR review.

[404] The core of Hawaii's Regulatory Flexibility Act (Hawaii Revised Statutes, Title 13, Chapter 201M) was Section 3 of the SBA model, with more explicit dollar cost requirements plus an explanation of how the agency involved small business in rule development. A departmental Small Business Advisory Committee was authorized. The Small Business Regulatory Review Board reviewed rules.

[405] Hawaii Small Business Regulatory Review Board Working Group, *Report Findings and Recommendations*, January 2009.

[406] Lingle, Administrative Directive No. 09-01, Policy and Procedure for the Adoption, Amendment, or Repeal of Administrative Rules, October 29, 2009.

[407] OSBA and SBRAC both do advocacy. There is a separate regulatory ombudsman. OSBA has a broad advocacy role that includes working with the legislature and with agencies at the pre-rule stage. SBRAC "focuses primarily on protecting business from over-regulation," working with agencies in rulemaking and rule review. Both work closely together, as is evidenced by a joint report.

[408] Office of Small Business Advocate & Small Business Regulatory Advisory Council, *FY 2009-10 Annual Report.*

[409] Office of Small Business Advocate, *Report on Small Business Issues and Recommendations*, September 2010.

[410] OSBA's recommendations were:

- Reduce overlap of state agency rules.

- Restrict regulations that add cost to doing business in Florida.
- Require the state regulatory costs for all combined business regulations to not exceed 7% of small businesses' adjusted gross revenue.
- Implement a law allowing businesses with fewer than 50 workers exempt from all new fees.

[411] SBRAC's report gave a sense of the scope of its activities.

- In FY 2009-10, agencies proposed over 1,000 rules, which SBRAC staff reviewed to determine small business impacts.
- SBRAC convened 24 meetings that reviewed over 275 sets of rules.
- SBRAC developed training on regulatory requirements and trained over 130 representatives of 17 state agencies.
- "On 41 occasions during 2009-10, SBRAC determined that new fees and expenses related to proposed rules were overly burdensome to small businesses and recommended that the agencies adopt lower-cost alternatives. Agencies responded positively in some cases but in many instances the agency declined to adopt SBRAC's recommendations."

[412] Office of Small Business Advocate & Small Business Regulatory Advisory Council, *FY 2009-10 Annual Report*, p. 7.

[413] Rick Scott, Executive Order 11-01, Suspending Rulemaking and Establishing the Office of Fiscal Accountability and Regulatory Reform, January 4, 2011.

[414] "The Office shall have the following responsibilities:

- Review proposed and existing rules to determine if they:
  - Unnecessarily restrict entry into a profession or occupation;
  - Adversely affect the availability of professional or occupational services to the public;
  - Unreasonably affect job creation or job retention;
  - Impose burdensome costs on businesses; and
  - Are justifiable when the overall cost-effectiveness and economic impact of the regulation, including indirect costs to consumers, is considered.
- Analyze, or require the analysis of, the impact of proposed and existing rules on matters of public health, safety and welfare, job creation, and other matters that may impact the creation or expansion of business interests in the state, and make recommendations for simplifying the regulations or regulatory processes of state agencies.
- Consistent with statutory provisions, require agencies to prepare a cost-benefit analysis, risk assessment, and analysis of the effect of proposed rules and regulations on the creation and retention of jobs in the state.
- Review actions taken by state agencies to improve program performance and meet program standards.
- Identify agency activities promoting economy and efficiency and benchmark such activities for other agencies.
- Identify fraud, waste, abuses, and deficiencies relating to programs and operations administered or financed by state agencies and make recommendations for corrective action.
- Investigate allegations of fiscal mismanagement.
- Consistent with statutory provisions, work with the Florida Small Business Regulatory Advisory Council, the Office of Small Business Advocate, the Rules Ombudsman, and the Florida Legislature, to identify rules and regulations that adversely or disproportionately impact businesses, particularly those relating to small business, and make recommendations that alleviate those effects." (E.O. 11-01, §3)

[415] Rick Scott, Executive Order 11-72, *Office of Fiscal Accountability and Regulatory Reform*, April 8, 2011.

[416] Rick Scott, Executive Order 11-72, *Office of Fiscal Accountability and Regulatory Reform*, April 8, 2011.

[417] Florida Supreme Court, *Whiley v. Scott*, No. SC11-592, August 16, 2011.

[418] Rick Scott, Executive Order 11-211, Superseding Executive Order 11-72; *Office of Fiscal Accountability and Regulatory Reform*, October 19, 2011.

[419] Janice K. Brewer, Memorandum, *The Governor's Regulatory Review Plan*, January 22, 2009.

[420] These included the following:

- A memorandum (April 30, 2009) extended the moratorium for another 60 days, and agencies were required to identify "administrative rules that:

(1) are no longer necessary due to changes in state or federal law or case law;

(2) are not effective;

(3) are inconsistent with current agency practice; or

(4) are not enforced."

The notice reminded agency directors of the statutory requirements for five-year reviews and related reporting.

- A memorandum (June 29, 2009) extended the moratorium until October 16, 2009. It also:
  - Directed agencies to submit requests for exemption in writing, and
  - Added regulations that "implement the ARRA, *or that are deregulatory*" to the exemption list.
- A memorandum (October 16, 2009) extended the moratorium until November 24, 2009.
- Legislation (HB 2008, which became effective on November 24, 2009) which established a similar moratorium on regulations during FY 2010 "to eliminate or replace archaic or illegal rules." It added regulations authorized by the Governor or required by legislation since January 1, 2009 to the list of exemptions.
- Executive Order 2010-13 (June 29, 2010) extended the moratorium until July 29, 2010.
- Legislation (HB 2260, which became effective on July 29, 2010) extended the moratorium through FY2011.
- Executive Order 2011-05 (June 30, 2011) extended the moratorium through FY2012. E.O. 2011-05 specified that the moratorium "does not apply to state agency rule making for any one or more of the following reasons:
  - To fulfill an objective related to job creation in this State.
  - To lessen or ease a regulatory burden while achieving the same regulatory objective.
  - To prevent a significant threat to the public health, peace or safety.
  - To avoid a violation of a court order or federal law that would result in sanctions by a court or federal government against an agency for failure to conduct the rule making action.
  - To comply with a federal statutory or regulatory requirement or a state statutory requirement...
  - To fulfill an obligation related to fees or any other action necessary to implement the state budget that is certified by the Governor's Office of Strategic Planning and Budgeting.
  - To promulgate a rule or other item that is exempt from [the ADA under] Arizona... Statutes
  - To address matters pertaining to the control, mitigation or eradication of waste, fraud or abuse within a state agency or wasteful, fraudulent or abusive activities perpetrated against a state agency."

  E.O. 2011-05 stipulated that "state agencies may continue a rule making that was authorized by the Office of the Governor on or after January 22, 2009" but prohibited agencies from conducting "any informal or formal rule making... without the prior written approval of the Office of the Governor.

[421] There one finds: "Editor's Note: This Executive Order is being reproduced in each issue of the Administrative Register until its expiration on June 30, 2012 as a notice to the public regarding state agencies' rulemaking activities."

[422] The alternative is: "Editor's Note: The following notice of Proposed [or Final] Rulemaking was exempt from Executive Order 2011-05 as issued by Governor Brewer. (See the text of the executive order on page [number].)"

[423] Grounds included:

- Necessity for compliance with federal regulations,
- Repeal of an existing regulation,
- Necessity on budgetary grounds, and/or
- Exemption from ADA provisions.

[424] One of the notices reviewed, for example, concerned a relatively routine updating of rules on pharmacy interns, related to internship training hours and reports, which was delayed nearly three years by the Moratorium.

[425] Four of the 22 notices reviewed cited the 5-year review – which has nothing to do with the Moratorium - as a significant factor leading to the rulemaking.

[426] Janice K. Brewer, Executive Order 2011-05, State Regulatory Rule Making Review and Moratorium To Promote Job Creation and Retention, June 30, 2011.

[427] MRP, Analysis of State Efforts to Mitigate Regulatory Burdens on Small Businesses, June 2002, p. 39.

[428] Considerably abbreviated, these steps were:

- For immediate relief from regulatory burdens, State agencies shall:
  - Engage in the "advance notice of rules" by soliciting the advice and views of knowledgeable persons from outside of New Jersey State government
  - Adopt the "time of decision" rule
  - Adopt rules for "waivers" which recognize that rules can be conflicting or unduly burdensome

  - Employ the use of cost/benefit analyses, as well as scientific and economic research
  - Detail and justify every instance where a proposed rule exceeds federal requirements
  - Take action to cultivate an approach to regulations that values performance-based outcomes and compliance
- For intermediate relief from regulatory burdens, State agencies shall:
  - In the first 90 days, identify those regulations and processes that impede responsible economic development
  - Within 180 days, redraft rules and processes identified in above to ensure that each rule and process is needed to implement the underlying statute
  - Within 180 days, reduce or eliminate areas of regulation where federal regulation now is adequate
  - Select for earlier review those rules or processes that appear to be least consistent with this Order.
- For long-term relief from regulatory burdens, State agencies shall:
- Draft all proposed rules and processes so that they promote transparency and predictability
- Adopt federally promulgated rules as written, except for specific New Jersey public policy goals
- Focus all proposed rules on achieving outcomes rather than on the process used to achieve compliance
- Draft all proposed rules so they impose the least burden and costs to business
- When possible and appropriate, provide stakeholders with compliance education and the ability to make compliance inquiries without risk of enforcement
- Waive penalties, when appropriate, for first-time or isolated paperwork or procedural regulatory noncompliance
- Engage in continuous regulatory process improvement including eliciting customer feedback
- Periodically evaluate their regulatory performance using measurable standards, data, or other objective criteria

[429] Kim Guadagno, et.al., *Red Tape Review Group Findings and Recommendations*, April 19, 2010.

[430] Legislative recommendations included

- Improve the administrative rule-making process under the Administrative Procedure Act,
- Provide for new and expanded powers to combat unfunded mandates,
- Eliminate unnecessary boards, task forces, study commissions and councils,
- Rationalize titles underway at the Civil Service Commission and provide a means for a municipal "opt-out,"
- Continue efforts to arrive at a more effective affordable housing policy that is fiscally less burdensome, and
- Examine unfunded mandates for both K-12 and higher education.

[431] Regulatory recommendations included:

- State agencies should adopt the "Common Sense Principles" for rule-making,
- State agencies should proceed with rule rescissions and modifications pursuant to the 90-day review of rules and 180-day review of rules, and
- Shortcomings of the Regulatory System should be addressed such as:
  - Archaic and anachronistic rules,
  - Rules that offend common sense, and
  - Rules that over-reach.

[432] Broader policy recommendations included:

- State agencies should adopt a culture change that results in a more customer-service oriented mentality.
- Endorse the creation of a new model for job creation/economic development, with creation of "one-stop" shopping for State permits for significant economic development projects as a central element.
- Adopt improvements to State Information Technology systems,
- Recognize the key strategic roles of the Office of Smart Growth and the State Planning Commission
- Establish an ongoing, transparent and bi-partisan Red Tape Review Group, and
- Rescind Executive Orders that confuse or impede economic development goals.

[433] Instead of just rhetoric about how burdensome regulation was, for example, the report cited two surveys that rated New Jersey 48th among states for job and business growth and 50th based on state policy climate for business and entrepreneurship.

[434] *Ibid*, p. 3.

[435] Membership include the Lt. Governor (or designee) as chair, four legislators (two from each house; two from each party), and "up to four (4) public members with experience and expertise in the regulatory process."

[436] This was a classic sunset provision: "it is appropriate that the new Review Commission be subject to reauthorization after three (3) years to determine whether it remains necessary, or whether it should expire at that time."

[437] "The Review Commission shall:

a. review existing administrative rules and regulations to analyze their impact on job creation, economic growth, and investment in New Jersey;

b. solicit both written and oral comments from the public;

c. conduct at least three (3) public hearings each year, one each in the Southern, Central, and Northern regions of the State;

d. issue periodic written reports to the Governor, making detailed findings and recommendations that include an analysis of the following issues, among others: existing rules, regulations and legislation that are burdensome to the State's economy; ways to improve the regulatory processes of State government; and on other areas relevant to administrative procedural reforms."

[438] Kim Guadagno, et.al., *Red Tape Review Commission: Findings and Recommendations*, February 2012. The report covered the following topics:

- History of the Commission;
- Status of the original Red Tape Review Group's recommendations;
- Red tape accomplishments to further compliance with the Common Sense Principles;
- Red tape legislative efforts; and
- Red tape recommendations.

[439] The original Red Tape Review Group, for example, had recommended modifying the Administrative Procedures Act to allow agencies to change a proposed rule in response to public comments without re-proposing the rule all over again (as New Jersey – like many states – had required). The legislation was enacted, and the amended rules had been proposed at the time of the Commission's report.

[440] In keeping with the whole concept of periodic regulatory review, Executive Order No. 41 states that "it is appropriate that the new Review Commission be subject to reauthorization after three (3) years to determine whether it remains necessary, or whether it should expire at that time."

[441] Susana Martinez, Executive Order 2011-001, Formation of a Small Business-Friendly Task Force; Establishing a 90-Day Review Period for All Proposed and Pending Rules and Regulations, January 1, 2011.

[442] One of the regulations caught in the suspension was an Environmental Improvement Board (EIB) rule mandating reductions in global warming emissions from large stationary sources, which had been adopted the previous November but not yet published. In late January, the Supreme Court ruled that the suspension of publication of these rules was improper. Governor Martinez dismissed all seven members of the EIB, and her representative explained that in adopting the cap-and-trade rule "the majority of EIB members have made it clear that they are more interested in advancing political ideology than implementing common-sense policies."

[443] "Its core mission is to advance New Mexico business and enterprise with expansion, retention, and growth by resolving challenging bureaucratic, intergovernmental, and public policy problems [and by] help[ing] small businesses break through regulatory roadblocks." (Office of Business Advocacy web page, http://www.gonm.biz/Office_Business_Advocacy.aspx)

[444] Economic Development Department, Small Business-Friendly Task Force Report, April 1, 2011.

[445] "The members of the task force either own their own small business, represent an organization that serves on behalf of several thousand New Mexico small businesses or are part of a company that contracts with local small businesses. Collectively these members represent more than ten thousand small businesses around the state."

[446] "The task force recommends reviewing current members of the SBRAC and their status. They also recommend having a full and fair review by economists from a neutral party such as Workforce Solutions to provide SBRAC with economic impact analysis of the regulations. This would allow for the use of investigatory dockets as part of the rule making process with the agencies. The task force recommends that state agencies adhere to their statutory responsibility to send rules and regulations from their department to the Economic Development Department to be reviewed by SBRAC."

[447] "An overarching theme small businesses have observed is the difficulty working with mid-level managers at NMED and other departments who have an anti-business agenda despite changes in leadership at the exempt-employee level. The recommendation is to have businesses facing problems with agencies call the Office of Business Advocacy."

[448] These included:

- Environment,
- Agriculture,
- Construction,
- Health and Human Services,
- Child care, and
- Small business procurement.

[449] Recommendations for Construction, for example, included:

- Revert building codes to national standards.
- Consolidate license categories in the building trades.
- Consolidate mechanical, electrical, and plumbing inspections.
- Standardize continuing educations requirements for different trades.

[450] The discussion on child care facilities, for example, noted that providers are often being written up for things that are not in the regulations and are sometimes trivial (such as not enough blocks of a particular type); self-evaluation tools are being used rather than standard assessment tools; and enforcement differs in different parts of the state.

[451] "Developmental Disability Waiver. Recommendation is to establish a task force comprised of a broad spectrum of stakeholders including Department of Health personnel, agency representatives, individuals served, and family members, to review the current rules to see what could be streamlined or eliminated of the 170 pages of regulations governing services provided by business in serving the 4,000 individuals on the Waiver."

[452] In the discussion of child care, "Examples are:

a. An adult has to always be present with the door open as children go to the bathroom.

b. Hand sanitizer isn't allowed even though the CDC says it is better than hand washing."

The hand sanitizer prohibition is genuinely obsolete. One of the basic principles of prevention of child sex abuse, however, is not to allow an adult and a child to be alone together in a private space – such as a bathroom with the door closed. (There may also be good reason for different continuing education requirements in different construction trades.)

[453] Brian Sandoval, Executive Order 2011-01, Establishing a Freeze on Regulations, January 3, 2011.

[454] Each regulatory body shall... assess the following:

a. the problem the regulation was established to address or, if the regulation does not address a specific problem, the value to the public of the regulation;

b. the impact of the regulation on the problem or the benefits provided by it;

c. the adverse impact, if any, the regulation has had on various groups— including, but not limited to, businesses of various sizes, small communities and government entities;

d. the cost of the regulation, including, but not limited to, the cost of enactment and enforcement;

e. whether the regulation remains necessary;

f. whether alternate forms of regulation may adequately address the problem;

g. whether the regulation is written clearly and concisely so as to achieve easy understanding and application; and

h. whether other regulations address the same problem.

[455] Paul R. Lepage, Executive Order 09 FY 11/12, *An Order to Improve Review of the Rule Making Process*, January 10, 2011.

[456] Paul R. Lepage, Executive Order 20 FY 11/12, *An Order Establishing Comprehensive Rulemaking Oversight*, August 24, 2011.

[457] These considerations include:

- The impact of the proposed rule on job growth or creation,
- The burden imposed by any fees included in the rule,
- The cost to the public in terms of time and money required to comply with the rule,
- The extent to which other state laws and regulations already address the subject matter of the rule, and
- The relevant Federal standards, if any, and the specific need for Maine's rules to differ from them if such a need exists.

[458] Sam Brownback, Executive Order 11-01, *Office of the Repealer*, April 10, 2012.

[459] Richard D. Snyder, Executive Order 2011-4, *Executive Reorganization*, February 23, 2011. Richard D. Snyder, Executive Order 2011-5, *Executive Reorganization*, February 23, 2011,

[460] The list of factors, which applies both to review of proposed rules and to review of existing rules, include:

- "The health or safety benefits of the rules,

- Whether the rules are mandated by any applicable constitutional or statutory provision,
- The cost of compliance with the rules, taking into account their complexity, reporting requirements, and other factors,
- The extent to which the rules conflict with or duplicate similar rules or regulations adopted by the state or federal government,
- The extent to which the rules exceed national or regional compliance requirements or other standards,
- The date of the last evaluation of the rules and the degree, if any, to which technology, economic conditions or other factors have changed regulatory activity covered by the rules since the last evaluation,
- Other changes or developments since implementation that demonstrate there is no continued need for the rules,
- The recommendations of any Advisory Rules Committees formed pursuant to this Order, which shall consider the factors set forth in paragraphs 1-7 of this Section III. D.,
- The recommendations of any departments or agencies that are or will be charged with the implementation or enforcement of the rules...
- Comments received from the public under Section III of this Order, [and]
- The nature of any complaints or comments the Office of Regulatory Reinvention receives, or any departments or agencies receive, from the public concerning the rules."

[461] These include:

- Complete a detailed cost-benefit analysis for all proposed rules that specifies the methodologies utilized in determining the existence and extent of the costs and benefits of the proposed rules as well as an assessment of any disproportionate impact of the rules based upon industrial sector, segment of the public, business size, geographic location, environmental resource, or other factors determined from time to time by the Office of Regulatory Reinvention.
- Establish broadly representative stakeholder advisory groups and seeking the input of these groups on proposed
  rules as the department or agency deems appropriate or as directed by the Office of Regulatory Reinvention.
- Detail all provisions in rules that exceed federal or regional standards and explain the rationale for the deviation and the specific costs and benefits of the deviation.

[462] "The mission of the Office of Regulatory Reinvention (ORR) is to simplify Michigan's regulatory environment by reducing obsolete, unnecessary and burdensome rules that are limiting economic growth."

[463] "Complete a detailed cost-benefit analysis for all proposed rules that specifies the methodologies utilized in determining the existence and extent of the costs and benefits of the proposed rules as well as an assessment of any disproportionate impact of the rules based upon industrial sector, segment of the public, business size, geographic location, environmental resource, or other factors."

[464] The scorecard is called the Dashboard for ORR. It gives the reporting period, the previous month's numbers, and the previous month's n umbers, as well as a Progress indicator (an arrow pointing up, down, or sideways) for

- Number of existing administrative rules,
- Existing rules reviewed,
- Number of Departments that have collected non-rule regulatory actions,
- Advisory Rules Committees formed,
- Number of Public Comments Received at www.Michigan.Gov/ORR,
- Number of rules rescinded,
- Number of rules amended, and
- Pages of non-rule regulatory actions eliminated.

[465] Colorado has a unique administrative structure in that all regulatory agencies are administratively within DORA. DORA has the dual role of consumer protection and support of business. DORA's Office of Policy, Research, and Regulatory Reform reviews regulations and may order a cost-benefit analysis.

[466] Department of Regulatory Agencies, *Cutting Red Tape in Colorado State Government*, Omnibus Report to the Governor on the "Pits and Peeves" Roundtable Initiative, December 2011

[467] Under Colorado statute, individual regulations nominally sunset before the end of the legislative session of the year after promulgation (or renewal), unless reauthorized by the legislature.

[468] Scott Walker, Executive Order # 50, Relating to Guidelines for the Promulgation of Administrative Rules, November 2, 2011.

[469] 2011 Wisconsin Act 21 and 2011 Wisconsin Act 46.

[470] Examples include:

- Setting out the details of obtaining the governor's approval of scopes of work and draft final rules (including electronic submission), and
- Encouraging an agency to form an advisory committee if a proposed rule is anticipated to have a significant economic impact.

[471] Where the statute requires "consultation with those businesses, business sectors, associations representing businesses, local governmental units, and individuals," for example, the executive order says how to this:

a. The agency shall compile a list of affected persons and economic concerns identified in the comments solicited by the agency.

b. The agency shall contact those affected persons to discuss economic concerns and give consideration to those concerns in its EIA determination.

c. The agency shall document in the EIA the affected persons who were consulted and whether the agency's determination is disputed by any of the affected persons.

[472] The board previously had members representing eight departments, six small-business representatives, and the chairs of the house and senate committees most concerned with small business. The reconfigured Board consists of seven small-business representatives and the legislative representatives.

[473] Six of these had multiple executive orders, but in five states (Utah being the exception) they had enough similarities to be treated as one.

[474] Georgia is excluded because the legislative initiative never really materialized. Half of these initiatives were related to an executive order.

[475] Arkansas, Missouri, and Tennessee.

[476] Georgia, Massachusetts, and West Virginia.

[477] Maine, Pennsylvania, and Utah (2011).

[478] Michigan, New Jersey, Ohio, and Wisconsin.

[479] Kansas, Oregon, Virginia, and Washington.

[480] Arizona, Florida, Nevada, New Mexico, and Utah (1980s). New Jersey temporarily froze pending regulations to institute a longer-term review and overhaul the rulemaking and review process. Washington also froze rulemaking, but immediately set conditions under which rulemaking could go forward again.

[481] Colorado, Florida (OSBA survey), Hawaii, New Jersey, New Mexico, and Tennessee.

[482] This is necessary but, as was discussed earlier, may not be sufficient.

[483] New Mexico is something of an exception, because it also had a short-term study.

[484] Massachusetts also had a substantially earlier executive order (1995).

[485] Florida's executive order directed OFARR to "work with" SBRAC, OSBA, and Ombudsman. Nevada's order required assessment of impacts on small entities, which was already required by statute.

[486] The "Small Business-Friendly Task Force," which claimed broad small business representation.

[487] Child care providers, for example, received considerable attention. The Task Force's strongest recommendations, however, were on environmental regulations and would primarily benefit large utilities.

[488] Washington defines a threshold for "minor cost" per business as the greater of 0.3% of annual revenue or $100, or 1.0% of annual payroll. Utah uses a back-up threshold of one day's annual average gross receipts.

[489] The date is usually less obscure than some electronic search criteria (e.g., the CAR number).

[490] There are practical limits to designing a new set of web pages for an agency that rarely promulgates regulations, but documents still should be presented on line in some manner.

[491] One of the features of RSS is that it updates automatically.

[492] These include Arkansas (which is supposed to have a Regulatory Review Committee), California (which effectively does not do regulatory flexibility), Colorado, and Michigan.

[493] Arizona is the exception.

[494] "Estimate the number of small businesses, classified by industry sector, subject to the proposed rule." (Indiana)

[495] "Identify any disproportionate impact the proposed rule(s) may have on small businesses because of their size or geographic location."

"Estimate the ability of small businesses to absorb the costs without suffering economic harm and without adversely affecting competition in the marketplace." (Michigan)

[496] Small Business Administration, Office of Advocacy, *Small Business Regulatory Flexibility Model Legislation Initiative*, September 2005, pp. 5-8.

[497] Arkansas Economic Development Commission, Small and Minority Business Development Division regulatory flexibility website, http://arkansasedc.com/entrepreneurs/regulatory-flexibility.

[498] (California Office of Administrative Law, *OAL Checklist Notice Review*, http://www.oal.ca.gov/res/docs/pdf/checklist/NoticeReviewChecklist.PDF)

[499] Department of Finance *Economic Impact Statement* (STD. 399), http://www.fgc.ca.gov/regulations/2009/671std399.pdf.

[500] Indiana Department of Environmental Management rules web page, http://www.in.gov/idem/4087.htm

[501] Legislative Research Commission, *Kentucky Administrative Regulation*, Informational Bulletin 118, June 2003. p. 15.

[502] Office of the State Register, *LAC Handbook*, October 2011, pp. 52-53.

[503] Office of Housing and Economic Development, *Small Business Impact Statement Overview and Guidelines*, http://www.mfbo.org/news%20&%20events/2012%20proposals/SBIS-%202012%20Intl%20Ener%20Cons%20Code%20-%20Commercial%20(item%208).pdf

[504] Office of Regulatory Reinvention, Administrative Rules Process Summary web page, http://www.michigan.gov/documents/lara/Admin_Rules_Process_353271_7.pdf.

[505] Office of Regulatory Reinvention, Regulatory Impact Statement and Cost Benefit Analysis web page, http://www.michigan.gov/documents/lara/Regulatory_Impact_Statement_401371_7.doc.

[506] Small Business Regulatory Fairness Board, Small Business Impact Statement Form web page, http://www.sbrfb.ded.mo.gov/pdf/ImpactSt.doc.

[507] Department of State, Division of Administrative Rules, Regulatory Impact Statement web page, http://www.dos.ny.gov/info/pdfs/FMT-RIS.pdf.

[508] Department of State, Division of Administrative Rules, Regulatory Flexibility Analysis for Small Businesses and Local Governments web page, http://www.dos.ny.gov/info/pdfs/FMT-RFA.pdf.

[509] Common Sense Initiative, CSI Business Impact Analysis Form web page, http://www.governor.ohio.gov/Portals/0/pdf/CSI/Business%20Impact%20Analysis%20%28.doc%29.docx.

[510] Independent Regulatory Review Commission, Agency Toolbox web page, http://www.irrc.state.pa.us/agency_toolbox.aspx.

[511] Legislative Research Council, *Guide to Form and Style for Administrative Rules of South Dakota*, Revised: April 10, 2012, pp. 60-61.

[512] Department of State, Division of Publications, *Rulemaking Guidelines*, July 2010.

[513] Office of the Attorney General, *HB 3430 Small Business Impact Final Guidelines*, June 2008. https://www.oag.state.tx.us/AG_Publications/pdfs/hb3430guidelines2008.pdf.

[514] Courts have not interpreted the meaning of "adverse effect" under § 2006.002. *See Unified Loans, Inc. v. Pettijohn*, 955 S.W. 2d 649 (Tex. App.—Austin 1997, no pet.). Websters Dictionary defines "adverse" as "1: acting against or in a contrary direction; verdict>." 59 (9th New Collegiate ed. 1990).

[515] *Texas Shrimp Ass'n v. Texas Parks & Wildlife Dep't,* 2005 WL 1787453, at *6 (Tex. App.—Austin 2005, no pet.) (not designated for publication) ("The requirements in section 2006.002 are not absolute, but rather are conditioned on the adoption of "a rule that would have an adverse economic effect on small business'," quoting the text of 2006.002(c) as it existed at the time.)

[516] An objective of statutes such as § 2006.002 "is to afford adequate notice—to place the agency's assessment before interested persons in advance in order that (1) interested persons might comment intelligently on the proposed rules and (2) the agency might exercise intelligently its responsibilities in arriving at the contents of the rule as finally adopted in stating reasons for and against adoption, and in formulating the reqired contents of the adopting order, including a 'reasoned justification' for the rule." *Unified Loans*, 955 S. W. 2d at 652.

[517] Courts have held that the federal Regulatory Flexibility Act, 5 U.S.C. §§ 601-612, applies only to direct economic impacts. See *Mid-Tex. Elec. Coop v. FERC,* 773 F. 2d 317 (D.C. Cir. 1985) (Regulations for generating utilities did not need to consider potential effect on transmission utilities); *American Trucking Ass'ns v. EPA*, 175 F. 3d 1027 (D.C. Cir. 1999) (EPA's ambient air quality standards did not have a direct impact on small entities which were regulated directly through state implementation plan s), *aff'd in part and rev'd in part on other grounds, Whitman v. American Trucking Ass'ns,*531 U.S. 457 (2001); *United Distribution Cos. v. FERC*, 88 F. 3d 1105, 170 (D.C. Cir. 1996) (Regulatory flexibility analysis provision applies only to small entities that are subject to the requirements of the rule and the agency had no obligation to analyze the effects on entities which it did not regulate).

[518] See *Southern Offshore Fishing Assoc. v. Daley,* 955 F. Supp. 1411, 1437 (M.S. Fla. 1998) (interpreting the federal requirement to examine impacts on small entities). One court required that a federal agency consider comments not submitted during the formal notice and comment period because the agency's proposed rule did not properly inform the regulated industry that its interests were at stake. *Northwest Mining Assoc. v. Babbitt*, 5 F. Supp. 2d 9 (D.D.C. 1998).

[519] See *Unified Loans*, 955 S.W. 2d at 652-654.

[520] Additional labor market and other information may be found at www.twc.state.tx.us/customers /rpm/rpmsub3.html.

[521] See U.S. Small Business Administration, Office of Advocacy, *State Guide to Regulatory Flexibility for Small Businesses* (March 2007) (Examining the regulatory flexibility programs of Rhode Island, South Dakota, and other states).

[522] Protection of the public health, safety, and welfare is part of the inherent power of a sovereign state. See *Barshop v. Medina County Underground Water Conservation Dist.*, 925 S.W. 2d 618, 633-635 (Tex. 1996); Blacks Law Dictionary 1178 (7th ed. 1999).

[523] Virginia Regulatory Town Hall User Manual, http://townhall.virginia.gov/um/toc.cfm.

In: State Regulation of Small Business
Editors: Lindsay Lockwood and Paul Garritano
ISBN: 978-1-62948-193-7

Chapter 2

THE RFA IN A NUTSHELL: A CONDENSED GUIDE TO THE REGULATORY FLEXIBILITY ACT*

Small Business Administration, Office of Advocacy

FOREWORD

When government takes small businesses into consideration in developing regulations, it saves time and money for a vital sector of the nation's economy, our small businesses.

This primer on the Regulatory Flexibility Act (RFA) is designed to be used by those interested in the basics of federal regulatory compliance with respect to the RFA and Executive Order 13272. For more detailed guidance on the RFA, federal agency rule writers and policy analysts should refer to the Office of Advocacy's step-by-step manual: *A Guide for Government Agencies: How to Comply with the Regulatory Flexibility Act* (www.sba.gov/advo/laws/rfaguide.pdf).

The chief counsel for advocacy of the U.S. Small Business Administration has been designated to monitor agency compliance with the Regulatory Flexibility Act.

INTRODUCTION TO THE RFA

The Regulatory Flexibility Act (RFA), enacted in September 1980,[1] requires agencies to consider the impact of their regulatory proposals on small entities, to analyze effective alternatives that minimize small entity impacts, and to make their analyses available for public comment. The RFA applies to three types of small entities:

- *Small Businesses:* Defined by section 3 of the Small Business Act.[2]

* This is an edited, reformatted and augmented version of a Small Business Administration, Office of Advocacy publication, dated October 2010.

- *Small Nonprofits:* Any nonprofit enterprise that is independently owned and operated and not dominant in its field.
- *Small Governmental Jurisdictions:* Governments of cities, counties, towns, townships, villages, school districts, or special districts with a population of less than 50,000.

The RFA does not seek preferential treatment for small entities, require agencies to adopt regulations that impose the least burden on small entities, or mandate exemptions for small entities. Rather, it requires agencies to examine public policy issues using an analytical process that identifies, among other things, barriers to small business competitiveness and seeks a level playing field for small entities, not an unfair advantage.

In essence, the RFA asks agencies to be aware of the economic structure of the entities they regulate and the effect their regulations may have on small entities. It requires agencies to analyze the economic impact of proposed regulations when there is likely to be a significant economic impact on a substantial number of small entities, and to consider regulatory alternatives that will achieve the agency's goal while minimizing the burden on small entities.

The Small Business Regulatory Enforcement Fairness Act (SBREFA), enacted in March 1996,[3] amended the RFA and provided additional tools to aid small businesses in the fight for regulatory fairness. The most significant amendments made by SBREFA were:

- Judicial review of agency compliance with some of the RFA's provisions.
- Requirements for more detailed and substantive regulatory flexibility analyses.
- Expanded participation by small entities in the development of rules by the Occupational Safety and Health Administration (OSHA) and the Environmental Protection Agency (EPA).

The goal of Congress in creating the RFA was to change the regulatory culture in agencies and mandate that they consider regulatory alternatives that achieve statutory purposes, while still minimizing the impacts on small entities. Regulatory flexibility analyses built into the regulatory development process at the earliest stages will help agency decision makers achieve regulatory goals with realistic, cost-effective, and less burdensome regulations.

This primer should be utilized by anyone interested in commenting on draft federal regulations on behalf of small business and as a short description of the basic requirements of the act.

FIRST STEPS: WHERE DO WE BEGIN?

If you had to break down the RFA into sections, there are really four main parts. It's easiest to think of them as four related questions:

- Does the RFA apply to this rule?
- Will this rule have a significant economic impact on a substantial number of small entities?
- What is the potential economic impact of the rule on small entities?
- What has been done to minimize the adverse economic impact of the rule on small entities that was described in the proposed rule?

The following sections explain how to answer those important questions.

DOES THE RFA APPLY?

One of the first decisions to make is whether the Regulatory Flexibility Act applies to a particular regulation. The RFA applies to any rule subject to notice and comment rulemaking under section 553(b) of the Administrative Procedure Act (APA)[4] or any other law. However there are times when a regulation or rule can be exempt from the APA notice and comment requirements, thereby exempting it from the RFA as well. Rules are exempt when any of the following is involved: (1) a military or foreign affairs function of the United States, or (2) a matter relating to agency management or personnel or to public property, loans, grants, benefits, or contracts.[5] In addition, except where notice or hearing is required by statute, the APA does not apply (1) to interpretative rules, general statements of policy, or rules of agency organization, procedure or practice; or (2) when the agency for good cause finds that notice and public procedure are impracticable, unnecessary, or contrary to the public interest.[6]

The RFA presents its own exemptions as well. Section 601(2) states that the RFA does not apply to rules of particular applicability relating to rates, wages, corporate or financial structures, or reorganizations thereof, prices, facilities, appliances, services or allowances.[7]

CAN YOU CERTIFY? THE THRESHOLD ANALYSIS

Once an agency determines that the RFA applies to their draft rule, it must decide whether to conduct a full regulatory flexibility analysis or to certify that the proposed rule will not "have a significant economic impact on a substantial number of small entities."[8]

In order to certify a rule under the RFA, an agency should be able to answer the following types of questions:

- Which small entities will be affected?
- Have adequate economic data been obtained?
- What are the economic implications/impacts of the proposal and do the data reveal a significant economic impact on a substantial number of small entities?

If, after conducting an analysis for a proposed or final rule, an agency determines that a rule will not have a significant economic impact on a substantial number of small entities, section 605(b) of the RFA provides that the head of the agency may certify, or promise, that the rule will not have this effect. The certification must include a statement providing the *factual* basis for this determination, and the certification must be published in the *Federal Register* at the time the proposed or final rule is published for public comment. A certification must include, at a minimum, a description of the affected entities and an estimate of the cost of the impacts that clearly justifies the "no impact" certification. The agency's reasoning and assumptions underlying its certification should be explicit in order to obtain public comment and thus receive information that would be used to re-evaluate the certification. Clearly, an agency should identify the scope of the problem and the impact of the solution on affected entities before moving forward with a regulatory proposal.

DEVELOPING THE THRESHOLD ANALYSIS

Certification analysis does not require the depth of analysis necessary in an initial regulatory flexibility analysis. Nevertheless, this "threshold" analysis can offer important insights into the nature of regulatory impacts.

The Office of Advocacy believes the threshold analysis should include the following items in order to support an adequate certification statement:

1) Description of small entities affected
   - A brief economic and technical statement on the regulated community, describing some of the following types of information:
     a) The diversity in size of regulated entities
     b) Revenues in each size grouping
2) Economic impacts on small entities.
   - A fair, first estimate of expected cost impacts, or a reasonable basis for assuming costs would be insignificant within all economic or size groupings of the "small" regulated community.
   - The rationale for the certification decision, based on the analysis presented.
3) Significant economic impact criteria.
   - The criteria used to examine whether first-estimate costs are significant.
4) Substantial number criteria.
   - The criteria used to examine whether the entities experiencing significant impacts constitute a substantial number of entities in any of the regulated size groupings.
5) Description of assumptions and uncertainties.
   - The sources of data used in the economic and technical analysis.
   - The degree of uncertainty in the cost estimates, when uncertainty is large.

After the 1996 amendment, the RFA now requires that certifications be supported by a "statement of factual basis." In amending the RFA, Congress intended that agencies should do more than provide boilerplate and unsubstantiated statements to support their RFA certifications. Courts will overturn an agency's final certification if it is not adequate.[9] Consequently, certifications that simply state that the agency has found that the proposed or final rule will not have a significant economic impact on a substantial number of small entities are not sufficient under section 605(b) of the RFA.

Definition of "Significant" and "Substantial"

A critical decision point in the threshold analysis is for the agency to determine whether there is a significant economic impact on a substantial number of small entities. The RFA does not define "significant" or "substantial." What is "significant" or "substantial" will vary depending on the problem that needs to be addressed, the rule's requirements, and the preliminary assessment of the rule's impact. The agency is in the best position to gauge the small entity impacts of its regulations.

Direct versus Indirect Impact

The courts have held that the RFA requires an agency to perform a regulatory flexibility analysis of small entity impacts only when a rule directly regulates them. Although it is not required by the RFA, the Office of Advocacy believes that it is good public policy for the agency to perform a regulatory flexibility analysis even when the impacts of its regulation are indirect. If an agency can accomplish its statutory mission in a more cost-effective manner, the Office of Advocacy believes that it is good public policy to do so.

When More In-Depth Analysis is Required: The IRFA

During the preparation of a proposed rule, an agency must prepare an initial regulatory flexibility analysis (IRFA) if it determines that a proposal may impose a significant economic impact on a substantial number of small entities. The RFA requires agencies to publish the IRFA, or a summary, in the *Federal Register* at the same time it publishes the proposed rulemaking.[10] The IRFA must include a discussion of each element required by section 603 of the RFA, and the agency must also send a copy of the IRFA to the Chief Counsel for Advocacy.[11] Executive Order 13272 requires agencies to notify Advocacy when the agency submits a draft proposed or final rule to the Office of Information and Regulatory Affairs (OIRA) under Executive Order 12866, or at a reasonable time prior to publication of the rule by the agency.[12]

Questions to Consider

Section 603 of the RFA requires agencies to perform a detailed analysis of the potential impact of the proposed rule on small entities.[13] Some of the important questions the agency should address in preparing an IRFA are:

- Which small entities are affected the most? Are all small entities in an industry affected equally or do some experience disparate impacts such that aggregation of the industry data would dilute the magnitude of the economic effect on specific subgroups?

- Are all the required elements of an IRFA present, including a clear explanation of the need for and objectives of the rule?
- Has the agency identified and analyzed all major cost factors?
- Has the agency identified all significant alternatives that would allow the agency to accomplish its regulatory objectives while minimizing the adverse impact or maximizing the benefits to small entities?
- Can the agency use other statutorily required analyses to supplement or satisfy the IRFA requirements of the RFA?
- Are there circumstances under which preparation of an IRFA may be waived or delayed?
- What portion of the problem is attributable to small businesses (i.e., is regulation of small businesses needed to satisfy the statutory objectives)?
- Does the proposed solution meet the statutory objectives in a more cost-effective or cost-beneficial manner than any of the alternatives considered?

The preparation of an IRFA should be coordinated with the development of the data and analysis the agency will use in preparing the proposed rule under the requirements of the Administrative Procedure Act. In doing so, the agency should be mindful of the requirements of the RFA and collect data based on size. The development of a rational rule will require the acquisition of data that describe the scope of the problem, the entities affected, and the extent of those effects. Without such information, the agency will be unable to develop a rational rule. When data are not readily available, the agency should consult with industry sources or other third parties to collect data. If the data collection is inadequate, then agencies should solicit the data as part of the proposed rulemaking. [14]

Elements of an IRFA

Under section 603(b) of the RFA, an IRFA must describe the impact of the proposed rule on small entities and contain the following information:

1) A description of the reasons why the action by the agency is being considered.
2) A succinct statement of the objectives of, and legal basis for, the proposed rule.
3) A description—and, where feasible, an estimate of the number—of small entities to which the proposed rule will apply.
4) A description of the projected reporting, recordkeeping, and other compliance requirements of the proposed rule, including an estimate of the classes of small entities that will be subject to the requirement and the types of professional skills necessary for preparation of the report or record.
5) An identification, to the extent practicable, of all relevant federal rules that may duplicate, overlap, or conflict with the proposed rule.
6) A description of any significant alternatives to the proposed rule which accomplish the stated objectives of applicable statues and which minimize any significant economic impact of the proposed rule on small entities.

The principal issues an agency should address in an IRFA are the impact of a proposed rule on small entities and the comparative effectiveness and costs of alternative regulatory options.

Significant Alternatives are the Key

The keystone of the IRFA is the description of any significant alternatives to the proposed rule that accomplish the stated objectives of applicable statutes and that minimize the rule's economic impact on small entities. It is the development and adoption of these alternatives that provide regulatory relief to small entities.

Analyzing alternatives establishes a process for the agency to evaluate proposals that achieve the regulatory goals efficiently and effectively without unduly burdening small entities, erecting barriers to competition, or stifling innovation. This process provides an additional filter by which the agency conducts rational rulemaking mandated by the APA.

Rather than focus on the overall costs and benefits of a particular regulation (as might be required by statute, such as the best achievable control technology, or by the regulatory analysis requirements of E.O. 12866), the RFA requires the agency to undertake an analysis that determines the impacts of the rule on small entities and then considers alternatives that reduce or minimize those impacts. Instead of analyzing the impacts of its regulatory actions on all relevant sectors of the economy, the IRFA narrows the scope of the particular review to small entities. The premise underpinning the IRFA is that, everything else being equal, the most rational alternative is often the one that achieves the objective of the agency at the lowest cost. Since small entities often have the highest costs to comply with a rule, while contributing the least to the problem the rule addresses, it makes sense to analyze them separately from all other regulated entities to determine if the rule can be made more cost effective by employing alternative standards for small entities.

The kinds of alternatives that are possible will vary based on the particular regulatory objective and the characteristics of the regulated industry. However, section 603(c) of the RFA gives agencies some alternatives that they must consider, at a minimum:

- Establishment of different compliance or reporting requirements for small entities or timetables that take into account the resources available to small entities.
- Clarification, consolidation, or simplification of compliance and reporting requirements for small entities.
- Use of performance rather than design standards.
- Exemption for certain or all small entities from coverage of the rule, in whole or in part.

Additional alternatives include adopting different standards based on the sizes of businesses or modifying the types of equipment required for large and small entities. In short, the agency should consider a variety of mechanisms to reach the regulatory objective.

Consistent with an agency's obligations under section 609 of the RFA, agencies should perform outreach to interested groups to help develop regulatory solutions. In doing so, agency personnel should recognize that different sectors of an industry may have very different perspectives on a particular regulatory approach. The agency, before adopting one approach, should ensure that it contacts small entities and their representatives as well as large entities and their representatives. This type of communication is not prohibited by the APA and will help the agency focus on potential benefits and costs of various approaches to small businesses.

THE FINAL RULE STAGE: THE FRFA

When it comes time to draft the final rule, the RFA requires agencies to either publish a certification statement with a factual basis as in the proposed rule, or a final regulatory flexibility analysis (FRFA). Agencies must prepare a FRFA unless the agency finds that the final rule will not have a significant economic impact on a substantial number of small entities or the final rule is issued under the APA provision allowing for good cause to forego notice and comment rulemaking.

The RFA mandates that agencies revise their initial regulatory flexibility analysis based on the public comments received. Agencies routinely create a summary of the public's comments to be published along with the final rules. In developing this summary, the agency should specifically summarize comments from small entities. Once the agency determines that it cannot certify the final rule under section 605(b), the agency must prepare a FRFA. If the agency determines that the rulemaking will not result in a significant economic impact on a substantial number of small entities, the head of the agency may so certify under section 605(b) of the RFA, and provide a copy of the certification to the Chief Counsel for Advocacy.

Questions to Consider

A number of important questions will assist the agency in preparing a final regulatory flexibility analysis under the RFA:

- Have all significant issues raised in the public comments regarding the IRFA been summarized and assessed and have any changes been made to the rule as a result of those comments?
- Has the number of small entities been estimated? If not, did the agency explain why?
- Has the adverse economic impact on small entities been minimized?
- Have all significant alternatives been reviewed?

Elements of a FRFA

Section 604(a) of the RFA outlines the central issues the agency must address in the FRFA. In short, agencies must evaluate the impact of a rule on small entities and describe their efforts to minimize the adverse impact. Agencies are required to publish a small entity compliance guide whenever they publish a rule that contains a FRFA. This must be done at the same time the final rule is published in the *Federal Register*.

The requirements, outlined in section 604(a)(1)–(5), are highlighted in italics below:

1) *A succinct statement of the need for, and objectives of, the rule.* The agency can cross-reference to a similar succinct statement in the supplementary information if the cross reference enables small entities to easily identify the need for and objectives of the rule.
2) *A summary of the significant issues raised by the public comments in response to the IRFA, a summary of the assessment of the agency of such issues, and a statement of any changes made in the proposed rule as a result of such comments.* Under the APA, agencies are required to respond to comments addressing relevant statutory considerations. Since the RFA constitutes a relevant statutory consideration, the agency is obligated under the APA to respond to comments on the RFA and relate how it changed the proposal, if at all, in response to the comments.
3) *A description and an estimate of the number of small entities to which the rule will apply or an explanation of why no such estimate is available.*
4) *A description of the projected reporting, recordkeeping, and other compliance requirements of the rule, including an estimate of the classes of small entities that will be subject to the requirement and the types of professional skills necessary for preparation of the report or record.*
5) *A description of the steps the agency has taken to minimize the significant adverse economic impact on small entities consistent with the stated objectives of applicable statutes, including a statement of the factual, policy, and legal reasons for selecting the alternative adopted in the final rule and why each of the other significant alternatives to the rule considered by the agency was rejected.*

A Word on Regulatory Panels

In 1996, SBREFA amended the RFA to include a number of important provisions. One of those was section 609, which requires, among other things, that certain agencies conduct special outreach efforts to ensure that small entity views are carefully considered prior to the issuance of a proposed rule. This outreach is accomplished through the work of small business advocacy review panels, often referred to as SBREFA panels.

Who Must Hold SBREFA Panels?

The statute requires that the Environmental Protection Agency (EPA), the Occupational Safety and Health Administration (OSHA) and the Consumer Finance Protection Bureau (CFPB) evaluate their regulatory proposals to determine whether SBREFA panels should be convened.

CONCLUSION

The RFA does not seek preferential treatment for small entities, does not require agencies to adopt regulations that impose the least burden on small entities, and does not mandate exemptions for small entities. Rather, as this guide has illustrated, the RFA establishes an analytical process for determining how public policy issues can best be achieved without erecting barriers to competition, stifling innovation, or imposing undue burdens on small entities. In so doing, it seeks a level playing field for small entities.

APPENDIX A: THE REGULATORY FLEXIBILITY ACT

The following text of the Regulatory Flexibility Act of 1980, as amended, is taken from Title 5 of the United States Code, sections 601–612. The Regulatory Flexibility Act was originally passed in 1980 (P.L. 96-354). The act was amended by the Small Business Regulatory Enforcement Fairness Act of 1996 (P.L. 104-121) and the Dodd-Frank Wall Street Reform and Consumer Protection Act of 2010 (P.L. 11-203)

Congressional Findings and Declaration of Purpose

(a) The Congress finds and declares that —

1) when adopting regulations to protect the health, safety and economic welfare of the Nation, Federal agencies should seek to achieve statutory goals as effectively and efficiently as possible without imposing unnecessary burdens on the public;
2) laws and regulations designed for application to large scale entities have been applied uniformly to small businesses, small organizations, and small governmental jurisdictions even though the problems that gave rise to government action may not have been caused by those smaller entities;
3) uniform Federal regulatory and reporting requirements have in numerous instances imposed unnecessary and disproportionately burdensome demands including legal, accounting and consulting costs upon small businesses, small organizations, and small governmental jurisdictions with limited resources;
4) the failure to recognize differences in the scale and resources of regulated entities has in numerous instances adversely affected competition in the marketplace, discouraged innovation and restricted improvements in productivity;
5) unnecessary regulations create entry barriers in many industries and discourage potential entrepreneurs from introducing beneficial products and processes;
6) the practice of treating all regulated businesses, organizations, and governmental jurisdictions as equivalent may lead to inefficient use of regulatory agency resources, enforcement problems and, in some cases, to actions inconsistent with the legislative intent of health, safety, environmental and economic welfare legislation;
7) alternative regulatory approaches which do not conflict with the stated objectives of applicable statutes may be available which minimizethe significant economic

impact of rules on small businesses, small organizations, and small governmental jurisdictions;

8) the process by which Federal regulations are developed and adopted should be reformed to require agencies to solicit the ideas and comments of small businesses, small organizations, and small governmental jurisdictions to examine the impact of proposed and existing rules on such entities, and to review the continued need for existing rules.
9) It is the purpose of this Act [enacting this chapter and provisions set out as notes under this section] to establish as a principle of regulatory issuance that agencies shall endeavor, consistent with the objectives of the rule and of applicable statutes, to fit regulatory and informational requirements to the scale of the businesses, organizations, and governmental jurisdictions subject to regulation. To achieve this principle, agencies are required to solicit and consider flexible regulatory proposals and to explain the rationale for their actions to assure that such proposals are given serious consideration.

REGULATORY FLEXIBILITY ACT[15]

Sections

SEC. 601. Definitions [Cite: 5 USC 01]

For purposes of this chapter—

(1) the term "agency" means an agency as defined in section 551(1) of this title;
(2) the term "rule" means any rule for which the agency publishes a general notice of proposed rulemaking pursuant to section 553(b) of this title, or any other law, including any rule of general applicability governing Federal grants to State and local governments for which the agency provides an opportunity for notice and public comment, except that the term "rule" does not include a rule of particular

applicability relating to rates, wages, corporate or financial structures or reorganizations thereof, prices, facilities, appliances, services, or allowances therefor or to valuations, costs or accounting, or practices relating to such rates, wages, structures, prices, appliances, services, or allowances;

(3) the term "small business" has the same meaning as the term "small business concern" under section 3 of the Small Business Act, unless an agency, after consultation with the Office of Advocacy of the Small Business Administration and after opportunity for public comment, establishes one or more definitions of such term which are appropriate to the activities of the agency and publishes such definition(s) in the *Federal Register*;

(4) the term "small organization" means any not-for-profit enterprise which is independently owned and operated and is not dominant in its field, unless an agency establishes, after opportunity for public comment, one or more definitions of such term which are appropriate to the activities of the agency and publishes such definition(s) in the *Federal Register*;

(5) the term "small governmental jurisdiction" means governments of cities, counties, towns, townships, villages, school districts, or special districts, with a population of less than fifty thousand, unless an agency establishes, after opportunity for public comment, one or more definitions of such term which are appropriate to the activities of the agency and which are based on such factors as location in rural or sparsely populated areas or limited revenues due to the population of such jurisdiction, and publishes such definition(s) in the *Federal Register*;

(6) the term "small entity" shall have the same meaning as the terms "small business", "small organization" and "small governmental jurisdiction" defined in paragraphs (3), (4) and (5) of this section; and

(7) the term "collection of information"—

A. means the obtaining, causing to be obtained, soliciting, or requiring the disclosure to third parties or the public, of facts or opinions by or for an agency, regardless of form or format, calling for either—

i. answers to identical questions posed to, or identical reporting or recordkeeping requirements imposed on, 10 or more persons, other than agencies, instrumentalities, or employees of the United States; or

ii. answers to questions posed to agencies, instrumentalities, or employees of the United States which are to be used for general statistical purposes; and

B. shall not include a collection of information described under section 3518(c)(1) of title 44, United States Code.

(8) recordkeeping requirement.—The term "recordkeeping requirement" means a requirement imposed by an agency on persons to maintain specified records.

(Added Pub. L. 96-354, Sec. 3(a), Sept. 19, 1980, 94 Stat. 1165; amended Pub. L. 104- 121, title II, Sec. 241(a)(2), Mar. 29, 1996, 110 Stat. 864.)

SEC. 602. Regulatory Agenda [Cite: 5 USC 602]

a) During the months of October and April of each year, each agency shall publish in the *Federal Register* a regulatory flexibility agenda which shall contain—
   (1) a brief description of the subject area of any rule which the agency expects to propose or promulgate which is likely to have a significant economic impact on a substantial number of small entities;
   (2) a summary of the nature of any such rule under consideration for each subject area listed in the agenda pursuant to paragraph (1), the objectives and legal basis for the issuance of the rule, and an approximate schedule for completing action on any rule for which the agency has issued a general notice of proposed rulemaking; and
   (3) the name and telephone number of an agency official knowledgeable concerning the items listed in paragraph (1).

b) Each regulatory flexibility agenda shall be transmitted to the Chief Counsel for Advocacy of the Small Business Administration for comment, if any.

c) Each agency shall endeavor to provide notice of each regulatory flexibility agenda to small entities or their representatives through direct notification or publication of the agenda in publications likely to be obtained by such small entities and shall invite comments upon each subject area on the agenda.

d) Nothing in this section precludes an agency from considering or acting on any matter not included in a regulatory flexibility agenda, or requires an agency to consider or act on any matter listed in such agenda.

(Added Pub. L. 96-354, Sec. 3(a), Sept. 19, 1980, 94 Stat. 1166.)

SEC. 603. Initial Regulatory Flexibility Analysis [Cite: 5 USC 603]

a) Whenever an agency is required by section 553 of this title, or any other law, to publish general notice of proposed rulemaking for any proposed rule, or publishes a notice of proposed rulemaking for an interpretative rule involving the internal revenue laws of the United States, the agency shall prepare and make available for public comment an initial regulatory flexibility analysis. Such analysis shall describe the impact of the proposed rule on small entities. The initial regulatory flexibility analysis or a summary shall be published in the *Federal Register* at the time of the publication of general notice of proposed rulemaking for the rule. The agency shall transmit a copy of the initial regulatory flexibility analysis to the Chief Counsel for Advocacy of the Small Business Administration. In the case of an interpretative rule involving the internal revenue laws of the United States, this chapter applies to interpretative rules published in the *Federal Register* for codification in the Code of Federal Regulations, but only to the extent that such interpretative rules impose on small entities a collection of information requirement.

b) Each initial regulatory flexibility analysis required under this section shall contain—
   (1) a description of the reasons why action by the agency is being considered;
   (2) a succinct statement of the objectives of, and legal basis for, the proposed rule;

(3) a description of and, where feasible, an estimate of the number of small entities to which the proposed rule will apply;
(4) a description of the projected reporting, recordkeeping and other compliance requirements of the proposed rule, including an estimate of the classes of small entities which will be subject to the requirement and the type of professional skills necessary for preparation of the report or record;
(5) an identification, to the extent practicable, of all relevant Federal rules which may duplicate, overlap or conflict with the proposed rule.

c) Each initial regulatory flexibility analysis shall also contain a description of any significant alternatives to the proposed rule which accomplish the stated objectives of applicable statutes and which minimize any significant economic impact of the proposed rule on small entities. Consistent with the stated objectives of applicable statutes, the analysis shall discuss significant alternatives such as—
(1) the establishment of differing compliance or reporting requirements or timetables that take into account the resources available to small entities;
(2) the clarification, consolidation, or simplification of compliance and reporting requirements under the rule for such small entities;
(3) the use of performance rather than design standards; and
(4) an exemption from coverage of the rule, or any part thereof, for such small entities.

(Added Pub. L. 96-354, Sec. 3(a), Sept. 19, 1980, 94 Stat. 1166; amended Pub. L. 104- 121, title II, Sec. 241(a)(1), Mar. 29, 1996, 110 Stat. 864.)

SEC. 604. Final Regulatory Flexibility Analysis [Cite: 5 USC 604]

a) When an agency promulgates a final rule under section 553 of this title, after being required by that section or any other law to publish a general notice of proposed rulemaking, or promulgates a final interpretative rule involving the internal revenue laws of the United States as described in section 603(a), the agency shall prepare a final regulatory flexibility analysis. Each final regulatory flexibility analysis shall contain—
(1) a succinct statement of the need for, and objectives of, the rule;
(2) a summary of the significant issues raised by the public comments in response to the initial regulatory flexibility analysis, a summary of the assessment of the agency of such issues, and a statement of any changes made in the proposed rule as a result of such comments;
(3) a description of and an estimate of the number of small entities to which the rule will apply or an explanation of why no such estimate is available;
(4) a description of the projected reporting, recordkeeping and other compliance requirements of the rule, including an estimate of the classes of small entities which will be subject to the requirement and the type of professional skills necessary for preparation of the report or record; and
(5) a description of the steps the agency has taken to minimize the significant economic impact on small entities consistent with the stated objectives of

applicable statutes, including a statement of the factual, policy, and legal reasons for selecting the alternative adopted in the final rule and why each one of the other significant alternatives to the rule considered by the agency which affect the impact on small entities was rejected.

b) The agency shall make copies of the final regulatory flexibility analysis available to members of the public and shall publish in the Federal Register such analysis or a summary thereof.

(Added Pub. L. 96-354, Sec. 3(a), Sept. 19, 1980, 94 Stat. 1167; amended Pub. L. 104- 121, title II, Sec. 241(b), Mar. 29, 1996, 110 Stat. 864.)

SEC. 605. Avoidance of Duplicative or Unnecessary Analyses [Cite: 5 USC 605]

a) Any Federal agency may perform the analyses required by sections 602, 603, and 604 of this title in conjunction with or as a part of any other agenda or analysis required by any other law if such other analysis satisfies the provisions of such sections.
b) Sections 603 and 604 of this title shall not apply to any proposed or final rule if the head of the agency certifies that the rule will not, if promulgated, have a significant economic impact on a substantial number of small entities. If the head of the agency makes a certification under the preceding sentence, the agency shall publish such certification in the *Federal Register* at the time of publication of general notice of proposed rulemaking for the rule or at the time of publication of the final rule, along with a statement providing the factual basis for such certification. The agency shall provide such certification and statement to the Chief Counsel for Advocacy of the Small Business Administration.
c) In order to avoid duplicative action, an agency may consider a series of closely related rules as one rule for the purposes of sections 602, 603, 604 and 610 of this title.

(Added Pub. L. 96-354, Sec. 3(a), Sept. 19, 1980, 94 Stat. 1167; amended Pub. L. 104- 121, title II, Sec. 243(a), Mar. 29, 1996, 110 Stat. 866.)

SEC. 606. Effect on Other Law [Cite: 5 USC 606]

The requirements of sections 603 and 604 of this title do not alter in any manner standards otherwise applicable by law to agency action.

(Added Pub. L. 96-354, Sec. 3(a), Sept. 19, 1980, 94 Stat. 1168.)

SEC. 607. Preparation of analyses [cite: 5 usc 607]

In complying with the provisions of sections 603 and 604 of this title, an agency may provide either a quantifiable or numerical description of the effects of a proposed rule or alternatives to the proposed rule, or more general descriptive statements if quantification is not practicable or reliable.

(Added Pub. L. 96-354, Sec. 3(a), Sept. 19, 1980, 94 Stat. 1168.)

SEC. 608. Procedure for Waiver or Delay of Completion [Cite: 5 USC 608]

a) An agency head may waive or delay the completion of some or all of the requirements of section 603 of this title by publishing in the Federal Register, not later than the date of publication of the final rule, a written finding, with reasons therefor, that the final rule is being promulgated in response to an emergency that makes compliance or timely compliance with the provisions of section 603 of this title impracticable.
b) Except as provided in section 605(b), an agency head may not waive the requirements of section 604 of this title. An agency head may delay the completion of the requirements of section 604 of this title for a period of not more than one hundred and eighty days after the date of publication in the Federal Register of a final rule by publishing in the Federal Register, not later than such date of publication, a written finding, with reasons therefor, that the final rule is being promulgated in response to an emergency that makes timely compliance with the provisions of section 604 of this title impracticable. If the agency has not prepared a final regulatory analysis pursuant to section 604 of this title within one hundred and eighty days from the date of publication of the final rule, such rule shall lapse and have no effect. Such rule shall not be repromulgated until a final regulatory flexibility analysis has been completed by the agency.

(Added Pub. L. 96-354, Sec. 3(a), Sept. 19, 1980, 94 Stat. 1168.)

SEC. 609. Procedures for Gathering Comments [Cite: 5 USC 609]

(a) When any rule is promulgated which will have a significant economic impact on a substantial number of small entities, the head of the agency promulgating the rule or the official of the agency with statutory responsibility for the promulgation of the rule shall assure that small entities have been given an opportunity to participate in the rulemaking for the rule through the reasonable use of techniques such as—
    (1) the inclusion in an advanced notice of proposed rulemaking, if issued, of a statement that the proposed rule may have a significant economic effect on a substantial number of small entities;
    (2) the publication of general notice of proposed rulemaking in publications likely to be obtained by small entities;

(3) the direct notification of interested small entities;
(4) the conduct of open conferences or public hearings concerning the rule for small entities including soliciting and receiving comments over computer networks; and
(5) the adoption or modification of agency procedural rules to reduce the cost or complexity of participation in the rulemaking by small entities.

(b) Prior to publication of an initial regulatory flexibility analysis which a covered agency is required to conduct by this chapter—
(1) a covered agency shall notify the Chief Counsel for Advocacy of the Small Business Administration and provide the Chief Counsel with information on the potential impacts of the proposed rule on small entities and the type of small entities that might be affected;
(2) not later than 15 days after the date of receipt of the materials described in paragraph (1), the Chief Counsel shall identify individuals representative of affected small entities for the purpose of obtaining advice and recommendations from those individuals about the potential impacts of the proposed rule;
(3) the agency shall convene a review panel for such rule consisting wholly of full time Federal employees of the office within the agency responsible for carrying out the proposed rule, the Office of Information and Regulatory Affairs within the Office of Management and Budget, and the Chief Counsel;
(4) the panel shall review any material the agency has prepared in connection with this chapter, including any draft proposed rule, collect advice and recommendations of each individual small entity representative identified by the agency after consultation with the Chief Counsel, on issues related to subsections 603(b), paragraphs (3), (4) and
(5) and 603(c); (5) not later than 60 days after the date a covered agency convenes a review panel pursuant to paragraph (3), the review panel shall report on the comments of the small entity representatives and its findings as to issues related to subsections 603(b), paragraphs (3), (4) and (5) and 603(c), provided that such report shall be made public as part of the rulemaking record; and
(6) where appropriate, the agency shall modify the proposed rule, the initial regulatory flexibility analysis or the decision on whether an initial regulatory flexibility analysis is required.

(c) An agency may in its discretion apply subsection (b) to rules that the agency intends to certify under subsection 605(b), but the agency believes may have a greater than de minimis impact on a substantial number of small entities.

(d) For purposes of this section, the term "covered agency" means the Environmental Protection Agency and the Occupational Safety and Health Administration of the Department of Labor.

(e) The Chief Counsel for Advocacy, in consultation with the individuals identified in subsection (b)(2), and with the Administrator of the Office of Information and Regulatory Affairs within the Office of Management and Budget, may waive the requirements of subsections (b)(3), (b)(4), and (b)(5) by including in the rulemaking record a written finding, with reasons therefor, that those requirements would not advance the effective participation of small entities in the rulemaking process. For purposes of this subsection, the factors to be considered in making such a finding are as follows:

(1) In developing a proposed rule, the extent to which the covered agency consulted with individuals representative of affected small entities with respect to the potential impacts of the rule and took such concerns into consideration.
(2) Special circumstances requiring prompt issuance of the rule.
(3) Whether the requirements of subsection (b) would provide the individuals identified in subsection (b)(2) with a competitive advantage relative to other small entities.

(Added Pub. L. 96-354, Sec. 3(a), Sept. 19, 1980, 94 Stat. 1168; amended Pub. L. 104- 121, title II, Sec. 244(a), Mar. 29, 1996, 110 Stat. 867.)

SEC. 610. Periodic Review Of Rules [Cite: 5 USC 610]

(a) Within one hundred and eighty days after the effective date of this chapter, each agency shall publish in the *Federal Register* a plan for the periodic review of the rules issued by the agency which have or will have a significant economic impact upon a substantial number of small entities. Such plan may be amended by the agency at any time by publishing the revision in the *Federal Register*. The purpose of the review shall be to determine whether such rules should be continued without change, or should be amended or rescinded, consistent with the stated objectives of applicable statutes, to minimize any significant economic impact of the rules upon a substantial number of such small entities. The plan shall provide for the review of all such agency rules existing on the effective date of this chapter within ten years of that date and for the review of such rules adopted after the effective date of this chapter within ten years of the publication of such rules as the final rule. If the head of the agency determines that completion of the review of existing rules is not feasible by the established date, he shall so certify in a statement published in the *Federal Register* and may extend the completion date by one year at a time for a total of not more than five years.
(b) In reviewing rules to minimize any significant economic impact of the rule on a substantial number of small entities in a manner consistent with the stated objectives of applicable statutes, the agency shall consider the following factors—
(1) the continued need for the rule;
(2) the nature of complaints or comments received concerning the rule from the public;
(3) the complexity of the rule;
(4) the extent to which the rule overlaps, duplicates or conflicts with other Federal rules, and, to the extent feasible, with State and local governmental rules; and
(5) the length of time since the rule has been evaluated or the degree to which technology, economic conditions, or other factors have changed in the area affected by the rule.
(c) Each year, each agency shall publish in the Federal Register a list of the rules which have a significant economic impact on a substantial number of small entities, which are to be reviewed pursuant to this section during the succeeding twelve months. The

list shall include a brief description of each rule and the need for and legal basis of such rule and shall invite public comment upon the rule.

(Added Pub. L. 96-354, Sec. 3(a), Sept. 19, 1980, 94 Stat. 1169.)

SEC. 611. Judicial Review [Cite: 5 USC 611]

(a) -

(1) For any rule subject to this chapter, a small entity that is adversely affected or aggrieved by final agency action is entitled to judicial review of agency compliance with the requirements of sections 601, 604, 605(b), 608(b), and 610 in accordance with chapter 7. Agency compliance with sections 607 and 609(a) shall be judicially reviewable in connection with judicial review of section 604.

(2) Each court having jurisdiction to review such rule for compliance with section 553, or under any other provision of law, shall have jurisdiction to review any claims of noncompliance with sections 601, 604, 605(b), 608(b), and 610 in accordance with chapter 7. Agency compliance with sections 607 and 609(a) shall be judicially reviewable in connection with judicial review of section 604.

(3) (A) A small entity may seek such review during the period beginning on the date of final agency action and ending one year later, except that where a provision of law requires that an action challenging a final agency action be commenced before the expiration of one year, such lesser period shall apply to an action for judicial review under this section.

(B) In the case where an agency delays the issuance of a final regulatory flexibility analysis pursuant to section 608(b) of this chapter, an action for judicial review under this section shall be filed not later than—

i. one year after the date the analysis is made available to the public, or

ii. where a provision of law requires that an action challenging a final agency regulation be commenced before the expiration of the 1-year period, the number of days specified in such provision of law that is after the date the analysis is made available to the public.

(4) In granting any relief in an action under this section, the court shall order the agency to take corrective action consistent with this chapter and chapter 7, including, but not limited to—

A. remanding the rule to the agency, and

B. deferring the enforcement of the rule against small entities unless the court finds that continued enforcement of the rule is in the public interest.

(5) Nothing in this subsection shall be construed to limit the authority of any court to stay the effective date of any rule or provision thereof under any other provision of law or to grant any other relief in addition to the requirements of this section.

(b) In an action for the judicial review of a rule, the regulatory flexibility analysis for such rule, including an analysis prepared or corrected pursuant to paragraph (a)(4), shall constitute part of the entire record of agency action in connection with such review.

(c) Compliance or noncompliance by an agency with the provisions of this chapter shall be subject to judicial review only in accordance with this section.
(d) Nothing in this section bars judicial review of any other impact statement or similar analysis required by any other law if judicial review of such statement or analysis is otherwise permitted by law.

(Added Pub. L. 96-354, Sec. 3(a), Sept. 19, 1980, 94 Stat. 1169; amended Pub. L. 104- 121, title II, Sec. 242, Mar. 29, 1996, 110 Stat. 865.)

SEC. 612. Reports and Intervention Rights [Cite: 5 USC 612]

(a) The Chief Counsel for Advocacy of the Small Business Administration shall monitor agency compliance with this chapter and shall report at least annually thereon to the President and to the Committees on the Judiciary and Small Business of the Senate and House of Representatives.
(b) The Chief Counsel for Advocacy of the Small Business Administration is authorized to appear as *amicus curiae* in any action brought in a court of the United States to review a rule. In any such action, the Chief Counsel is authorized to present his or her views with respect to compliance with this chapter, the adequacy of the rulemaking record with respect to small entities and the effect of the rule on small entities.
(c) A court of the United States shall grant the application of the Chief Counsel for Advocacy of the Small Business Administration to appear in any such action for the purposes described in subsection (b).

(Added Pub. L. 96-354, Sec. 3(a), Sept. 19, 1980, 94 Stat. 1170; amended Pub. L. 104- 121, title II, Sec. 243(b), Mar. 29, 1996, 110 Stat. 866.)

The following is an excerpt from the Dodd-Frank Wall Street Reform and Consumer Protection Act of 2010 (P.L. 11-203), amending the Small Business Regulatory Enforcement Fairness Act of 1996 (P.L. 104-121).

Sec. 1100G. Small Business Fairness and Regulatory Transparency

(a) PANEL REQUIREMENT.—Section 609(d) of title 5, United States Code, is amended by striking "means the" and all that follows and inserting the following: "means—
"(1) the Environmental Protection Agency;
"(2) the Consumer Financial Protection Bureau of the Federal Reserve System; and
"(3) the Occupational Safety and Health Administration of the Department of Labor.".
(b) INITIAL REGULATORY FLEXIBILITY ANALYSIS.—Section 603 of title 5, United States Code, is amended by adding at the end the following:

"(d)(1) For a covered agency, as defined in section 609(d)(2), each initial regulatory flexibility analysis shall include a description of—

"(A) any projected increase in the cost of credit for small entities;

"(B) any significant alternatives to the proposed rule which accomplish the stated objectives of applicable statutes and which minimize any increase in the cost of credit for small entities; and

"(C) advice and recommendations of representatives of small entities relating to issues described in subparagraphs (A) and (B) and subsection (b).

H. R. 4173—738

"(2) A covered agency, as defined in section 609(d)(2), shall, for purposes of complying with paragraph (1)(C)—

"(A) identify representatives of small entities in consultation with the Chief Counsel for Advocacy of the Small Business Administration; and

"(B) collect advice and recommendations from the representatives identified under subparagraph (A) relating to issues described in subparagraphs (A) and (B) of paragraph (1) and subsection (b).".

(c) FINAL REGULATORY FLEXIBILITY ANALYSIS.—Section 604(a) of title 5, United States Code, is amended—

(1) in paragraph (4), by striking "and" at the end;

(2) in paragraph (5), by striking the period at the end and inserting "; and"; and by adding at the end the following:

"(6) for a covered agency, as defined in section 609(d)(2), a description of the steps the agency has taken to minimize any additional cost of credit for small entities.".

SEC. 1100H. Effective Date

Except as otherwise provided in this subtitle and the amendments made by this subtitle, this subtitle and the amendments made by this subtitle, other than sections 1081 and 1082, shall become effective on the designated transfer date.

End Notes

[1] Regulatory Flexibility Act, Pub. L. No. 96-354, 94 Stat. 1164 (codified at 5 U.S.C. § 601)

[2] 15 U.S.C. § 632. The North American Industry Classification System (NAICS) breaks down industry sectors and is used to identify the industry, governmental and nonprofit sectors an agency intends to regulate. Size standard regulations specifying size standards and governing their use are set forth in Title 13, Code of Federal Regulations, 13 CFR §121.

[3] Small Business Regulatory Enforcement Fairness Act of 1996, Pub. L. No. 104-121, 110 Stat. 857 (codified at 5 U.S.C. § 601 et seq.).

[4] 5 U.S.C § 553(b).

[5] Id .at § 553(a).

[6] Id. at § 553(b)(A).

[7] 5 U.S.C. § 601(2).

[8] 5 U.S.C. § 605(b).

[9] See North Carolina Fisheries Ass'n v. Daley, 27 F. Supp. 2d 650 (E.D. Va. 1998).

[10] 5 U.S.C. § 603(a).

[11] Id.

[12] Exec. Order No. 13,272, § 3(b).

[13] 5 U.S.C. § 603(b)-(c).

[14] Bowen v. AHA, 476 U.S. 610, 643 (186); National Ass'n of Home Health Agencies v. Schweiker, 690 F.2d 932, 949 (D.C. Cir. 1982); Chocolate Mfrs. Ass'n v. Block, 755 F.2d 1098, 1103 (4th Cir. 1985).

[15] Source: Title 5, Part I, Chapter 6 from U.S. Code Online via GPO Access [wais.access.gpo.gov]

INDEX

D

E

F

G

H

N

O

P

Q

R

S

T

U

V

W

Y